Therapy with God

Wonderful Counselor, Comforter, Friend

Why art thou cast down, O my soul? And why art thou disquieted within me? Hope thou in God: for I shall yet praise Him, who is the health of my countenance, and my God.
(Psalms 42:11 KJV)

I came that they may have life, and have it abundantly
John 10:10b

Susan Henderson McHenry

xulon
PRESS

Copyright © 2008 by Susan Henderson McHenry

Therapy with God
Wonderful Counselor, Comforter, Friend
by Susan Henderson McHenry

Printed in the United States of America

ISBN 978-1-60477-587-7

All rights reserved solely by the author. The author guarantees all contents are original and do not infringe upon the legal rights of any other person or work. No part of this book may be reproduced in any form without the permission of the author. The views expressed in this book are not necessarily those of the publisher.

Unless otherwise indicated, Bible quotations are taken from the New American Standard Bible. Copyright © 1960, 1962, 1963, 1968, 1971, 1972, 1973, 1975, 1977, 1995 by The Lockman Foundation Used by permission. (www.Lockman.org).

Quotations by Henry Blackaby and Claude King taken from *Experiencing God: Knowing and Doing the Will of God.* **Used by permission of Holman Publishers, 2004**

Quotations by Jon Courson taken from the *Application Commentary: Old Testament Volumes I and II, and Application Commentary: New Testament.* **Copyright © 2005, 2006, 2003 Used by permission of Thomas Nelson, Inc.**

Other Scripture Quotations are from:

The Holy Bible, King James Version. New York: American Bible Society: 1999; Bartleby.com, 2000. www.bartleby.com/108/.

Scripture quotations marked NLT are taken from the Holy Bible, New Living Translation, copyright 1996, 2004. Used by permission of Tyndale House Publishers, Inc., Wheaton, Illinois 60189. All rights reserved.

Quotations by Mary Southerland
Copyrighted by Mary Southerland
www.marysoutherland.com
Out of the Darkness
(Harvest House Publishers 2006)

cover photograph taken by:
© susan henderson mchenry

www.xulonpress.com

DEDICATION

This book is dedicated to all of my family and friends who reviewed it and gave me their invaluable feedback, and to all those who have encouraged me all along the way.

It is dedicated to my courageous clients who honored me by allowing me to be a part of their transformation at the hands of Jesus Christ.

It is dedicated to my wonderful husband, Stuart, who has encouraged me when I felt insecure, lifted me up when I felt down, and pushed me along when I needed that shove. I feel loved by him, and I love him from the bottom of my heart.

But it is mostly dedicated to God the Father who called me, to the Holy Spirit who guides me, and to the Lord of my life, Jesus Christ, without whom I would still be living in the dark. To God be the glory.

* * *

My heartfelt and humble 'thank you' to you all.

Readability Statistics:
Flesch Reading Ease: 70.4
Flesch-Kincaid Reading Level: 7.1

TABLE OF CONTENTS

SECTION 1 — INTRODUCTION
I. Introduction 11

SECTION 2 — FOUNDATIONAL ISSUES
II. Defining Mental Health 27
III. What is The Bible? 43
IV. Falling in Love with Jesus 49
V. Final Christian Concepts 57

SECTION 3 — TECHNIQUES
VI. How I Read the Bible 71
VII. Thinking About What I Read 89
VIII. Memorizing Scripture 95
IX. Old versus New Testaments 103
X. Chatting with Jesus 111

SECTION 4 — APPLICATION
XI. The Seven Biblical Freedoms 117
XII. The Seven Joy-Robbers 141
XIII. The Issue of Self Esteem 167
XIV. Bible-based Therapy 175
XV. If Only I Had More Faith 235
XVI. Victory in Trials 241
XVII. What is God's Will for My Life? 271

SECTION 5 — EXAMPLES
XVIII. Examples for Reflection..285
XIX. Topical Examples: Old Testament................................295
XX. Topical Examples: New Testament...............................321

SECTION 6 — SUMMARY
XXI. Summary..349

APPENDICES

Appendix A - The Gospel of Jesus Christ 357
Appendix B - I'm a new Christian — Now What? 365
Appendix C - How to Select the Right Bible..........................369
Appendix D - How to Use the Bible..377
Appendix E - References and Recommendations 387
Appendix F - Introduction to the Author................................389

Notes

SECTION 1

****

INTRODUCTION

I — INTRODUCTION

"And Your words became for me a joy and the delight of my heart" (Jeremiah 15:16).

I have experienced something amazing in my work with clients that I would like to share with you. Reflect on this profound truth for a moment:

Jesus Christ is the best mental health therapist on the face of the planet, and His Holy Bible is the best mental health book.

See Him that way, regard His book that way, invite Him to change you and change your life, and you will never look back.

Meet with Jesus in the pages of His Holy Book. Seek His counsel, rely on His judgment, and lean on His shoulder — not weekly, but day by day and minute by minute — and your life will be transformed. That transformation is there for you, and you can do it. Bask in the restorative powers of your ever-deepening relationship with Jesus, and watch it happen. I know it can happen for you. I've seen it. I've taught it. I've lived it.

This book is about change. It is about replacing what is wrong in your life with what God has to offer: peace, contentment, and unspeakable joy. It is about walking with Jesus and hearing Him whisper tender words of healing into your ear. It is about emotional renewal, and it is about mental health victory.

This book will help you change how you relate to God, Jesus, and the Bible, and will help you cultivate those new relationships to effect profound changes in your life. Jesus wants to work with you - not judge or condemn you - if you will let Him. He will encourage you gently and lovingly, over time, to help you see yourself and your world through His eyes. Through this new perspective, you will develop a deeper knowledge of God, the world, your own purpose, and your place in His kingdom. This knowledge will then build your faith, and you will learn to trust that He is there, He loves you, and He will see you through all of your trials. Start slowly and give yourself a lot of grace as you work through this process. Don't give up. Remember that you are addressing ways of thinking and habits that have years of roots in your soul.

What Is The Purpose Of This Book

On the surface, this may look like a guidebook to teach you how to read your Bible. Learning how to read the Bible is a certainly a big part of the process, but the purpose is much larger than that. The purpose is to have you open your Bible and find Jesus everywhere you look. It is to draw you into a closer understanding of who He is and what He can mean to you. It is to invite you and guide you into His healing arms.

The ultimate purpose of this book is to help you find that unspeakable joy in 'the land of promise,' the land flowing with milk and honey that God talks about in the Old Testament: the "Christian Promised Land," so to speak, of an extraordinary relationship with Jesus Christ Himself. It is intended to shed light on the following dilemma:

> "I have always heard that if I give my life to Jesus Christ, I will have the solution to every problem I could ever face. I know the Bible has the answers, but I don't know where to go or how to find them."

As a nation, we spend millions of dollars annually on what we refer to as 'self-help' books. They teach us to rely on our own strength and become self-sufficient and independent of God, hence the name 'self' help. We keep spending and reading because we are looking for answers in all the wrong places. Like bad relationships, they make us feel better for a season — until the next crash. Because the solution does not include God, we're no better off than before. The crash is because their advice sends us off in the wrong direction — a direction toward 'self' that takes us farther and farther away from God, and farther and farther away from the real answer to our questions.

So why do we keep turning to the self-help books? Because we don't know where else to turn; we don't know how to use the Bible that way. We have a Creator who knows us better than we know ourselves, but we don't know how to go to Him. He knows how we tick. He knows how we react. He knows what we want and what we really need. He knows what satisfies us and gives us peace and joy. If we could only sit with Him and talk to Him, maybe He could give us the answers to our deepest questions.

To really experience God's best, we need to connect with Him on a spiritual level, and learn to think, feel, react, and love as He does. Since He does know us better than we know ourselves, He can transform our lives if we let Him. Remember that God loves you and wants your heart overflowing with his Spirit — His true blessing[1] and the source of true joy. Like any good Father, He's miserable when you're miserable (Judges 10:16), He wants to guide you into a life of peace and contentment and purpose, and He has painstakingly created for you His divinely-inspired guidebook to lead you through that process. It is in those glorious pages where you can seek and find the person Jesus Christ to love you and mentor you toward that God-filled, joy-filled life.

We all crave that wonderful relationship with Jesus, and we know that the Bible shows us the way. But sometimes, it just seems too daunting, frightening even, like a river running too fast. *Therapy with God* will help you wade in slowly enough to feel safe and comfortable, and yet deeply enough to allow true changes to permeate your life.

The purpose of this book is to point you to Jesus — it is not a self-help book or another therapy technique. It is to help you find the ultimate Counselor, Jesus Christ. It is in His arms alone where you will find true and lasting relief.

Why I Wrote This Book

I started my private practice as a Christian Mental Health Therapist in early 2005 after having dedicated my life to the Lord in 2001. The idea for this book started to take shape in my thoughts shortly after I began my practice with Christian clients. After several years as a secular therapist, it was astonishing to me how rapidly using Scripture and working with the Holy Spirit could move my Christian clients to recovery. Therapy with God worked, and it worked miraculously. Today, my practice is exclusively Christian-based. As a Christian Mental Health Therapist, I see the power of God at work daily, and I could never go back to a secular approach of therapy without God. I love what I do, and it works. It is extremely exciting to witness the power of Scripture and the intervention of the Holy Spirit transforming lives before my very eyes. The look of awareness in my client's eyes, then the healing, often instantaneous, all attest to the power of God's healing hand.

But what I came to realize was that before we began our work together, most of my clients did not understand the power they held in their hands and in their hearts. I knew that Jesus has the answer — *is* the answer — to every single problem we face in our lives. My clients knew that as well, but they didn't know how to find those answers through their relationship with Him. I realized that if they knew what I had learned about Jesus and Scripture, they would be set free. It was far more than I could communicate to them in weekly 50-minute sessions, so I knew I had to write it down.

So what was it that I knew? What is it that I know? Through my studies, I have come to realize that every story and every character in both the Old and New Testaments can, in some way or another, be applied to our lives today. The practical applicability of every single page of Scripture is nothing short of miraculous. These stories and the people in them visually bring to life the Christian principles that Jesus taught and lived while He was with us in the flesh. They teach us who God is, who we are, how we can serve Him, and how we can live our lives to the fullest. Let the Holy Spirit teach you how to personalize what you read. Let Him show you how to weave the Old Testament stories into the New Testament truths. Let Him lead you through the door into a deeper understanding of how you can apply those amazing truths to your life.

Reading Scripture is a grand and glorious treasure-hunt. Seek those wonderful, life-changing moments when you hear directly from God through Scripture. Let Him fill that treasure-chest in your heart with the knowledge and the fullness of Him. When you and the Holy Spirit find the buried treasures together, your faith will grow, your love for Christ will grow, and you will sing praises to God. As you go through the pages of this book, you will learn how to do just that.

This book is a compilation of what I've learned working with clients, my personal experiences and research, and the journey I've taken with Jesus. I have included my own interpretation and applications of what I've learned as a Mental Health Therapist in general, and incorporated what I have learned through the influence of endless sermons, books, conversations, and personal encounters with God, Himself. Many people have influenced what ended up in these pages, and to the extent it serves to bring people closer to Christ, I give them all thanks, and God gets the glory.

So those of us who are privileged to call ourselves Christian Mental Health Professionals will continue to try to be Jesus with skin on for you, but we will never come close to the Master. It is my prayer that once you understand the process of studying your Bible from a <u>personal</u> perspective and experience its transforming power, Jesus will become your every-day therapist, and your life will never be the same.

Who Should Read This Book

So who is my target audience? I've narrowed it down to four broad groups of people. I was each of you at one time or another, so I welcome you all.

1. People who suffer and are hungry for answers from God,

2. Professionals who want to help those people find those answers,
3. Seekers trying to understand more about God, and
4. The curious non-believer who just wants to listen in.

I currently fall into a couple of those categories, and I'm assuming that since you're reading this book, at least one of them applies to you as well. Frankly, I don't know anyone who hasn't suffered at some point in their life, and likely will again.

Mental health is a difficult problem in our complex and secular world. Being filled with joy, contentment, and complete satisfaction in our station in life is virtually impossible without the Spirit of God. Looking to Jesus for the answers will bring you peace, and this book is to show you how to use your Bible in that way.

Now I can hear some of you saying, "But I don't know anything about the Bible. What if I can't do it?"

Please hear me: *You can do it.* Yes, this is a book about mental health and the Bible, but for those of you without psychology or theology degrees, be comforted. This is a down-to-earth, roll-up-your-sleeves, practical guidebook for learning, in a step-by-step fashion, how to improve your mental health God's way. It's for you. It is not about what you know about the Bible or mental health or anything else: *It's about having a heart for God.* I will give examples, specific instructions that you can follow, explanations of terms you might not understand, and an encouraging 'peering over your shoulder' as you work.

There is no question that it involves some effort, but if you went so far as to pick this book up in the first place, I know that you are ready to work. Neither this book, nor the work itself is above anyone's head. All that it requires is a desire to draw closer to God and a Bible in your hands. It is the *desire* that will propel you, and it is the Holy Spirit who will guide you. You cannot lose, and you cannot fail.

I will say this, though: Anyone can read this book and gain an understanding of how Christianity helps Christians, but to really understand this book and apply the lessons to *your* own life, you need to know Jesus Christ personally. You need to have His Holy

Spirit living in you. You need to love Him and be submitted to Him — however loosely or inadequately — or it won't make any sense at all. If you believe you are not a Christian but would like to be, or if you're just not sure if you are or not, then please stop now and read Appendix A, "The Gospel of Jesus Christ." In it, I describe what the word 'Gospel' means and how you can become a Christian. That's the first step toward allowing Jesus and the Bible to change your life.

A Word About Style

I have written this book in conversational style. I don't use fancy language, and some of it may even be grammatically incorrect to make it more natural to read. It's not meant to impress the scholars. I want it to be casual and comfortable, like an old pair of jeans.

One of the things you will notice as you read this book is that you will occasionally find some repetition. I do that for a couple of reasons. The first is because it's a good teaching technique. Repetition means the student will likely learn the lesson faster and retain it better. The second reason, and actually the more important one for this book, is because there are illustrations and Scripture verses that simply apply to more than one section. To have left them out would have been to leave you with less understanding and depth in the section than was optimum. So if you find yourself saying, "Didn't I read this before?", then you may very well have. I tried not to do it too much, but what is in here is intentional.

Also, just as a personal preference, I don't like the common use of the pronouns 'him/her,' 'himself/herself,' and 'he/she' with the slashes. When I need to use personal pronouns to make the sentence make sense, I will alternate between 'he' and 'she' and 'him' and 'her,' etc. When you see one of those pronouns, please know that I am generally referring to both genders. When I'm not (as in the case of husbands and wives), you'll know.

So relax, put your feet up, grab a cup of something hot, and join me in some fun and exciting Bible time.

How To Read This Book

Now, go ahead and grab your Bible. It'll be a bit before we actually get into it, but just get used to having it next to you as you read. You can use any translation you'd like. If you don't have a Bible and don't know what I mean by 'translation,' then go to Appendix C, "How to Select the Right Bible." You'll definitely need one to get the most out of this book, so please don't skip this critical step.

My Bible is the New American Standard Bible, NASB. Unless I say otherwise, it's the one I'll be using wherever I include quotes. Your translation may be different in terms of the words it uses, but the meaning should essentially be the same.

Now, there is something important about this process that you need to be aware of. I would love it if this was a book you could read reclining in bed as you drop off to sleep, but it's really not. If you approach it that way, you're not going to get nearly as much out of it as you could. This is just a little instruction manual on how to draw close to Jesus and to use the Bible in a unique way. It's that relationship with Christ and your use of the Bible that will transform your life, and if you don't use the Bible as you read, you are cheating yourself.

If you just don't know where to begin, I have included a lot of information you may find useful in the Appendices. Check them out to see if there is anything there you could use to help you with this process.

I refer to the Bible frequently, and include many references to specific verses in parentheses. It looks like this (John 3:16). When you get to those notes, stop and read the verse(s) in your Bible. That's a critical part of this process. Read the verse. Please don't skip this step.

And whenever you've been referred to a specific verse, remember your mother's advice: *Look both ways before crossing the road.* Don't just read the single verse itself and expect to really understand it. *Always* read a few verses above and a few verses below to understand what they call 'the context.' Some of the most damaging 'truths' that have been drawn out of the Bible are at best misleading, and at worst heresies because they've been taken so badly out of context. Don't let that happen to you. Get a sense of what the author is trying to say in the section — not just the single verse.

Remember that the Bible is not there for you to interpret any way you choose. You need to try to understand what the *author* meant. In the end, the author is God working through the human authors, so you're trying to learn from and understand God.

Please know that this approach means that it is going to take you a little longer to get through this book than you might have originally thought. The whole purpose here is to help you incorporate some very important changes into your day that will radically improve your mental health. Although this book will give you ideas to help you, it's the changes in your life patterns that will make the big difference, and the biggest changes will be in your relationship with Christ and in how you use Scripture. You have to actually *use* it to get that life-changing benefit out of it.

If you don't know how to use your Bible at all, then stop here and go to Appendix D, "How to Use the Bible." In it I explain, step by step, how to navigate around your Bible. I explain how to find the different books of the Bible and the specific verses I'm referring to. I explain some of the codes, cross-references, and other items of curiosity you'll find when you get in there. If you're totally new to Bible reading, that's the place to start.

I have not included most of the text of the verses themselves for several reasons:

1. I want the Holy Spirit to have a chance to speak to you directly from Scripture,
2. If you're not already, I want you to get proficient at looking them up yourself,
3. I want you to learn to regard your Bible as a comfortable, old friend,
4. I don't want to impose my version on you, and
5. They would take up way too much space.

Even if you see yourself as being familiar with the Bible and its verses, please do not skip the readings. The deeper understandings of the subject won't come from my writings — they come from

God — and you never know what God is going to tell you through a particular verse *this* time. I've seen it happen way too many times where people release years of pain because they followed this simple guideline, and came across the one verse that set them free. God wants to speak to you through these verses — don't muzzle Him by not reading them. A single encounter with the holy God can change everything.

Except for the Appendices, read the chapters in order. The book builds on lessons and concepts, and you might miss something critical that you need for later chapters.

Let me suggest that you stop now and read through the short Footnotes section in the back of the book. There are some footnotes that you won't care about because they're just the references to the sources of information in the text, but there are others you will find interesting. If you pre-read them, then when you get to that section, you'll have some memory that there was something interesting about it and go back and look. Otherwise, you'll tend to just ignore the footnotes altogether (like I usually do) and miss some interesting stuff.

Also, have a pen and paper handy. You may have thoughts, insights, questions you need to look up later, whatever. Have it handy so you don't have to break your train of thought to find something to write on. I've also included some blank pages in the back of the book. If you'd like to personalize it, you can jot down some notes there as well.

Get a partner, if you'd like, to work through the process with you, or use it in your small group studies. You can support one another, you can help each other with questions as you go, and you can hold each other accountable for working the process. But the biggest benefit to the partnership approach is that it will be a lot of fun. Christian fellowship is always a very good thing.

I have included an "Intermission Verse to Ponder" periodically throughout the book. It has no particular relationship to anything in the surrounding text; it us just meant to give you a break and give you something Scriptural to think about for a moment. Read them, and see if there's something there that God can speak to you through about your own life.

Finally, before we get started, a friend of mine once told me that before people are going to be interested in what I have to say, they're going to have to know a little about me personally. To that end, I have included my testimony and some information about my history in Appendix F, "Introduction to the Author." If you are curious about who I am and where I am coming from, that's where you'll find it.

My Disclaimers

If you have read Appendix F, "Introduction to the Author," then you know that I am not a Bible scholar. I'm just an ordinary Christian who loves the Lord, just like you. And just like you, I have a lot more to learn. There are many concepts and precepts that aren't included here, most of which are because I have yet to discover them myself. The opportunities for discovery are endless. I pray that you will join me on my continuing journey with Jesus, to find more treasures, more faith, more love, and more of Him through His holy Word.

My apologies to any pastors, Bible scholars, theologians, etc., who might honor me by reading this book. I know there are a lot of things that I have missed because I don't have the training you have. My heart, though, is to keep it simple and personal. I want anyone with a heart for God and a desire to draw closer to Him to understand it and grow from it. I want this to inspire people to start looking deeper on their own with the many resources that are available, and know that they can do it without the formal training. There are people for whom formal training is simply not an option, but there is much that they can gain from a deeper study on their own. My hope in writing this book without that formal training is to personally demonstrate to them that that is true.

And finally, I know there are going to be some who are going to read this book and exclaim, "Yeah, but you don't understand my situation!" That's so true. I don't. I can't. Even if you and I were sitting in the room together, I couldn't really, really understand what your unique situation is doing to you inside your head and inside your unique life. No one can. But what I ask is that you understand that these are general precepts meant to give you a different way of looking at your situation and some additional tools in dealing with it, regardless of what it is. I pray that they will be helpful to you in some way. If you feel like this misses a point that is unique to you, then again, please see a professional Christian therapist. Let them help you navigate your stormy waters and get from this book what helps you. There is much that you can learn here, even if it doesn't completely resolve your issue. As my mother-in-law says, "Take the chicken and leave the bones."

How This Book Is Organized

Section 1 — Introduction: Chapter 1 — This is the chapter you are reading now. It gives my thoughts about the purpose of this book, how to proceed reading it, and for whom it is intended. But you already knew that.

Section 2 — Foundational Issues: Chapters 2-5 — This section offers my thoughts about what the phrase 'mental health' means, how I define the Bible and how I think about it, who the Holy Spirit is, and what spiritual gifts are to the believer. It also includes my thoughts on the importance of falling in love with the man Jesus of Nazareth, and how that can be accomplished. These chapters are meant to ensure that you know my position regarding some foundational Christian concepts.

Section 3 — Techniques: Chapters 6-10 — This section provides specific techniques for reading and studying Scripture with a mental health perspective. These chapters represent the 'meat' of this book, including how to read the Bible and think about what you are reading, and why memorizing Scripture is so critical as it relates to mental health. It presents some examples of how to read the Bible a little differently, as well as some specific suggestions regarding prayer from a mental health perspective.

Section 4 — Application: Chapters 11-20 — This section provides practical applications for specific situations. It includes examples of how to apply the lessons to your life, including how to increase your faith, how to deal with trials, and how to know God's will for your life. This is where you will learn how to apply the techniques you've been studying and gives you specific examples of how to change 'boring' Old and New Testament stories into life-changing experiences. This is where the real change will begin.

Section 5 — Summary: Chapter 21 — This chapter brings it all home in a concise, easy-to-reference synopsis. It is where you go when you hear yourself say, "Now, what was it she said to do?" It also contains a message to professional counselors, and how they might be able to use this book to help their clients.

Appendices — The Appendices provide some basic Christian information intended for those of you who don't see yourselves as Christians, or for the brand-new Christians who don't know how to proceed. It presents the Gospel of Jesus Christ, and some suggestions on how to select the right Bible and how to use it once you have it. It offers 'Now What?' guidance for new believers, and a Bibliography, References, and Recommendations section for additional reading and Internet browsing. It ends with my history and testimony.

An important note: If you consider yourself to be seriously depressed or in some other significant crisis, then see a professional Christian therapist and ask them to help you work this process, encourage you, and pray with you. You need connection, understanding, and a loving heart to join you in the journey. You will find those things in Christ, but if you're in crisis, this process may be too overwhelming initially if you try to do it alone. Second Corinthians Chapter 1 says that, "we comfort others as we are comforted by God." It is in His plan that we comfort when we can, and get comfort when we need to. Get help.

As a final thought, a precious client read this book before its publishing, and shared her thoughts with me about how I should end this chapter. I offer them to you from her:

> "The only suggestion I might have is to add a bit about the process — what's going on...like God getting into our deepest thoughts and secrets, that it's going to be a challenge, that we have pretty stubborn patterns that need to break, and that no matter what, God is holding out His hand to walk us through."

Remember that the idea of this book is to help you draw closer to God and into the arms of Jesus, and to realize that the study of Scripture can be the most exhilarating experience you will ever have.

Ok then, enough about the book. Let's get started.

SECTION 2

****

FOUNDATIONAL ISSUES

II — DEFINING MENTAL HEALTH

Pathology Versus Dysfunction

The term 'mental health' conjures up many pictures. It spans the gamut from mild, situational-dependent depression to life-altering Schizophrenia and other major illnesses. In this chapter, I'd like to set up some parameters and definitions.

Pathology is a term that refers to a disease. For some of the serious mental illnesses such as Major Depressive Disorder, Bipolar Disorder, Obsessive Compulsive Disorder, Panic Disorder and others, there seems to be a strong genetic component to them, as well as some environmental factors. This means that the tendency to have them may come from your parents, but your environment could either cause them to develop in the first place, or could certainly exacerbate them when they do develop. In this way, there is a difference between the more serious, pathological, mental health disorders like those I've listed above, and some of the other behaviors and attitudes that wreak havoc on our lives.

I do not claim that the application of Biblical principles will cure Schizophrenia, Personality Disorders, or some instances of Major Depressive Disorder.[2] These are likely candidates for medication along with long term therapy. I believe there is scriptural support for the judicious application of psychotropic medications at the right time, depending on the individual situation. The purpose of these medications, whether temporary or permanent, is to stabilize the client emotionally and mentally. They will then be better able to apply Biblical principles to their attitudes and behaviors, glorifying God and enhancing their own lives to the greatest extent possible.

It is also my deep conviction that, regardless of the existence or seriousness of underlying pathology, there are ways of thinking, habits, and life patterns that we pick up that will either add to or detract from our lives. If they detract, I call them *dysfunction.* No one is immune to dysfunction, but **everyone can be helped when Biblical principles are applied**, regardless of the underlying pathology.

Examples of dysfunction include anger, poor relationships, loneliness, bitterness, irresponsible behavior, lack of motivation to function, hopelessness, and purposelessness.

These issues are usually the result of environmental factors rather than pathology, or they can occur in conjunction with pathology. In either case, the dysfunction makes life extremely difficult for the client, as well as those around him.

The Bible addresses all of these issues and gives us direct guidance on how to resolve them. It's *never* a condemning boney-finger pointed and wagging in your face. It doesn't say, "get with the program and shape up." It doesn't say, "just pick yourself up by your bootstraps." God demonstrates and guides with an occasional gentle poke in the side to get our attention, and then gives us practical and loving instruction. His way is to ask for a series of baby steps, and then celebrates with us when they come. The only time Jesus admonishes someone severely is:

- when they impose legalistic rules that do people harm (Mark 3:5, Luke 13:15-16),
- when they impede other people from getting close to Him (Mark 10:14),
- when they cause His children to stumble (Matthew 18:6-7),
- when they dishonor the Father (John 2:13-16).

He reaches out to those who are poor, suffering, or have sinned; so don't be afraid to take His hand.

How Our Past Affects Our Present

Many of us have a terrible life history. There is so much abuse in this country, it boggles the mind. I won't go into statistics here, but please be assured that if you are a survivor of abuse, you are not alone. In any given room of 20-30 people, you will probably have 10 or more who have some sort of abuse in their past. It's horrible, it's tragic, it's infuriating, and it's terribly, terribly sad.

If you are a survivor of abuse and have never been treated by a trauma therapist, then in all likelihood, you are still experiencing some effects from it. The common reactions include: anger or rage (overreacting to negative situations), relationship difficulties, often some hopelessness, boundary issues (e.g., people walking on you and taking advantage of you, you being overly vulnerable to people, you being either sexually promiscuous or sexually closed off and fearful, etc.), as well as anxiety, depression, panic attacks, and other symptoms.

On the other side of the spectrum, some people find themselves feeling better than everyone else. They come across as smarter and more important than other people. They often become excessively high achievers, are driven to perfection, only associate with the best or most important people, attend only the best universities. They tend to come across as 'better than...,' well, you get the idea. Believe it or not, these are also often symptoms of abuse as well. If you see any of these symptoms in yourself, get help. If you know someone like this, chances are good that you don't like them very much because of their air of superiority. They need help as badly as the person who is rageful or depressed. Encourage them, if you can, to get that help. Way down deep inside, they're miserable. They just hide it differently.

The good news is that none of this is a life sentence. If you are a survivor of abuse and are still suffering, please understand that your trip to recovery is going to be a little slower and tougher than what some others might experience. You have a tough battle to wage, but be uplifted — *it is a winnable battle*! So be patient with yourself and know there is light at the end of the tunnel — and that Light is Jesus Christ. You and He together can defeat the enemy!

Note: At this point I would like to say, if you're a survivor of severe abuse or trauma and are still suffering, try to find a Christian therapist who has special training in trauma. Bible-based therapy will bring you through it, but you shouldn't do it alone. You'll need guidance to help you deal with some memories that might crop up, some emotional reactions that might surprise you, or even some resistance to the apparent 'simplicity' of this approach. Please get the help you need in order to get the most out of this book.

Sin Versus Circumstance[3]

I pray that this section is received with the love and compassion with which it is offered. Jesus was described as the "Rock of Offense" (Rom 9:33, 1 Pet 2:8) and sometimes what must be said is simply what must be said. Please be assured, however, that it is not intended to offend or lay a guilt trip on anyone. This is intended to help you understand the relationship between sin and mental health, and to help you understand just how much power you actually have over your own mental health. It is intended to set you free.

First, let me state my disclaimer: There are absolutely circumstances over which we have no control, and which have directly caused or exacerbated our state of mental distress. The death of a loved one, loss of a job and the family welfare, failure to achieve our life goals, major changes in our lives, a history of abuse or trauma, etc., are each circumstances which could be out of our control and which could cause depression or other mental distress. The resulting distress is normal, and I am not going to minimize these events' impact on our mental health and the devastating effects of them on our lives. Nor is it my intention to make you feel guilty for having those feelings. This is about regaining the power through Christ to have the lives we want and that He wants for us — the life abundant (John 10:10).

I would also like to say that many people will tell you that your depression, grief, anxiety, etc, are the result of an underlying lack of faith and not trusting God, and that this is sin. Be careful with this one. I agree that when our faith and trust improve, our obedience will become more consistent, we'll have a better relationship with Jesus, and our mental health will improve. I would also say, however, that our walk with Christ is about building our faith progressively through our relationship with Him, and that it isn't helpful to beat ourselves up for our lack of faith and to call it sin. I spend an entire chapter on that issue later in the book, but for now, understand that your faith is what it is, and although there are lessons you'll be learning as you go through this process that will help you build your faith, give yourself a break now and don't allow the enemy to condemn you for your apparent 'lack of faith.'

Sin that is foundationally a lack of faith and sin that is willful disobedience to God are two different things, although they are related, and both will have an impact on your mental health. The fact is that there are many habits which we have picked up that, in the final analysis, are sin and cause us mental distress. We will deal with many of them in this book, and hopefully the Holy Spirit will help you see where they apply to you and you can find the courage to confront them head-on. In the mean time, remember that this is about God's *grace*.

Fibromyalgia

For those of you who don't know, fibromyalgia is a disease where the sufferer has chronic, widespread pain in muscles and soft tissues surrounding their joints, as well as fatigue, and sometimes terrible fatigue. Very often, it will control their lives in a devastating way.

I recently went through special training on Trauma Therapy.[4] The instructor said, "I'm not saying it's not possible, but so far, I've never met a single client who had fibromyalgia who did not also have a history of trauma. When we deal with the trauma, the symptoms of fibromyalgia are either significantly reduced, or vanish altogether."

For those of you who are fibromyalgia sufferers, as you work through this book and implement the processes into your life, you may find that your physical pain will begin to diminish. Many of my clients have told me that their doctors view their fibromyalgia symptoms as partly psychological, which means that their stress, anxiety, anger, unforgiveness and the like are causing their muscles to stay in a more contracted position much of the time, thus increasing their pain. If you can learn to find peace, contentment, forgiveness, and relief from anger and bitterness through a renewed relationship with Christ, then I am convinced that as your mood and demeanor relax, your muscles will relax, and you will feel a significant reduction in your fibromyalgia pain (Psalm 42:11; Proverb 4:20-22).

Please stop now and read Psalms 42:11. It's on the inside title page of this book, or you can look up both of the referenced passages in your Bible. It is pivotal to the essence of this book and your physical and mental health.

What Does Good Mental Health Look Like?

If a person is mentally healthy, what would they look like? There are some specific characteristics that are common in people who are the healthiest mentally.

I need to draw a distinction here for mental health as it pertains to believers and non-believers. For a Christian to have good mental health, they must have a healthy relationship with Jesus. Many of the characteristics below will naturally improve as your relationship with Him improves and as He works with you through His Holy Spirit. Without that relationship, some of these characteristics are very difficult to attain and some are virtually impossible. In all cases, a relationship with Jesus facilitates the characteristic and gives the believer the strength to achieve it. I have tried to address what the characteristic is, and then how a relationship with God helps the believer achieve that characteristic.

The clearest indication of good Christian mental health is **contentment with any circumstance**. The Apostle Paul said, "I can do all things through Christ Who gives me strength" [Phil 4:13]. People misunderstand that as meaning, 'I can perform any *task* through Christ' and certainly it is true that all things are possible with God. But what Paul was talking about here was being able to live in wealth or poverty, hardship or comfort, chaos or peace, prison or freedom. It means He is totally content no matter his circumstances, or what life situation he encounters or what gets thrown his way. He wrote that while chained to guards in a prison cell.

If you are not content with your life circumstance — bad job, bad spouse, bad home environment, or bad health — then God can help you through your study of His Word. Please don't misunderstand this as saying, "just deal with it." That's not what this means at all. Studying His word can provide a deep, penetrating contentment where you *know* that God is in control and that He loves you. Scripture can enhance your trust that God has some purpose for allowing it, and He's with you through it. You can handle this situation through Christ who gives you strength. This is inner peace in the midst of the storm.

People who identify themselves as being mentally healthy and happy generally **get along well with people**. That doesn't mean they always get their own way. It means they've learned to navigate a difficult situation in such a way as to either negotiate an equitable solution, or they have simply resolved to be flexible enough to put it into its proper perspective and let it go. The goal of a mentally healthy person in interpersonal issues is peace, resolution, harmony — not winning. Winning takes a distant back seat.

That's also not to say they're milk toasts and doormats, however. Mentally healthy people have **solid boundaries** as well. That means that they know what's in the best interest of the situation and aren't afraid to say 'no' when 'no' is the most appropriate answer. They also know how to 'let in' what people say that is helpful (even if it hurts), and 'keep out' what people say that is harmful (even if it feels good, e.g., a flattering compliment that is untrue and meant to manipulate). Their boundaries form a door to their hearts over which they have total control.

Mentally healthy people **aren't offended easily**, and when they are offended, they seek resolution quickly. They aren't afraid to confront someone who has offended them, they quickly accept apologies offered, and they aren't afraid to apologize and make restitution to those whom they have offended. Again, the relationship is the goal — not winning or being 'right.'

Mentally healthy people tend to be **more open and honest** about their perspective and feelings. They aren't afraid to speak their minds because their hearts are pure and they understand that the ultimate goal is to love one another. Communication then becomes a means of enhancing that goal, and the fear of hurting someone's feelings is subordinated to the higher goal of honoring God through open and healthy interpersonal relationships. Jesus said that people will know we are His by our love for one another (John 13:35). Unless we communicate openly and are willing to share our feelings with a loving, gentle, and quiet spirit bent toward resolution, we cannot have that love. Mentally healthy people know that, and they know how to do it.

Mentally healthy people know that it **isn't about them**, and they're okay with that. God says it's about Him, and He's made it about our fellow man. We are to love one another (1 John, many references; Romans 13:8; 1 Thessalonians 4:9, others) and regard others as more important than ourselves (Philippians 2:3). Much of our dysfunction comes from our natural tendency to make everything about us, and to react negatively when *they're* trying to make it about them. It becomes a dog-eat-dog world for us, and we feel the need to defend our rights.

Mentally healthy people have **submitted their rights to God**, so there's nothing to defend.

Mentally healthy people have **purpose in their lives**. Rick Warren popularized the concept of the purpose-driven life in his book by the same name. God gave us the need to have value, to find purpose in our lives. In *The Purpose-Driven Life*, Pastor Rick gave us a framework for purpose that applies to *all* Christians. This is a critical component of having a fulfilling Christian life, and if you haven't read it, it is a must-read.

The Purpose-driven Life doesn't try to address, however, another very important component of purpose, and that is our *individual* purpose in God's world. Mentally healthy people feel a very profound and penetrating sense of **their own, unique, individual purpose**. They know where they're going and why, or they're excited and motivated to find out what it is. They know God placed them in this world for a purpose, and they're content with that alone. As driven as they are to accomplish their God-given purpose, though, they also understand that God is their driver and their power-source, and they are to partner with and depend upon Him. With the arms and oars God gave them, they row the boat and trust that God is steering.

Mentally healthy people are **resilient in dealing with trials**. Trials are a fact of life, and becoming a Christian doesn't immunize you from them. Mentally healthy people can see that their trials are not personal, that God isn't 'out to get them' or punish them for some distant past sin, and that with a proper perspective, they can use the trial to grow. Mentally healthy people understand — in the midst of the trial — what the atheist Fredericke Neitchze stumbled onto when he said, "That which does not kill us makes us stronger." (Clearly, the truth he missed was that even that which *kills* us makes us stronger, as well! Praise God for that.)

Mentally healthy people **don't gossip**. They don't need to prove their own importance by knowing what other people don't know, or by seeming to be 'better than' others who have flaws. They know they're sinners, and they exhibit grace and mercy and not condemnation and judgment. They remember that words have meaning, and they also have the power of life and death. They use their words very carefully to encourage and strengthen the body of Christ.

Mentally healthy people **tend not to complain**. That's not to say they *never* complain. I've never met anyone who never complains (including me). It's just that they complain far less, what they complain about is generally shorter term or pertains to less significant issues, and they typically catch themselves early on and resolve the complaint in their minds in a different way. They understand that complaining is prideful, and that it says, "I'm a better judge of this situation than God is, and I don't trust that He could help me out of it if He wanted to, or that He would if He could." Rather than complain, mentally healthy people turn to God and cry out to Him for help.

Mentally healthy people **tend not to ask "Why."** They know that "It is what it is," and resolve to figure out how to deal with the reality of it rather than plague themselves with questions about why it is happening. Asking "Why" says, "I don't trust you, God. I have to understand what you're doing here to feel safe and at peace." It says, "If you don't explain it to me, I'm not going to be content, I'm not going to learn the lesson, and I may not even cooperate with the trial." God says, "Trust Me, even if you don't understand."

Mentally healthy people aren't afraid to **do things anonymously** because they aren't about getting their own glory. God gets the glory and they're thrilled.

Mentally healthy people understand that **obedience to the will of God equals happiness**. If you truly crave happiness, then purpose in your heart to be obedient to Him. Read His Word, figure out what it is He's asking you to do today, and do everything you can to do that. When you spend a minute with Him in the morning, remember to say, "God, please speak to me today so I know how You want my day to go. Please give me clear direction, and guide my steps. I promise to be obedient to Your still small voice."

God wants us to be blessed and joy-filled because it draws people to us, and thus to Him. As you love Him through your obedience to Him, He will bless you by filling your heart with all spiritual blessings, and you will see these wonderful characteristics of sound mental health manifested in your life.

It is an absolute truth that:

The more obedient you are — the more joy-filled you are.

Thoughts and Feelings

Mentally healthy people know that **thoughts and feelings are two different things**. This is a huge issue, so I gave it its own section here. We often confuse the two. We either think that they're the same thing and that the phrase 'thoughts and feelings' is redundant, or we let our feelings run our lives rather than our thoughts, thinking that if we *feel* something is true, then it must *be* true. If we *feel* like someone doesn't like us, then clearly they don't. If we *feel* that God is angry at us, well then clearly He must be. If we *feel* unhappy, then clearly we have something to be unhappy about.

Please hear me: Thoughts and feelings are two different things.

Many people yield to their feelings because they don't know they have a choice, but doing so can be paralyzing and destructive to your mental health. I would like to offer you a different way.

Think about your feelings, and decide if they serve you or hurt you. I'm not trying to tell you that your feelings aren't real — they certainly are. But what I am telling you is that very often, our feelings are a result of what we're thinking, how we're interpreting our world, our baggage from the past, and the meaning we've given to our circumstances.

"I don't believe that!" you say. No? Consider this:

> You have to go to the Department of Motor Vehicles to get your license renewed. The line is wrapped halfway around the room and it takes you 30 minutes just to get to the counter. Then the elderly lady behind the counter seems distracted, disinterested, and rude, and suddenly you understand why the line is so long. She takes forever and makes mistakes, increasing the time it takes to get this frustrating chore accomplished. Then to top it off, when you say something about the long line, she treats you like you're an inconvenience to *her* and she snaps at you. Inside, you're now raging, and you might have even snapped back at her. You leave, cursing her under your breath, angry and frustrated at the audacity of her to treat you that way. You grew up in a family where your mother treated you that way, and the *last* thing you're going to do is to take that attitude from some DMV clerk. Who the heck does she think she is, anyway?!
>
> Then on your way out, someone you know is coming in and you chat. In the course of that conversation, your friend tells you that the clerk you just dealt with has recently been told that her husband of 30 years is dying of cancer, he's in a great deal of pain, and there's nothing they can do. Furthermore, she can't even get off of work to go visit him in the hospital because she's used all of her leave already. When she's not at work, she lives at the hospital. Suddenly, the inconvenience you've just experienced seems trivial, shallow, and insensitive.

Dare I surmise that your feelings about the experience might change? My guess is that you would be feeling guilty for your reaction, and you'd probably start praying for the woman you were

Therapy with God

just cursing. The situation hasn't changed a bit, but your feelings certainly would.

Your feelings ended up being more the result of what you assumed about the woman, the meaning you'd given her attitude, and your own baggage than about the actual situation itself. Your thoughts drove your feelings. When your thoughts changed, so did your feelings.

Let me repeat that: Your thoughts, misguided as they initially were, drove your feelings.

Ok, now that I've proven to you that your feelings can be the result of your thoughts *about* a situation rather than the actual situation itself, consider another example that strikes a little closer to home, but may be a little tougher.

Let's say you're dealing with someone at work who rubs you the wrong way, and you go home every day anxious and angry, and it seems to be escalating. The guy is just a total jerk and means to make your life miserable, and furthermore, it's working, right? You've tried and tried, but there's nothing you can do to change the situation.

You then read in your Bible that "God causes all things to work together for good to those who love God" (Romans 8:28). Do you really believe that God is in control? You now have a choice: You can either think this guy at work is just a total jerk who means to ruin your life, or you can choose to think he's been placed there by God to help you develop your character and learn how to deal with difficult people in preparation for something (or someone) bigger down the road. It's a choice you now have to make. Whether you go home angry and anxious or at peace is at stake. Whether your witness improves or suffers is at stake.

If you *feel* your way through the situation, then you'll convince yourself that he's just a total jerk. But if you *think* your way through it, you can see this irritating person as a 'gift' from God to train you for some future battle. Then you'll focus on honoring God's purpose for their place in your growth, and less on the irritating nature of their personality. You'll work at learning how to deal with them productively, reducing the negative affect they have on you.

Therapy with God

What you choose to *think* about their role in your life will have a huge affect on how you *feel* at the end of the day.

See, the fact is that you have a lot more control over your feelings than you think you do. We've been trained by society to think that our feelings *just are what they are*. We've been told that our feelings are *valid*, and as part of the secular mental health therapy approach, we seek to have our feelings *validated* by others. We are taught that for our feelings to change, the situation needs to change.

Hear me now — that is *a lie straight from the pit of hell!* Not every feeling you have will be valid. Was your feeling about the DMV clerk valid? Based on what you thought, maybe, but based on the reality? I'd say not. Satan wants you upset, anxious, angry, offended. It serves *his* purpose for your life for you to be feelings-driven because it ruins your witness and drags you farther from God.

God has a better way. Change your thoughts and perspective that you have *about* the situation and your feelings about it will change, too.

Boot-camp and Battles

Let's try a very tough example. Let's say you're in a dead marriage. Your spouse never pays attention to you and you're lonely. You've tried every trick in the book, but nothing brings your spouse around, and for years you've remained in this state.

Now, let's just say I have some inside word from God. I happen to know that God is working on you through this difficult marriage. He's paying very close attention and has a very difficult job He needs to assign to you years down the road. There's a child who is going to grow up one day and be in a marriage very similar to yours. To survive her marriage and draw closer to God, she is going to have to have some very wise and loving counsel from a Godly woman who's been there. That woman is you.

To help this young woman, you need tremendous patience and you need a very close relationship with God yourself, where you have learned to love Him and lean on Him in all sorts of circumstances. If you can succeed at this future job, the young woman's life will be transformed, her children's lives will be transformed, her husband will come around, God will be glorified, and people will come to Him by watching this transformation take place. Many people's future depends on you performing this one job. It's a critical job that He feels you're the most qualified to handle, but He has some 'boot camp' He needs to put you through before He can assign this extremely important job for you to do.

If you *knew* that was true, would it make a difference to you in your current situation? If God asked you to go through boot-camp so you could have a significant impact on many people's eternal destination for Him, would you be willing to do it?

Well, I'm here to tell you that that's one of the primary things our trials are about (James 1:2-4; 1 Peter). Very often, they're 'boot camp' preparing us to accomplish our divine purpose. He can't send you into battle with a machine-gun in your hand until you've gone under the ropes in the training field.

As an illustration of how important this belief-system is, imagine a soldier who refuses to work hard at his training. Oh, he'll half-heartedly go through the motions, but he'll complain the whole time and refuse to do anything more than what will keep him out of trouble with his superiors. He'll get through basic training and be sent off to war, but is that the soldier you want fighting next to your brother or father or son or daughter? Is that the soldier you want fighting next to you? What are his chances of returning safely home again? He missed the opportunity to be prepared by not taking his basic training seriously.

If you think about your current environment as an inconvenience or a burden on your life, then you leave yourself open to the attacks of the enemy and will be in bondage to your feelings. But if you view it as basic training for God's battles to come, does it help you put your life into a different perspective? Does it take the edge off of your feelings somewhat?

Mentally healthy people know that **life is a series of boot camps and battles**, more training and tougher battles.[5] If you don't view it that way, you'll be ill-prepared when the battles come — and they *will* come, again and again.

Summary

Now, in case I've totally depressed you with this chapter, please understand that this is the ultimate — the *goal*. I've never met anyone (including myself) who exhibits all of these qualities, and I doubt I ever will this side of Heaven. This list, however, should give you an idea of the areas in which you need God's help to grow. We are God's work-in-progress. He delights in the 'baby-steps' we take as we learn to lean on Him more and more. Stick with it. Stay the course. You won't regret a minute of it.

In general, mentally healthy people tend to be content, well-centered, successful in life (as defined by God — not man), relational, purpose-filled, and epitomize what God means by *peace* and *joy*. Jesus, as you study His life, exemplified all of the elements of good mental health I've defined above. We will discuss some of these attributes as we go through the following chapters, but first, let's review some characteristics about the Bible.

III — WHAT IS THE BIBLE?

What It Is

The Bible is a collection of 66 books written over a period of 1500 years, by 44 different authors, over three separate continents, chronicling the lives and history of the Jewish people, and then Jesus and the early Christian church.

But it is so much more.

The Bible is God's word. That means that although it was written by 44 different individuals, those individuals were influenced by God in such a way that every single word of it came directly from the mouth of God. The Bible refers to itself as having been inspired by God (2 Timothy 3:16). That means that God literally "breathed" the words into the minds of the human authors. When you read the Bible, understand that it has all the authority of God, written in a way that you can comprehend it and apply it to your life.

The Bible is a history of the origin of the world, the origin of sin, the subsequent destruction of the world (except Noah and his family), and the repopulation of the planet.

It is the history of the Jewish people, from their origins with their father Abraham in 2000 BC, through many wars and tribulations, to the destruction of the temple in A.D. 70 and beyond.

It is a book about Jesus Christ, as the single plot throughout, with Him as the ultimate hero, from the first "In the Beginning" on page one of the Old Testament to the last "Amen" in the Book of Revelation.

It is a book about a fallen people's restoration and salvation by a sovereign and loving God, referring both to the people of Israel as well as to the sinful people of the rest of the world today. It is about treachery, betrayal, adultery — all against a loving God.

It is a book about forgiveness, restoration, mercy and grace.

The Bible is a book of lessons on how to live your life.

It is the prophesy of the coming Messiah and its fulfillment.

The very existence of the Bible is a miracle. The documentary, "The Forbidden Book," shows the historical attempts to destroy the Bible. God sovereignly and miraculously saved the Bible for us.

The Bible describes itself as sharper than any two-edged sword (Hebrews 4:12; Revelation 1:16). In this way, it can help one divide and distinguish (visualize a swift cutting action) between selfish motives and Godly ones, between fleshly lusts and desires and a heart bent toward God, and between good and evil. It protects us against temptations and spiritual forces. The Bible is a book of revelation and prophesy, instruction and illumination, love and encouragement, and a wonderful vehicle for getting to know the Lord. It's personal. It's God's love letter to me, and to you.

Learn to regard the Bible that way — written personally and uniquely to you — and you won't be able to put it down. Then, it will miraculously transform your life.

What It Isn't

The Bible is not a book to be used to beat people up. Convict, yes. Show the difference between good and evil, no question. Help you discern the path you're on, absolutely. But it is *never* to be used as a weapon to hurt people. That's not God's way, and when Moses struck the rock twice after God told him to *speak* to it, God forbade Him to go into Canaan, the land of promise, the land flowing with milk and honey promised to their fathers by God (Numbers 20:12). By striking the rock, Moses showed God as an angry God bent on punishing His children when they're disobedient. He mischaracterized who God is. That's not God's heart, and it's not His way.

God will show us the error of our ways, and sometimes we don't like His methods. Sometimes He needs to crank up the heat on us to get our attention. Sometimes, His methods may even result in our deaths, but God does not punish. He disciplines, He rebukes, and He allows natural consequences. But He *does not* punish. The difference is huge. Discipline says, "I love you enough and want you to grow enough to suffer with you as you learn the hard way not to go down the wrong path." Punishment speaks of vengeance and the self-serving agenda of the punisher. Discipline is for the benefit of and yields a positive result in the one disciplined. Punishment is for the gratification of the punisher.

God's discipline is pure and perfect. He loves us more than we love ourselves or even our own children, and His Word reflects that over and over and over.

How The Bible Is Organized

Briefly, the Bible is physically organized into two major sections: The Old Testament and the New Testament, each of which are made up of many of what we call 'books.' Most likely, you already knew that.

What I really want you to understand, though, is that the Bible is *One Book*, not 66, and not even two. You cannot separate the two Testaments and view them apart from one another and have either of them make sense. The Old Testament, the history of the Jews, is actually a progressive revelation of the character and purpose of Jesus Christ. It leaves us with the question, "Where's the Lamb" (Genesis 22:7) who will finally and completely save mankind from doom? The New Testament is the answer to that question. Without one side of this equation, the other side stands in curious isolation, without real meaning or completeness.

God told Moses, "Tell them I AM sent you" (Exodus 3:14). Moses could have legitimately asked "I AM?? You are *what*?" or "You are *who*?" It's a strange name. God left the readers of the Old Testament with that curious unanswered question. Jesus, throughout the New Testament, answers that question. "I am the Bread of Life," "I am the Light," "I am the Way and the Truth and the Life," "I am the Good Shepherd." The phrase "I am" is repeated over and over and over in the New Testament by Jesus as if to say, "I am the answer to your question."

Jesus *is* the answer to our questions. All of them. Regard the Old and New Testaments as a single book, and you'll be amazed at how it all comes together and comes to life.

Symbolism In The Bible

One of the things that persuades me that the Bible is supernaturally inspired by God is the simplicity and complexity of it, all at the same time. A child can read it and understand who Jesus is and what it means to be going to heaven, and yet the greatest scholars of all time can spend a lifetime studying it and never reach the end of their work.

The symbolism in the Bible is one of the miraculous things God used to convey, on a gut level, the truths about Christ. I think it would be worthwhile at this point to show you some of the symbolism in the Bible and spend a minute seeing how it works.

Consider, for example, Moses. You know the story. Moses went into Egypt to rescue the Jews and bring them out of captivity. Remember Charlton Heston's, "LET MY PEOPLE GO!" Chilling. In addition to being an historically accurate account of what happened in Egypt, consider the parallels between that story and our own salvation.

Think of Egypt as being symbolic, a 'picture' if you will, of the world system and its sin, and Moses is a symbol of Jesus. Just as Moses rescued the Jews out of Egypt, Jesus rescued us out of a life of sin in the world. Moses' rescue of the Jews from Egypt is then a perfect picture — a physical illustration — of the Gospel of Jesus Christ. As they become more and more complex, these symbols and illustrations in the Old Testament give us a deeper understanding of New Testament concepts. The story of Moses and Egypt is an extremely simple example just to give you an idea of how it works. Every story in the Old Testament can be seen through that lens to be an important lesson to us of how we should live our lives, some New Testament doctrine or truth, or of a character quality of Jesus

Therapy with God

Christ Himself. Finding them and figuring them out is one of the most exciting treasure hunts on which you will ever embark.

I heard a sermon recently where the Pastor described the Old Testament as a 'Video' of the New Testament instructions.[6] Much like a video might enhance the five-page assembly instructions of the toy you bought your ten-year-old son for Christmas, so the Old Testament illustrations enhance the instructions and concepts of the New Testament.

For example, in many of the stories, as was the case with Moses, Egypt can be seen as symbolic of the world system and our sinful nature. Noah, Moses, and Joshua can be understood to teach us something about Christ and how we are to relate to Him. Rocks and stones can often be used to illustrate something of Christ and His role as the Rock upon which we build our spiritual house, and the Rock upon which the Church is built. There are others as well, too exhaustive to treat fully here. As you get deeper and deeper into your own study of Scripture, you will start to see the patterns unfolding, and you will hear God telling you through your readings some special concept He wants you to reflect on *today*. The stories can be life-changing once you see them as relevant today, and more particularly, as relevant to you. I present some examples later in the book to give you a better idea as to how you can find these stories and apply them to your life.

Having now been introduced to the concept, let me give you another very simple illustration I will draw on later in the book. Joshua (an image of Christ in this story) goes through the Jordan River, parted by God, to take the Jewish people to the land of promise. This is a beautiful 'video' of Christ taking us through the Bible to get us to our Christian Promised Land, a deeper and more personal relationship with Him.

The more you read and study Scripture, including the Old Testament, the more you'll know Jesus, and the more you'll discover the peace and joy — "the land flowing with milk and honey," the "abundant Christian life" — that God has promised us. As Joshua had to wage war against the Canaanites and others in the land of promise, so must we wage war against the evil forces of our world to acquire the 'land' that God wants for us. Even though the Jews were 'saved' (e.g., rescued from Egypt) they spent 40 years in the wilderness, and many of them died there. Even though we're 'saved' because of our acceptance of Christ's sacrifice, we can spend an entire lifetime in our spiritual wilderness if we never 'cross the Jordan River' through God's Bible into the Promised Land of peace and joy in our lives.

Moses' rescue of the Jews from Egypt is a perfect picture of salvation. Joshua bringing the Jews into the land of promise and fighting the bad guys is a perfect picture of what we call *sanctification*, that is, the purification and separation of God's people for God's Holy purpose. While the Jews were in the wilderness, they were not accomplishing God's purpose for their lives. The same applies to us. They had a river to cross and wars to wage, and so do we.

When you say, "Why should I read the Bible?," also ask yourself, "Why should the Jews cross the Jordon River into Canaan?" It's the same question, with the same answer. You certainly don't have to, but that's where you will find God's Promised Land.

Each story in the Old Testament, as we will see as we study, is a picture of something God wants us to understand about Him, about ourselves, and about our ultimate relationship with Jesus.

Think about that concept. I will be using it again as we go through the following chapters.

Summary

The Bible, in a single volume, is many, many truths all rolled up in one. As you come to appreciate the miracle that it is, the miraculously inspired Word of God, you will see it from deeper and deeper levels. The more you understand that God is the author, the more you will trust what it says, the more you will purpose to be obedient to Him, and the more peace and joy you will experience.

IV — FALLING IN LOVE WITH JESUS

What Is Love?

This is a critical step, but one wrought with confusion and anxiety. Good Christian people will lament that they don't 'feel' the love for God they think they should, and so question their salvation.

A client once said to me that "love is a decision" and revolutionized my thinking and my life. Instinctively, I knew he was right. But how did that square with the messages we receive from Hollywood about love? Something was amiss.

I had to turn to the Greek to find the answer. If you never learn another word of Greek, learn this.

The Greeks have several different words for the word the Bible calls 'love.' I'll only describe two of them here, but the others are fascinating if you're so inclined. The two I'm going to describe are agape (pronounced uh-GAW-pay) and phileo (pronounced fih-LAY-oh). Sometimes when the Bible says, "love," it means agape, and sometimes it means phileo. Not knowing that there's a difference when you read the word 'love' in Scripture can be misleading in some cases. For now, though, just learn the meanings.

Agape is God's love for us. It's that self-sacrificial love that says, "Your needs are more important to me than my needs." Jesus' death on the cross was an act of agape love. It's not based on feelings and emotion, but a decision of the will simply to conduct your life putting someone else's needs before yours. It's unconditional. Your decision is not based on their behavior, their appreciation of your sacrifice, their reciprocal focus on your needs, your feelings, nothing. With agape love, you don't need recognition or reward of any kind. That's what it means to be unconditional. There are absolutely no conditions. My *agape* love for you is completely a decision of mine to make it *about and for you*. The emotions of agape love are *as a result of* the acts of love, not the source of them.

So, agape love is:

- God's Love
- Unconditional
- Self-sacrificial
- Not based upon your feelings for the other person
- Doesn't require familiarity — You don't even have to know them
- Action-based — It's something you *do*, not something you feel
- A choice
- Endless, "Love never dies"
- Not commonality-based — You don't have to have anything in common with the other person)
- Totally about the other person — My agape love for you is totally *about you!*

The feelings associated with agape love spring from the acts of love as you experience the joy of pure, selfless giving. The feelings are separate, though, from the love itself. If I'm agape loving you, then I am thrilled at the opportunity to serve you. Your being in my life gives me an opportunity to look outside of myself into the needs of another person and respond to those needs in a way that glorifies God. That helps me grow, and that pleases God, so it pleases me.

If I am agape loving you, you are making me a better person. That's not the same thing as you making me a happier person, although that certainly comes. You are making me a better person because I'm learning how to be selfless, I'm learning how to recognize another's needs, I am learning how to put myself into proper perspective, and I am learning how to be a Godlier person. I love

Therapy with God

you because I *choose* to love you regardless of what you do or how it benefits me from the world's standards. I choose to make that love about you. Again, Jesus was agape loving us from the cross.

If you saw the movie *Bruce, Almighty*, you'll remember the scene in the very end when Bruce and God were talking. Bruce had just been hit by a truck and supposedly died, and was in the presence of God. God asked Bruce if he wanted his girlfriend back. Bruce looked reflective, and said, "No. I want her to be happy. I want her to have someone in her life who treats her the way she deserves to be treated. If that's me, then so be it, but if it's not, then I just want her to be happy." God said, "Now, that's a prayer." That was agape love.

Phileo, on the other hand, is quite different. It says, "I really enjoy being with you. We have common goals and interests, our personalities mesh well together, you make me feel good, you make me feel good about me." As Jerry McGuire said, "You complete me." It is totally based on emotion and feelings. My phileo love for you will continue as long as we have common goals, interests, and the like. My phileo love for you is therefore, *very* conditional. My phileo love for you is absolutely based on my feelings, and is about *me* and how you make *me* feel. I call phileo love, "like on steroids."

So phileo love is:

- Brotherly love — Philadelphia is called 'The City of Brotherly Love, right?
- Commonality-based — You have things in common with the other person, goals, interests, personality styles, etc.
- Feelings based — When it's there, it feels *great,* and the feelings make me want more.
- Familiarity based — This is where they say, "You can't love someone you don't know."
- Conditional — It can die if the conditions change
- The Hollywood, "You complete me" kind of love
- 'Like' on steroids
- About me

My phileo love for you says, "I really enjoy your company. I enjoy being with you. You make me feel good about my life, about my day, about myself. I need you." So who's all that about? *Me!* There's not a shred of you in there.

When someone proclaims their undying love for you and your caution light is on, find out which kind of love they're talking about. It's a very important issue. Ask them to tell you what love means to them. Is their love about them, or about you? If it's about them, if it's purely the phileo love, then as soon as you no longer have common goals and interests, the love will start to fade. When you no longer complete them, the love will grow cold. As soon as you are no longer serving their needs, the love will die. I know many of you will understand what I mean. I've just described your life. Now you know why.

Now of course agape love is the goal, but I don't want to disparage the phileo love here. Phileo love is wonderful and it feels great. Both agape and phileo love are critical for a fulfilling relationship, whether that relationship is a marriage, a friendship, family, business partnership, anything. If one person is an agape lover and the other person is a phileo lover, then the agape lover will be sucked dry and eventually the relationship will implode. What every good relationship needs is the balance of both. A 'marriage made in heaven' has both, and that's a very good thing.

A marriage with nothing more than agape love on both sides lacks the thrill of the companionship. A marriage with nothing more than the phileo love on both sides will manifest itself in two people fighting for their rights and that their needs be met. You need balance for it to work.

Let me offer you a thought about parenting: The very sad thing is that all too often, our parents' love for us is more phileo than it is agape. If you feel like one or both of your parents weren't there for you or that something was missing, and yet you still feel that they loved you, then maybe they loved you in the only way they knew how. Maybe they loved you with the love that they received from their parents. Agape love is learned through experiencing it, and if we never experience it, it's extremely difficult to have it for others. It becomes an 'I have to take care of myself' world. Maybe all they had to give was phileo love. That's an extremely painful thing to consider. You may need help in learning how to deal with that. Get that help so you can understand it, forgive them for their shortfall, and learn to love them anyway with the agape love you're receiving from God. You will feel your inner core heal as you forgive them and release them.

Loving And Being In Love

God commands our love and He commands us to love our neighbors and our brethren. With those two definitions in mind, which *love* is He talking about? Of course, He's talking about agape. He commands you to *agape love* Him and them, but there's nothing in there about *phileo* loving anyone. You don't have to like them to agape love them. You don't even have to know them to love them. That's the miracle and the mystery of God's agape love.

He wants our unconditional love that is based on a decision of the will, not the fickle love that comes and goes with the changes of the conditions and our mood.

Love never dies? That's agape love, because it's a decision of the will, not something we're helpless victims of as our emotions wax and wane with the conditions. Agape love never dies. You can kill it off by making a different decision, but it doesn't die.

When we agape love God, we're saying "Lord, your needs are more important to me than my needs. I will sacrifice the life I think I want for the life You have for me because, if it's Your will for my life, it will glorify You, and that's all I need."

Falling In Love With The Man, Jesus

So how does that relate to falling in love with Jesus? If you've given your life to Christ, if you're truly saved, then you've already made the decision to agape love Him.[7] That's a done deal. You are *loving* Him to the extent that you give up your will and your ambitions for Him. It's a decision of the will to love Him through your dedication, sacrifice, and obedience to Him. You don't have to have the Hollywood love feelings to have arrived at that place.

But to be *in love* with Him, you need to look to the phileo form of love. Do you enjoy His company? Do you seek to be with Him? Do you think about Him often? Remember that High School sweetheart? You wrote his name in the covers of your books. You scratched her initials on the trunk of a tree. You thought about him all the time. You wanted to talk to her on the phone for hours without ceasing.

God commands that we agape love Him, but Jesus *invites* us to fall in love with Him.

John 16:26-27 In that day you will ask in My name, and I do not say to you that I will request of the Father on your behalf; **for the Father Himself loves you, because you have loved Me** and have believed that I came forth from the Father.

In 1 John 4:19, John said, "We love because He first loved us," but here, John is saying, "the Father loves us because we love the Son." Doesn't that sound contradictory? Who loved first, the Father or us? The answer lies in the Greek forms of the word 'love' in each of these two passages. Essentially, these verses say this:

"We have the capacity to agape love because the Father first agape loved us (1 John 4:19), but when we phileo love His Son, God will phileo love us back (John 16:26-27)."

Jesus says that if we fall in love with Him, God will fall in love with us. Incredible.

Do you want that with Christ? You can have it. It's totally different from the agape love you already have for Him. It's the difference between being 'saved in the wilderness' or being in the wonderful land of promise. To truly be in the Promised Land of your Christian faith, fall in love with Jesus.

You can agape love someone you don't know. You can give a homeless person a meal or an Ethiopian family a goat. If it's a sacrificial gift, that's agape, and you don't have to know a single thing about them.

But you can't phileo someone you don't know. To fall in love with Jesus, you have to learn *about* Him, spend time *with* Him, learn *from* Him, and really get to *know* Him. The person Jesus of Nazareth is an amazing man. He's someone you can *really* fall in love with once you get to know Him.

So just how do I do that? Well, that's the topic of most of the rest of this book, but briefly, talk to Him through prayer and through His word and feel Him talk back to you in your Spirit. Work for Him in ministries and see how He responds to you and teaches you and visits you there. Rejoice with Him through your good times and your bad. Worship Him in church and at home and when you walk down a dirt road. Thank Him endlessly.

As we go through the lessons in the following chapters, my intention, more than any other single goal, is to help you learn how to fall in love with Jesus. I know many Christian who love the Lord, but are not 'in love' with Him. They are missing an amazing opportunity to transform their life experience. My theory is this: If you fall madly in love with Jesus, you'll crave to spend time with Him in His Word, and you'll delight in being obedient to Him just because you know it delights Him. Therein lies your mental health. I've heard it said, "When Jesus is all you have, that's when you discover that Jesus is all you need." So true.

Ok, we're close to being able to look at the techniques I use to study Scripture. Before we get there though, there are a couple of additional concepts you need to understand about being a Christian and living a Christian life. We get to those in the next chapter.

V — FINAL CHRISTIAN CONCEPTS

Who Is The Holy Spirit?

The Holy Spirit is not an 'it,' He's a 'He.' He is a separate entity, the third person of the Trinity: God the Father, God the Son, God the Holy Spirit.

The Holy Spirit is the Spirit of God who 'indwells' us at the moment of our salvation (John 20:22; Acts 2:38), the moment we repented of our sins and gave our lives to Christ, the moment we were 'born again.' The word 'indwell' means that the Holy Spirit literally takes up residence — *abides* — in our physical bodies, intermingled with our own spirit with which we were born. If you're truly a Christian, you literally have the Spirit of God living inside of you. Amazing.

So, what does that do for us? The Holy Spirit who lives in us serves several critical functions. First of all, He brings to us God's divine blessing, the presence and fullness of Himself. As He fills us with His Holy Spirit, He sets us free from the things of this world. To the degree that we dedicate ourselves to Him, change our priorities, and allow Him to fill that 'treasure chest' in our hearts, we will be liberated from the worldly slave-masters that hold us in bondage. Then, as we face the challenges of the world, He is there to be our leader to help us build character and fulfill His purpose for our lives.

Then, as our indwelling leader, the Holy Spirit guides us and helps us in several specific, very practical ways. First, He communicates directly from our spirit to God (Romans 8:26, 27). He intercedes and intervenes. When the Bible talks about "going boldly before the throne of grace" (Hebrews 4:16), it's the Holy Spirit that does that work for us. It is because He lives in us as our intercessor, our representative, that we can go before God with the confidence that our prayers will be translated to God in such a way as to bless and please God. He ensures that we will be heard, understood, and responded to, regardless of how poorly the words come out of our mouths or our thoughts.

The Holy Spirit also guides us (John 16:8). As we go through life as Christians, we will occasionally get what I call, "The Holy Spirit poke in the side," bringing our consciousness to an alert status that something in our behavior or thought-life is amiss. Some people call it 'conscience,' but it's deeper than that. Your conscience leaves you feeling like you have a choice to make, and you are the one to whom you are responsible for that choice. The Holy Spirit's intervention definitely leaves you feeling 'busted.' You know you've done something wrong, and you haven't gotten away with it. As much as you feel like you're doing it in secret, you know that somebody knows, and that somebody is God. The Holy Spirit will lovingly remind you of that, and work with you to turn it around.

The Holy Spirit will also instruct you as to what the Bible means and how it applies to you (also John 16:8). He is very selective on what He will reveal to you at any given time, so be patient with Him and with yourself. If you find yourself reading a section of the Bible and you have, "no idea what it means," relax. It's not for you today. The Holy Spirit will tell you when it is, and it will be unmistakable.

That's why Bible reading is so critical. God literally *speaks* to you through what you're reading or have read. Your very relationship with God depends on your reading what He has written. Oh, that's not to say you can't hear from Him through a sermon or a daily devotional — you certainly can. But that's like having a friend read a letter from a loved one and describing it to you. If you really want to know what they're saying in their letter — *read the letter*! Read God's letter, and you'll hear Him speaking directly into your heart. His voice may seem a little different at first, so you might not recognize it right away. But don't give up. Keep listening, and pretty soon you'll learn to recognize that voice for Who's it is, and you'll be hearing the very voice of God directly into your spirit.

To illustrate what I mean, I have often found myself reading a section of Scripture I've read many times, only to have it jump off the page 'this time' and transform my heart and my life. Those are times that I know God is truly speaking to me through the Bible. It's an amazing experience. If you haven't had it yet, just wait. You will.

But even if you feel like most of it is 'over my head,' press on. Do *not* give up on it. Keep reading. Even if it isn't getting into your head, it is absolutely getting into your spirit. It isn't about head-knowledge anyway. It's about the heart. Society will tell you that it can't get into your heart until it gets into your head first, but that's wrong. The Spirit gets it first, and feeds your head as He sees fit. Just be patient and work with Him.

In the movie *Jesus of Nazareth*, Judas, thinking he was doing Jesus a favor, got him an audience with a member of the political leadership of the day, the Sanhedrin. Jesus did not succumb to the man's political pressure, and Judas exclaimed, "Master, why did you offend him? He's one of the most open-minded people in the Sanhedrin!" Jesus responded, "Open your heart, Judas, not your mind."

Allowing Scripture to enter your heart is far more important than having it enter your head. The Holy Spirit, in collaboration with your spirit, will bring it into your heart even if your head doesn't have a clue. Conversely, you can have memorized entire books of the Bible, but if they've never touched your heart, if they've never transformed you inside, then you might as well be reading the phone book. Press on, and you will come to feel its presence in your heart, and that's where you want it.

Ok, my scholarly friends, I hear you. Let me address your concerns right now. Yes, you definitely want to study it, and you definitely want to learn to understand it. My point is not to minimize the power of understanding — it is to give those who aren't there yet the confidence to keep reading without feeling like it's a waste of their time. Yes, study. Look up the definitions of words you don't understand. Look words up in the Greek[8] if you're so inclined. Check the commentaries if you want to see what they say. But first and foremost, no matter what you understand, or even if you don't understand a single thing in your head — don't stop reading. You're getting a whole lot more out of it than you know.

The other thing the Holy Spirit will do is to remind you of what you've read in the Bible (John 14:26). If you find yourself in a situation, and all of a sudden something you have read comes to your mind as being relevant to this situation, or suddenly something you read makes sense now when it didn't this morning when you read it, that's the Holy Spirit talking to your spirit. He will bring the right Scripture to your mind at exactly the right time to show you the path you need to take. The degree to which you hear that voice is dependent upon the degree to which you read your Bible. Learn to listen, and learn to hear.

The Holy Spirit will teach you what to say (Mark 13:11). Jesus told his disciples that when they are arrested after He's gone not to worry about what to say. Relax. The Holy Spirit will tell them what to say. The trick is to 1) learn to hear when He is trying to guide your words, and 2) obey. We tend to let our pride get in the way. "They can't treat me that way! I won't let them talk to me that way!", and we say what *we* want to say. Learn to hear the Holy Spirit giving you words, use them, and watch what happens in your situation. You'll learn to trust Him and His guidance as you do what He tells you to do and observe the results. Your heavenly Father knows best.

The Holy Spirit is also your comforter and your companion (John 14:16, 26; 15:26; 16:7) and your direct connection to the heart of God. As you go through your difficult times, learn to pray to the Holy Spirit and to God. The Holy Spirit has already brought you peace and comfort just by His presence in your heart. However, if someone gives you a gift, but you never pick it up off the table or open the box, what good is it to you? You have to actually 'receive' the gift for it to become yours. Receive the comfort and peace that is inherent with the presence of the Holy Spirit in your heart. We will address how you do that a great deal in the coming chapters of the book.

The Holy Spirit seals you as a child of God (Ephesians 1:13). When the old merchants were going to ship a crate of cargo, they would 'seal' it with an official seal that would uniquely identify it as their own. This way, once the cargo was received on the other side, they would know if anyone tampered with the contents of the crate. The Holy Spirit is our 'seal' from God, so no one dare 'tamper' with us. As God promised, we will arrive at our final destination with Him. The Holy Spirit is God's formal declaration that we are His personal possession. The demons know this, and are powerless against it.

The Holy Spirit is the 'down payment' for our inheritance in heaven (2 Corinthians 1:22; 2 Corinthians 5:5; Ephesians 1:14). When you prepare to buy a house, the first thing you do is give them a substantial amount of money as a 'down payment.' This is your pledge that you're serious about the purchase, and it seals the contract. This is the same word 'pledge' that God has used to describe His intention for us. He has given us the Holy Spirit as a pledge, proving His intention to bring us into His Kingdom when we die.

The Holy Spirit points us to Jesus. As Jesus constantly gave God the credit for everything He did on earth, so does the Holy Spirit give Jesus and God credit for what He does through us. You know that because the Holy Spirit was the mechanism God used to inspire the writings of the Old and New Testaments. You never see the Holy Spirit getting credit for doing any miracles. His function is to direct us upwards and point us to Christ. It is a wonderful example of humility and that precious agape love.

The Holy Spirit brings with Him what Scripture calls the "Fruit of the Spirit." This fruit is made up of several distinct but blended qualities or characteristics, made up of the following: love, joy, peace, patience, kindness, goodness, faithfulness, gentleness, and self-control (Galatians 5:22). In addition to being significant contributors to our mental health, these characteristics form the weapons that we use to defeat Satan's warfare against us. We cover this concept in more detail in Chapter 14, "Bible-based Therapy."

The Holy Spirit gives us power to do the work of God (Acts 1:8) and endure the trials we face (2 Corinthians 12:9). God's grace, which comes through our relationship with the Holy Spirit, is, among other things, the power we need to be obedient to His commands and to do His will regarding our purpose in life. With His grace, we have the perseverance to keep going when our flesh screams that we want to quit, we have the love in our hearts to forgive those who offend us and ask forgiveness of those we offend, and through Him, we can find peace and joy in the midst of the storm.

Learn who the Holy Spirit is, listen to Him, trust Him, pray to Him, and allow Him to transform your life.

What Are Spiritual Gifts?

There is some controversy in the Christian world concerning exactly what the Spiritual Gifts are. I'm going to give you a higher-level explanation, but understand that as you do some research, you'll find some additional information, and possibly some differences, especially between Christian denominations.

In essence, a Spiritual Gift is a supernatural ability that God has given you to equip you to do something extraordinary for Him. It's an ability that you have that you may not have had at all prior to giving your life to Christ, or it may have been a talent you always had but now you have profoundly more of it.

It's important to remember, though, that God's gift isn't about you. It isn't for the purpose of making you look good, help you earn money, make you popular or powerful or anything else about you. And you didn't earn it because you're a better Christian than somebody else. The gift has specifically been given to you to serve God, other Christians, and the non-believing world to draw people to Christ.

Every Christ-follower has at least one Spiritual Gift and some have more than one. How many you have is totally up to God, and is determined by Him specifically to give you the ability to perform the unique function He has for you to do. You've always heard, "God has a purpose for your life." Well, it's true. He does. And your Spiritual Gift has been given to you to help you fulfill that purpose.

So what are they? Romans 12:6-8 lists them as:

1. Prophesy — Proclaiming God's truth
2. Service — Serving the practical needs of people with your physical efforts (dinner for the sick, day care, etc.)
3. Teaching — Teaching the doctrine and underlying principles of God's word
4. Exhortation — Applying God's word to people's lives in a life-changing way
5. Giving — Serving the practical needs of people and the church by sacrificially giving
6. Leadership — Serving the Christian community through Leading and Administration
7. Mercy — Serving people by connecting with their pain in such a way as to help relieve it

First Corinthians Chapter 12 has a list of what the Apostle Paul calls 'manifestations of the Spirit' (1 Corinthians 12:7) and some churches regard these as gifts. Ephesians 4 has a list of positions or job titles, and some churches regard these as gifts as well. Who is right is less important than whether or not you are functioning in your gift(s) in a way that blesses God.

If you read the book *SHAPE* by Erik Rees, he's listed many spiritual gifts. The exact number or nature of the list isn't the final point: Finding out what God has given you and how He wants you to use it to serve Him and His people is.

Every Christian has an extra measure, supernaturally, of at least one of these gifts. If you don't know which one you have, it is important to find out. That will help you determine where God is planning on using you and you won't spend a lot of time getting involved in things that have no part in God's plan for you.

So how do you find out? Start with your pastor. Like I said, your denomination might have a slightly different list and may approach it slightly differently. You need to trust your leadership and the church where God has placed you and follow their lead regarding the gifts. If you don't have a pastor, then you definitely need to get one. Do some research and get involved in a church,[9] then follow their lead regarding Spiritual Gifts. If your church doesn't believe in Spiritual Gifts, then refer to Romans Chapter 12 and pray about whether or not that's the right church for you.

Remember, though, that the purpose for the spiritual gifts is to serve God, your Christian brothers and sisters, and the world (Ephesians 4:12). They're not about you.

Spiritual Warfare

This is just a very short treatment of the concept of spiritual warfare to introduce you to the problem. Many young Christians are skeptical about Satan and demons, believing that they are probably just figures of speech to infer the evil tendencies of mankind. Don't believe it. Satan would love for us to believe he isn't real because it keeps us off guard. Jesus spoke of them and to them often. He would not have had a conversation with a figure of speech.

I have heard many different sermons on the spiritual battle being waged inside and outside of our hearts. They all agree that there is one, but there is much disagreement as to how we are to handle it. Some say we need to be very aware of Satan's tactics and be on high alert, and others say to marginalize Satan by not giving him any credit or attention. If you have any questions, please see your pastor for guidance.

The important thing to remember about the devil is this:

James said, "Submit therefore to God. Resist the devil and he will flee from you. Draw near to God and He will draw near to you" (James 4:7-8a).

God has provided us defensive armor to protect us against the attacks, or "flaming arrows," of the enemy. He describes them in Ephesians Chapter 6:

"Therefore, take up the full armor of God, so that you will be able to resist in the evil day, and having done everything, to stand firm. Stand firm therefore, HAVING GIRDED YOUR LOINS WITH TRUTH, and HAVING PUT ON

THE BREASTPLATE OF RIGHTEOUSNESS, and having shod YOUR FEET WITH THE PREPARATION OF THE GOSPEL OF PEACE; in addition to all, taking up the shield of faith with which you will be able to extinguish all the flaming arrows of the evil one. And take THE HELMET OF SALVATION, and the sword of the Spirit, which is the word of God. With all prayer and petition pray at all times in the Spirit, and with this in view, be on the alert with all perseverance and petition for all the saints..." (Ephesians 6:13-18)

We use these shields and weapons to protect ourselves, as defensive weapons, when the enemy launches an attack. In addition to defending ourselves, Jesus said, "I also say to you that you are Peter, and upon this rock I will build My church; and the gates of Hades will not overpower it" (Matthew 16:18). To attack the gates of Hades, we will need more than shields and armor. We will need offensive weapons as well. I describe these offensive weapons in detail in the "Bible-based Therapy" chapter, but for now, just understand how the enemy works.

To help you with this, I offer the chart on the next page showing some of the battle issues in the fight between us and Satan. Look over this list and familiarize yourself with the items that are on the left, and those that are on the right. There are certainly many more than are listed, and this is intended to be nothing more than an introduction to the idea. You fill in the missing elements with your life, but just remember to filter them all through Scripture as you go.

As you review "Jesus' Weapons" on the right-hand side on the top of the chart, you may notice that this is from Galatians 5:22, where Paul is describing the "Fruit of the Spirit" (this is described in detail in Chapter 14, "Bible-based Therapy." As you look over this list, remember that it isn't "fruits." It's singular. It's a one-weapon deal. When you open fire on the enemy, you get all of the power all at once.

*** The BATTLE: Satan Verses GOD For My HEART & SOUL ***

Satan's Weapons ——— Actions Taken ——— Jesus' Weapon

"It's all about you" Hype	Love
Difficult Life Circumstances	Joy
Frightening Future Possibilities	Peace
Fast Lifestyle	Patience
'Tough guy' Persona is Idolized	Kindness
Selfishness is Normalized	Goodness
Sin is Tempting, Fun, Gratifying	Faithfulness
Irritating Circumstances/People	Gentleness
Addictions, You Deserve it Now!	Self Control

Worldly — Strategic Objectives - Our Perspective — Eternal

Covet Material Valuables 'Expectation'	Cherish God's Fullness
Giving	Anonymous Giving
Treasure Material Wealth	Sacrificial Giving
Prestige / Pride	Humility
Power Over Others	Serving Others
Circumstantial Happiness	Seek God's Joy
Judging People	Extending Grace
Sinful Anger & Rage	Purposeful Anger Towards Sin
Deceit Through Partial Truth	Exposing Deceit & Revealing Truth

Self ——————— Battle Plans - Our Focus ——————— Jesus

You Are in Control	Knowing He is in Control
Independent Spirit	Dependence on God
You Make Your Own Rules	Complete Submission to Him
Unbridled Lusts And Gluttony	Passion for His Word
Suffering, Negativity	Purpose in Suffering and Faith
Eternal Damnation	Eternal Reward

Satan — — **Victories In The Battles - Our Obedience** — — God	
Telling Even a 'White' Lie Taking Offense Nursing a Bad Thought Complaining / Negativity Anxiety / Fear Sense of Injustice (Not Fair) Impatience	Truth In Spite of Consequences Forgiving the Offense Capturing And Expelling it Giving Thanks for <u>All</u> Things Total Contentment Knowing Everything Has Purpose Extending Grace
Hell — — — — — — **Victories In The War** — — — — — — Heaven	
Darkness Bondage Emptiness Death Torment	Light Freedom Complete Satisfaction Eternal Life Joy

Well, congratulations! You've struggled your way through the introductory stuff. Now we're ready to see exactly how we do it.

Intermission Verse to Ponder: "A gentle answer turns away wrath, But a harsh word stirs up anger" (Proverbs 15:1).

SECTION 3

****

TECHNIQUES

VI — HOW I READ THE BIBLE

What Is The Bible To You?

There's so much guidance on how to read the Bible, some people get frustrated and feel like nothing they do is the 'right' way, so they just give up. Please, don't do that.

I've discovered that reading and studying the Bible is the most fun I've ever had in my whole life, and I've had an extremely exciting life. The most important thing about reading the Bible is to approach it with the right perspective. If you can do that, everything else will fall into place.

Okay then, so what perspective is that?

When I first started reading the Bible, I thought it was a good resource for learning what Jesus was all about. Then I realized that no, it's more than that. It's also a history book about the Jews, and I was fascinated with that. As my reading progressed, I realized that, no, it was actually a lot more than even that. I could learn a lot about how to live my life by paying attention to how these people lived theirs. Some of the stories were good examples of what to do, and others were good examples of what not to do, but they were all helpful. Once I started applying some of them to my life, I started to realize how relevant they all were, first to society, and then to me. I started to notice that they seemed to be about me in some very strange, and sometimes disturbing, ways. I saw myself in there more and more, became more and more convicted of what I needed to work on, and I finally realized that what my sister-in-law had told me before I was even a believer was true: He knows me!

Then it hit me. This was no accident. This was no coincidence. This was a book authored by God, and He wrote it to me. He wanted me to take it personally. Wow, my own personal instruction book from God! Unbelievable.

As I thought about the idea that God had me in mind when He inspired the human authors, and if I could just apply what He's saying to my own heart, how much more wonderful my life could be. I could see it so clearly, and I got so excited! Obedience to His commands wasn't just to get me to be a good girl — it would actually transform my life into a life of peace and great, unspeakable joy! He wants me to be joy-filled and he's told me how to do it!

Oh, my gosh! It isn't an instruction book at all — *it's a love letter*! A *love letter* from the Creator of the universe!

Just reflect on that for a moment. Close your eyes and let that sink in.

Now consider this: What if your spouse, boyfriend, girlfriend, or someone else precious to you was away for an extended trip? One day you receive a 10-page letter from them professing their undying love for you. You open the letter, call someone you know, and ask them to come over and read it for you. They read it, and then they read a sentence here and a sentence there to you — and then they describe to you, in their words, whatever they feel is important for you to know. And then you put the letter on the shelf where it proceeds to gather dust.

Imagine then that your loved one calls and asks you if you've been reading their letter. You respond, "Not as much as I should. I know I need to. I'm going to. I just haven't had the time." Then you feel guilty and purpose in your heart to get up early in the morning and start reading the letter. You do this for 10 minutes or so a day for several days in a row, then you oversleep one day, then the next, and finally the letter is back on the shelf.

Of course, you would never do that. You would rip it open and devour it. You'd probably read it several times. It would certainly never gather dust.

Yet that's what we do with the Bible — God's love letter.

To really get spun up about the Bible, you have to see it as personal, to you, individually and personally. Page after page after page He declares His undying love for you.

Now, if you saw the Bible that way, would I have to encourage you to read it? Would you need discipline? Do you see the problem? It isn't your discipline or your techniques that are the problem. It's your perspective of the book you're holding in your hands. As long as you regard it as a history book about the Jews and early Christians, or worse, a book of rules and regulations, you'll look forward to reading it about as much as you do your company's policy manual.

Change the way you think about the Bible, and your feelings about reading it will change, too. God wants your heart, not your discipline. If you don't have the heart yet, then discipline will have to suffice for now, so don't stop reading waiting for that heart. It's just not God's best for you. Learn to love the Bible as a love letter from God and you'll be drawn to it like a moth to a flame. Love it, and it will no longer be discipline that opens those glorious pages.

Gently Turning The Corner

Without burdening yourself with standards and more rules, there are some basic patterns that you can use as 'red flags' to indicate that your perspective of Christ and the Bible is slipping. If you're not following these patterns, then you need to lovingly examine yourself and see where your heart is.

Now this next part is critical, so note it carefully: If your heart isn't right, do not reprimand yourself, admonish yourself for your lack of discipline, or feel guilty. Quietly and gently, turn your heart back to Christ and pick up where you left off. Pray to Him, confess that you've been distant, feel Him smiling at you with His arms open wide, and crawl back into His lap.

Stop Reading The Bible

Ok, but I need to make a radical change here. This is going to shatter a paradigm or two, so brace yourself. We are no longer going to read the Bible. Bet you didn't expect that from me, did you? That's right. You need to stop reading your Bible.

From now on, rather than reading your Bible, you will be visiting with the Lord there.

Look at it this way: Think about when you've been to a Bible study with a good friend who knows more than you do. You grab your Bible and a cup of coffee, and the two of you open your Bibles up to — say — the Gospel of John. You would never just sit there, the two of you, reading quietly to yourselves starting in verse 1 and then reading to the end of the first chapter, close the book, and get up and leave. You would converse about what you're reading. You would explore the meaning of "In the beginning" together and realize that it's not referring to the same "In the beginning" as Genesis 1:1, but that it's referring to the very beginning when there was no beginning when God and Jesus were together as One for all of eternity. It far pre-dates the Genesis "In the beginning," going back to the beginning of all eternity. You would discover that together, or your friend would point it out to you, and you would both marvel together at the implications of that simple phrase.

If you don't make your time in the Bible about talking with the Lord, then you're missing the best part, and I'd go so far as to say, you're missing the whole point.

Now of course I'm going to continue to use the word "read" when I talk about the Bible, but the little secret between us is that when you see that word, think "visit with the Lord."

So here we go. Here is my personal "How I talk with the Lord" list. You may develop some differences as you go, but here's mine.

1. Read Daily.

You've heard it a thousand times — read your Bible daily. "Why?" we say. "I don't understand a lot of it anyway, and I'm really busy. Besides, I want *practical* guidance on how to fix my problems, not some pie-in-the-sky holier-than-thou lecture from some old gray-haired guys."

If that were what it was, I would totally agree. But it's not. A bunch of old gray-haired guys put the words on paper, but the words they put down came right out of the heart of God.

To allow the words of Scripture to change your heart, you need to totally believe that God wrote them, and not just some old gray-haired guy who might have written Jesus' words down wrong or remembered Israel's history wrong. You need to believe it down to your core — not just in your head because somebody told you to believe it. It can't be Christian brainwashing — it has to be yours, and it can be.

But really, deeply and profoundly *knowing* that the Bible is the actual, literal word of God can only come through many hours of reading it. There's no other way. You have to read and read and read and read and read.

This is important enough to repeat: **You have to read and read and read and read and read**.

Visit with Jesus there every day. *Pray Him into the room.* Oh, of course He's always in the room because He's always everywhere, but to pray Him into the room is your conscious reminder to yourself that He's with you, He's available, He's listening, and your point is to visit with Him and learn from Him. By praying Him into the room with you, you become more aware of His presence. So since He is there, talk to Him like He is. The more you do that, the more it's going to sink deeper and deeper into your heart that it is truly His voice speaking directly to your heart as you read.

Make the goal of your daily reading to discover who Jesus is, to meet with Him in those precious pages, and to allow the reality of the Bible's authorship to sink deeply into your heart.

One of my primary initiatives with all of my clients is to get them into the habit of reading Scripture daily. This is a tough habit to start, even though they're good Christian people and love the Lord. They mean well, but they're just really busy people like the rest of us and they have little, if any, experience with the regenerating power of the Bible. They're not motivated because they can't see the value. It's just another homework assignment they can't spare the time for and wouldn't understand anyway.

If that describes you, what you need to remember is that the miracle of Scripture is that it's a Spirit-to-spirit communication. I know I'm repeating myself here, but it isn't about head-knowledge. It's about God's Spirit communicating with your spirit directly. Oh, it would be wonderful if your head got it, too, but if it doesn't, it's not a show-stopper. The *real* work is going on anyway.

I tell my clients, I don't care if you don't understand a single word of it. What I want you to do is to take some time every day — and I don't care how much time — and just let your eyeballs roll over the top of the words. Don't worry about comprehension or understanding at first. If you can't understand it, then just let the words touch your eyes. That's all you need to do for now.

If you do that every day and invite Jesus into the room with you when you do, then little by little, you'll start to get more and more out of it. Regardless of what you understand in your head, you'll start to see the most amazing transformation you could imagine. You'll start to feel some changes in your heart. You'll start to understand a word here, or a phrase there, and then one day you'll pick up the book and say, "Oh my gosh!! This really IS written by God! It really does apply to me! He really does know me!" And it will have truly sunk in. You'll own it. It will no longer be something you learned from your parents or some mantra you learned in Sunday School. It'll be yours. And you'll start to really experience that transforming touch.

Please just trust me on this. I've seen it over and over, so I know it's true. Until you experience it, though, you'll be doubtful. *Please* trust me and find a way to read daily — not because somebody *told* you to, but because you want to know Jesus and you want to be transformed by Him. It's the only way.

I can't wait to get up in the morning to read. It's the best part of my day. The house is quiet and I'm at peace in my mind because I don't have the day's work to think about yet. I try to get in an hour or two if I can, and it always goes way too fast. I'm never ready for it to end when I have to stop at 8:00 am to start my day.

Now, having said all of that, please don't get legalistic with this. Of course there are those days when I can't do it for some reason. I know that Jesus knows it isn't because I don't enjoy His company or that I don't want to be there. Things just happen sometimes. I would say that happens, say, once every week or two at most. I'm not legalistic about my reading because I don't have to be. I love it, and the Lord and I both know my heart.

I strongly caution you, though, that if your heart isn't there yet, be very careful about skipping time with the Lord. If it isn't yet a passion for you, then each time you skip it, you have a greater chance of skipping the next time, and then the next. Pretty soon, you'll wonder when the last time you spent time with the Lord was. Ever try to get involved in an exercise program? Did you stick with it? One skipped day leads to the next, and so forth. Until you love it, you run the risk of it exterminating itself.

Once you love it, though, your 'skipping' days will leave you with a feeling in your stomach: not a feeling of guilt, but a feeling of loss. You will *miss* Him. You'll miss your time with Him. You'll feel it all day, and it won't be discipline that gets you up tomorrow. You won't be *able* to skip it for the anticipation of your daily, quiet, intimate conversation with the Lord.

2. **Relax, Don't Get Frustrated.** (Jesus said, "My yolk is easy and My burden is light" (Matthew 11:28-30), remember?)

Many people find that when they don't understand something in the Bible, they get frustrated and feel like their efforts are a waste of time. Let it go. If it doesn't touch you, it isn't for you today. Again, let the Holy Spirit work with your spirit to get what you need and let the rest go. Trust Him. He's right there guiding you and teaching you. That's a promise from God. Let it be easy and light, not frustrating.

Now, having said that, there may also be times when God wants you to dig deeper and search harder for the truth of His message to you. Pray about it, and determine through your relationship with the Holy Spirit whether this is one of those times when you are to let it go or dig deeper. Be open to His promptings and obedient to His direction, and He promises you that the burden will be light. I've actually found it to be *a blast*! The deeper I dig, the more treasures I find.

3. **Pray First, Ask Questions Often, Chat With Jesus.**

When you sit down to read, pray first, and ask the Holy Spirit to guide you. I literally invite Jesus to join me in my living room and visualize Him sitting on the couch next to me. When I read, I chat with Him about what I'm reading. "I don't understand that one, Lord. Why did you say that?" If someone were eavesdropping on me, they'd think I'd totally lost my mind. But I love it. Just me and the Lord, enjoying a cup of tea and morning devotions together. I'm open to His teachings and He teaches. I'm not trying to squeeze meaning out the Scripture on my own. I'm letting Him teach me as I go. He's faithful, He tells me when I need to look something up, and He teaches me unbelievably exciting new and amazing truths. I treasure my quiet, personal time with Him each day.

If you struggle with this, my guess is that you're just trying to go too fast. If your mind is revved up with the words that are flying across your eyes, then the Lord doesn't have a chance to get a word in edgeways. You need to 'pause' in your reading every few verses so He doesn't have to interrupt your thoughts. He's a gentleman, remember.

4. **Slow Down, But Don't Bog Down.**

Some people like the Bible-in-a-year approach. They've done it that way for many years, and they've read the Bible cover-to-cover many times. That's a very successful approach for them, and I applaud them for their discipline and the dedication to the Word.

Personally, though, I've tried it, and I don't like the forced scheduling aspect of it. My pattern has been to allow the Holy Spirit to guide me day by day, and when He tells me I'm done with a section, I move on to the next. This past year, for instance, He had me 'camped' on the Sower of the Seed (Luke 8:5-15) parable for several days. I know I spent 10-12 hours on that short section alone. I was amazed at what He showed me, and I've been able to use it with clients several times in a life-altering way. The draw-back of that approach, obviously, is that it will take me longer than a year to get through it all.

Now, when I say that I allow the Holy Spirit to guide me day-by-day, I'm not referring to the pop-corn approach to Scripture reading where you just pop the book open and read where it falls. I'm in a specific book, and I read it from Chapter 1 verse 1 until I get to the end of it. To really understand Scripture, that's critical. He guides me, however, on how many verses I read today, what I pass over and what I look up in the Greek or commentaries or whatever. I may go over that same section of Scripture several times until I get the big point He wants me to get, or I may read it more casually and not dig any deeper than the surface message. I listen for His guidance on exactly how to handle each day's readings. When I feel like I have a certain amount to 'cover' to keep up with a schedule, I tend not to hear from Him as well. I don't like that, and it just doesn't work for me.

Both the scheduled approach and the slower approach have their pros and cons. They may even have their seasons, meaning, one approach might work for you this year, while another approach works better next year. I encourage you to find your own niche and do what the Holy Spirit guides you to do. If you're not sure what He wants you to do yet, just pick one at random and you'll know before long whether or not it fits you. But whichever approach you choose, make sure it brings you the joy that comes from spending time with Him.

5. Observe Carefully.

Watch what you're reading. Is there a word that's repeated over and over in a short section? Words like "love," "world," "righteousness," and others will often be something of a theme in a particular section. You can tell they're a theme because the same word will be repeated several times in a brief piece.

Also, watch for words like "But," "Therefore," "And," "However," and so forth. These kinds of words will indicate transitions, comparisons, contrasts, etc. If you're not in tune to them, then you might miss something that brings the whole piece together.

This exercise is especially true in the beginning of a chapter. We often miss some of the biggest truths in the Bible because we fail to realize that the chapter we've just started is actually a running thought from the prior chapter. When you start a new chapter, always go back into the prior chapter and see if there's a linkage. As often as not, there is.

The old adage is "If you see the word 'therefore,' check to see what it's there for."

Be observant. Be an analyst. Look for treasures and listen for the voice of God.

6. Become The People In The Stories.

As you read, I want you to see yourselves as the heroes and villains you're reading about. Pretend that you're actually them - in the scene. What would it be like to be Mary Magdalene at the open tomb? What would it be like to be the Pharisees when Jesus is doing the "Woe to you, Pharisees" speech (Matthew 23)? What would it be like to be one of the people who got healed, or Peter when he denied Jesus?

Imagine their feelings in that scene. Imagine the faces of the other people in the scene as the events are unfolding. See it as a video in your head. Try to *be* there at the time.

When you read the Old Testament and you become more familiar with the people there, do the same thing. See yourself as Esther saying, "If I perish, I perish" (Esther 4:16) and meditate on what that must have been like for her at that moment. Think about how frightened she must have been, how courageous she was, and how important her faith in God must have been.

The truth is that you *are* Esther.

Like Esther, God has a plan for your life. Like Esther, God wants you to make sacrifices and take risks for Him and His people. You are Esther. You are also Abraham dedicating your most precious things to God (Genesis 22:1-19). We all are. We are Lot's wife, tempted to look back at our old lives with longing (Genesis 19:26). We are Adam, blaming God and whomever else is around when we are really the ones to blame (Genesis 3:12). We are Saul, proud, rebellious, compromising, disobedient, and paying the consequences for it all (1 Samuel 15:17-29, 1 Samuel 18:12, 1 Samuel 31). We are

Gideon, that "mighty man of valor" as the Angel of the Lord called him while he was cowering in his shed in fear (Judges 6:11-12). We are that same Gideon, overcoming our fears and following the Lord into battle (Judges 7). We are Jeremiah proclaiming the word of the Lord fearlessly while we are being persecuted by those who don't understand our message (Jeremiah). We are the people of Israel, struggling with our relationship with a Holy God, and feeling His discipline and His grief through it all.

We are all of those people we read about. Become them, and your experience in reading the Old Testament will be transformed, and it will transform your life.

7. Personalize What You Read.

Whenever you read Scripture, become the person to whom the text is written. When you are reading Philippians, don't read it as if it were a letter written from the Apostle Paul to the church of Philippi; read it as if it were a letter written from God to you. I call that "personalizing" Scripture. Sometimes the reading can be a little awkward because of the structure of the text, but persevere. You'll get the hang of it, and you will hear God speaking to you through these verses. Let me give you a couple of examples:

In Philippians, Paul is trying to encourage the people at Philippi. When you read it, read it like this (assume your name is Kathy):

> "I thank my God in all my remembrance of you, Kathy, always offering prayer with joy in my every prayer for you, in view of your participation in the gospel from the first day until now. For I am confident of this very thing, Kathy, that He who began a good work in you will perfect it until the day of Christ Jesus" (Philippians 1:3-6).
>
> "Indeed, the Lord will comfort Kathy; He will comfort all her waste places. And her wilderness He will make like Eden, and her desert like the garden of the Lord; Joy and gladness will be found in Kathy, Thanksgiving and sound of a melody" (Isaiah 51:3).

Also, whenever you read stories about the Old Testament people, try to ask yourself, "Do I do that?" When Adam is blaming both God and Eve for him eating the fruit, ask yourself, "Do I blame others when I do something wrong?" When the Israelites turn away from God when things are going well in their lives, say, "Do I forget my morning devotions, do I stop going to church, or does my prayer life suffer when things in my life are going well?" Whenever you read and meditate about what is going on in the Bible, think about the 'human' aspect of the story, what is happening and what each of the individuals are doing, and ask yourself that penetrating question - "Do I do that, too?" You'll be a amazed at what God will show you.

As you read, remember to see it as a love letter from God to you. Put your name in there and see yourself as both the villain and the hero to hear God speaking the words of love and restoration directly into your heart.

8. Meditate, Pray, And Apply It To Your Life.

Meditation (Josiah 1:8; Psalms 1:2), and including Jesus in that meditation, is absolutely the key that unlocks the door to Scripture. Without meditation, what you're reading won't sink in to your soul and change your heart. Meditation is the difference between reading the Bible and talking with the Lord. Without meditation, you'll miss out on the miraculous regenerating power of the Word.

So what is meditation? The Greek word for the word the Bible calls meditation means, "To growl, groan, sigh, mutter." It's the same word they use to describe the growl of a lion or the cooing of a dove.

So how do I apply that to myself practically? The practical definition is to focus thoughtfully. If you were mumbling Scripture out loud as you read, it would be a lot harder to day-dream, and you'd pay more attention. Reflect on what you're reading as if you were mumbling it audibly. I actually do mumble it audibly. That just works for me. Stop on a verse long enough to roll it around in your head. Don't rush through it just to get it done. Taste it. Smell it. Talk to Jesus about it, and let Him guide you on how it applies to you.

I've heard it said, "I'd rather you read a single verse and apply it to your life than memorize the entire Bible, cover to cover." I wish I knew who said that. So profoundly true.

I read an article on the Internet where a Bible teacher had told her students to take a single verse out of Proverbs, write it on a sheet of paper, and leave it next to them wherever they went for a few days. Read it over and over, think about it, write down their thoughts, and bring them back to class next week. The discussions and life-changing experiences that went along with that assignment were astonishing.

Slow down, meditate, and pray. Then, apply it to your life.

9. Write In Your Bible.

If you can't write in your Bible, get another Bible. As you read, jot thoughts down in the margins, underline or highlight stuff, draw big stars and happy faces next to verses that really delight you and arrows from one verse to another if they relate, etc. Make the book yours. Personalize it with your thoughts. The next time you run across this section or that verse that has your thoughts written down, it's fun to see what you thought last year or the year before, and sometimes you'll remind yourself of some special insight you might have missed this time.

It can also be humbling when you read what you thought *last* year and go, "Ugh, I can't believe I thought that." Humbling is good.

Writing in your Bible is invaluable, and even if you're one of those neurotic types who "<u>never</u> writes in books!" (like me), you'll find you love it after a while. So if you can't write in your Bible, get another Bible.

10. Keep A Journal.

A journal is just a book that allows you to jot down some particularly notable or profound thoughts you have as you read. I like to use my journal to record when I believe the Holy Spirit has really said something to me that is uniquely and particularly to me or about me. It enhances my meditation to be able to record how this verse is going to shape my heart and my life. (I've put some of my journal entries on a blog site called "Biblical Therapy" that you can link to from my web site at http://www.suemchenry.com).

11. Camp When Prompted By The Holy Spirit To Do So.

Like meditation, I think 'camping' is a crucial part of Biblical study. Camping says that the Holy Spirit is really working with you closely, and has something specific He wants you to get. I can tell He wants me to camp when I've read a section of Scripture and feel very drawn to it for some reason. It'll make perfect sense to me as I'm reading and I feel focused on it, but the very next section of Scripture might as well be in Chinese and I just can't focus. I find myself going back over it over and over and over again, and it's never any clearer the fourth or fifth time than it was the first time.

But when I go back to the section immediately preceding the Chinese section, I can focus again. That says to me that that's where He wants me right now. There's something there for me that I missed the first time through, so I camp there. That's His way of slowing me down.

Camping, for me, means reading slowly, looking at each clause in the sentence in its own light, reading with a different emphasis on different words to see if the meaning changes.

"MY grace is sufficient for thee."
"My GRACE is sufficient for thee."
"My grace is SUFFICIENT for thee."
"My grace is sufficient for THEE."

Does the meaning change? What might the author have meant? Which emphasis is actually correct? Does it matter to the text? Does it matter to your life?

Think about what might have been going on at the time in the scene or culturally. Who is there? Who is talking? Is this for the Jews or the Gentiles? What's just happened in the paragraph or page or chapter before this scene? Is this early in Jesus' ministry, or later? Why do you think the speaker is saying what He's saying?

Has anybody else said that? In other words, is Paul or James quoting Jesus? Is Peter saying something here because he denied Jesus three times and has some special insight into failure? Ponder these things as you camp.

I always know when He's done with me and I've gotten what He needs me to get because the Chinese section isn't Chinese any more.

12. Cross-Check With Other Versions Of The Bible And Other Versions Of The Gospel.

There are many different versions of the Bible. For a more detailed explanation of some of them, refer to Appendix C, "How to Select the Right Bible." There are many more than I could cover there, but it gives you a sampling.

For the purposes of this text, however, having different versions might help with understanding. First of all, if you're looking verses up in different versions, then you're slowing down, and that's a good thing.

Second, some versions are extremely accurate to the Greek, but lose some of the understandability as a result. Other versions aren't as strict in their translation, but have captured something of what the authors meant that the more literal translations can't capture without taking liberties with the wording that they haven't wanted to take.

Compare these two as examples from John 1:16:

NASB: For of His fullness we have all received, and grace upon grace.

NLT: We have all benefited from the rich blessings he brought to us — one gracious blessing after another.

The NASB version is more accurate to the Greek, but in this example, the New Living Translation makes it clearer to the English-speaking reader what the author was trying to say.

Whether the accuracy or readability appeals to you more is a personal preference. In either case, though, doing some cross-referencing has wonderful benefits.

A Word of Caution: There are many examples where the simpler, more 'understandable' version has lost something in the translation.

Some of them even come a little too close to heresy for comfort. Just be very careful about relying solely on the 'more understandable' versions, and always compare them with the KJV, NASB, or NKJV versions to be sure.

While we're talking about versions, I also wanted to bring to your attention that there are four different versions of the Gospel Story: Matthew, Mark, Luke, and John each wrote their own perspective of Jesus' life.

So as you're studying a particular story in a particular Gospel, look up that same story in the other Gospels. Compare the differences and talk to Jesus about what the differences mean. Don't get caught up in the hype that says, "Since they're different, that must mean they can't be inspired because otherwise they'd be identical." The scholars have crawled all over those differences and every time I've questioned one, I've always come away convinced that the difference is one of perspective and not fact. If you and your spouse both wrote a story about your latest Thanksgiving Dinner, I'd bet you would each remember different details, and have different perspectives. It wouldn't mean either of your accounts was inaccurate.

So as you're reading and comparing, just know that they're both accurate, but see what the differences tell you. We'll talk more about this in the chapters with the examples later in the book.

13. Read, But Don't Rely On Commentaries.

There are some fabulous commentaries out there that will aid in your understanding of Scripture, particularly some of the more difficult passages. Be very careful, though, that you not allow the commentaries to become a stand-in for the Holy Spirit.

I use commentaries with great care. I will always read the passage first, meditate, and pray, and allow the Holy Spirit to guide me through that process. Once I feel like I've exhausted what I might glean myself, I refer to commentaries to make sure I'm not off-track with my understanding or my application. When I do so, however, I will always refer to more than one to get a more rounded perspective. Each commentary writer is analyzing the Scripture from his own perspective, with a particular target audience and focus for research, and with a particular goal in mind. Spread the wealth and allow the sum of the parts to influence, but not drive, your analysis of the passage. In the end, the Holy Spirit is your best and final commentary. The others should be used just to be sure you haven't gone too far afield with your own interpretation.

Remember, it's not about what you or anyone else thinks the verse means. It's about what the original author meant it to mean, and the original author is God.

14. Avoid The 'Flip And Point' Technique.

When I first became a Christ-follower, I occasionally enjoyed the 'flip and point' technique of Biblical study. For those of you who've never done it, it's where you blindly flip the Bible open to some random page, and with your eyes closed, point to a verse and start there. The logic is, "I'll allow God to choose what I read today."

That's all well and good for when you have a couple of minutes to burn at the doctor's office and you just want to read something brief. But for serious study, you can't get the context and deeper meaning God intends.

Serious Bible study requires starting at the beginning of a book and studying it verse by verse. You have a lot of flexibility as to which book to start with, but read each one beginning to end. It's just too important to get the context and perspective.

So this ends the process and perspective-shift of studying the Bible. Now I'd like to talk about the more internal processing of the material — how to think about it.

VII — THINKING ABOUT WHAT I READ

Lose The 'Shoulds'

The biggest mistake Christians make when embarking on a study of the Bible is in how they regard the very activity itself. I can always tell when someone needs a bit of an adjustment in their way of thinking when I ask the question, "How much time do you spend in your Bible?" If they say, "Not as much as I should," I know we have a perspective-shift to make.

First of all, let's lose the "should" and replace it with "I can't wait," or "I get to." I know that seems strange at first, kind of like saying "I can't wait to get to my homework!" They'd lock you up. The fact is that that's the way many people regard Bible study — as homework.

Bible study is *not* homework — it's the greatest opportunity in your lifetime to get to know your Lord and transform your life. It's a thrilling adventure in which *you* are a grand and glorious participant! As we go through this chapter, I want to help you see yourself *in* the pages of the book you hold in your hands rather than as a passive, distant observer of events long ago. You're not high on the hill watching the events unfold: You're in the battlefield!

The Bible is *today* and you are one of its heroes. Regard it that way, and you are well on your way to "I can't wait!"

Think Outside The Ancient Box — What God Wants *You* To Learn.

Let's go back to the concept of the love-letter from God. After I let that wash over me for a while and basked in the wonder of it, I started to think about the practical application of that to my life. Here I hold in my hands God's love letter to me telling me how I can live a life filled with joy and peace and wonder, regardless of my personal circumstances. How do I receive that? How do I make that happen in my life?

The answer is this: Stop seeing the Bible as an instruction book. Stop seeing it as a history book about the Jews. Stop seeing it as a revelation of the Lord Jesus Christ. It is decidedly all of those things, but if you want it to transform your life, you have to start seeing it as a letter written *to you*. Every single verse has something God is trying to tell *you*. What *is* that? What does He want you to learn with *this* passage *today*?

Approach it as a love letter written to you, and you'll approach it with anxious anticipation that today, He might have something life-changing just for you!

Let me give you an example so you'll see what I mean.

> Jesus has sent the disciples across the Sea of Galilee to go to the other side and He stayed on shore (Mark 6:45-52). Many hours later (at least six, and possibly as many as nine), after they had struggled and strained at the oars because of the terrible wind, Jesus walked on the water toward them. The part most people miss because they're reading too fast is the next phrase: *And He intended to pass by them* (v 48).
>
> What?? You intended to pass by? What does *that* mean? Why would You *do* that? They were in trouble. Why wouldn't You stop to help them, Lord? I don't understand.
>
> Notice the details and ask questions of the Lord as you go. Then see how it fits your life.

Can you apply that to your life? Are there times when you feel like He hasn't stopped to help you? Do you sometimes feel abandoned and alone? What did the disciples do next?

They cried out. Once they did, He got into the boat, calmed the storm, and they went to the other side, which is where He told them they would go all along. If he said it would happen, it will happen. The question is, how much effort will you put into it, how much pain will you suffer, and how much fear will you experience before you finally cry out?

Jesus is a gentleman. If you don't ask Him into your situation, He won't force Himself in. The lesson I can learn from this story, if I slow down, talk to the Lord, and apply it to my life, is this: The quicker I cry out to Jesus to come into my situation, the quicker the storm will calm down, and the quicker I can accomplish the work He wanted me to accomplish all along.

You could have read that as an interesting story about the disciples and Jesus walking on water, but if you had, you'd have missed the whole point.

Let me give you another example of how to apply it to your life. For this one, I'll go to the 'boring' Old Testament.

Gideon was an Israelite during the time of the Judges (Judges Chapters 6-8). The Israelites had been heavily into idol worship, so God "delivered them into the hands of the Midianites." As a result, the Midianites would raid the Israeli lands every year at harvest time, stealing the fruit of the Israelites labor and starving them. They did this for seven years.

On the seventh year, God told Gideon He was going to deliver the Midianites into the Israelites hands, and commissioned Gideon to lead the army. It's a great story, and I highly recommend you read the entire thing.

I'm going to leave out the details, but after some back and forth dialogue and events between God and Gideon, Gideon was left with an army of 300 men against the Midianite army

Therapy with God

of 135,000 men. God wanted to make sure that everyone knew that the victory was His, not Gideon's.

What God told Gideon to do was to have each of the 300 men take a torch, hide the torch inside a clay jar, and bring a trumpet. They surrounded the Midianite army, blew the trumpets, broke the clay pots, and shouted. The Midianites, believing that each light represented 1,000 soldiers,[10] became so frightened of the army of what they thought was 300,000 men, that they began attacking one another and finally fled while Israel stood and watched from a distance. Israel finally chased them down, and defeated them soundly. Brilliant military maneuver.

On the surface, on first reading, it's just another boring Old Testament story about another Israeli battle. Trumpets, clay pots, torches — it all seems so arbitrary and meaningless. That's your clue that there's something else going on. That's the red flag that there's a deeper message for you.

Let's think about symbolism in the Bible again. Light refers to the light of Jesus (I am the light of the world — John 8:12; 9:5), and the clay pot refers to us ("We are the clay, and You are the Potter" — Isaiah 64:8; Jeremiah 18:6; Romans 9:21). In addition, trumpets are symbolic of the Gospel of Jesus Christ, shouting forth the truth of God's word and love.

Inside each one of us who have the Holy Spirit living in us is the light of Christ. You already know that. It isn't light we generate, we get it from Christ. In Gideon's case, what did they have to do to let the light shine forth to defeat the enemy?

They had to 1) blow the trumpet, and 2) break the clay pot.

When does the light of Christ shine most brightly out from us? When are we most effective in defeating the enemy? When we are preaching the Gospel and the love of God in the middle of our brokenness. When we are broken and proclaim the love of God, people notice, and the enemy is defeated, regardless of how outnumbered we see ourselves to be. When you're broken, do you complain, or do you demonstrate the love and provision and protection of our Lord? If you proclaim the Gospel and God's love in your brokenness, the enemy will run for his life.

In a similar example, consider Job. When your life is going well and life is good, as was the case with Job before Satan got to him, people will say, "Sure you love God. Who wouldn't? Look how well He's taken care of you." Satan said to God:

> "Does Job fear God for nothing? Have you not made a hedge about him and his house and all that he has, on every side? You have blessed the work of his hands, and his possessions have increased in the land. But put forth Your hand now and touch all that he has; he will surely curse You to Your face."

Did he? Did Job curse God? Of course not. God knew he wouldn't, and he became an incredible witness to the rest of us.

It was because Job was broken that his love for God became the example to the world.

It is when you are broken that people will really sit up and take notice of your love for God in spite of the trial, through it, and because of it.

So here is the list of how you can directly apply the stories you read to your life and make them about you and your transformation.

- Think about how the situation is affecting people in the scene.
- Think about how it would affect you if you were there.
- Compare this Gospel account with another Gospel account — note, meditate on, and ask Jesus and the Holy Spirit about any differences.
- Learn about how the culture would affect what's going on.
- Picture the scene as a video in your head.
- See if there is any 'symbolism' as we learned earlier.
- Remember to alternate word emphasis to get more insight as to the possible meaning.
- See yourself as the characters, and consider how their experiences apply to your life
- Think about the alternative ways of thinking about the story (see example below).

Most of the above list is either self-explanatory or we will touch on it later, so I won't waste space here going into more detail. The final item, though, which suggests thinking about alternative explanations, could use an example for illustration.

In the story at the Pool of Bethesda (John 5:2-18), Jesus saw a man there who had been crippled for 38 years. He went up to him and said, "Do you want to get well?" He healed the man, who picked up his pallet and left.

In our mind's video of the scene, we hear Jesus with a loving, gentle tone inviting the man to enjoy the fruits of physical healing. Then we see the man leaping up, hugging everyone at the pool, picking up his pallet, and dancing home filled with joy.

But read the story again, all the way through. First of all, the man never asked Jesus to heal him, even when Jesus asked him if he wanted Him to. He just made excuses for why he was still sick after all these years and blamed everyone else.

Second, the story never even suggests that the man leapt up for joy and danced home. Quite the contrary. It says he went to the Jews and reported what happened, and as a result, the Jews wanted to kill Jesus.

So in the video in your head, change Jesus' tone from one of a gentle Lamb to a loving confrontation. "Do you *want* to get well?? If you do, then stop making excuses, stop blaming everyone else, pick up your pallet, and get on with your life."

Does that change how it applies to you? How about you? Are you making excuses? Are you blaming others for your life? Jesus just might have something to say to you about that, if you read this story just a little differently than you might at first.

Allowing yourself to mentally explore alternative ways of thinking about a story is where the Holy Spirit will speak to you personally. He will show you, if you listen to Him, how it applies to you, but you have to slow down, meditate, and pray.

Slow down, meditate, pray, and then apply it to your life. It's worth repeating again. Slow down, meditate, pray, and apply.

That's the key, and you'll hear me say it over and over and over again throughout this book.

VIII — MEMORIZING SCRIPTURE

Why Should I Memorize?

Uh, oh. Homework.

Your Sunday School teacher assigned 'memory verses,' and so did your Bible teacher if you went to a Christian School. Memory verses seem like homework. Yuk. "As if I don't have enough pressure on me already, now you're going to add to my already too-busy day and tell me to memorize Scripture??"

Yep. That's what I'm going to do. This is the *work* part of the work.

When I was in my early years in the 70's, we had this wonderful 'new' way of boosting our wounded self-esteem. We called it "positive affirmations." The idea was that if you say something positive and uplifting to yourself often enough, you'll eventually believe it, and you'll feel better.

If you grew up in a home where you received a lot of negative messages about yourself, you eventually took them on board as your own and believed them. They then became the source of much of your dysfunction and poor decision-making in later life.

Without thinking about it, fill in this blank with a descriptive adjective about yourself: I am _____. Whatever you filled that blank in with, whether it was positive or negative, I guarantee you that if you think about it for a minute, you'll come to realize that it came from one or more of your primary care-givers. My guess is that there are a whole lot more adjectives than just that one, and a lot of them are negative.

So to 'undo' those negative messages, we would memorize and repeatedly recite positive things we wanted to believe about ourselves over and over and over again throughout the day. "I'm a good person," "I'm lovable," "I'm worthy of love," "I'm bright," "I'm a winner, not a loser," etc.

Strangely enough, it worked. The more we repeated the positive messages over time, the better we felt about ourselves. Our self-esteem grew and grew through the power of the spoken word. God said that words have the power of life and death (Proverbs 18:21), and we used that to our advantage.

It worked because that's the way God made us. If we hear a message often enough, we'll eventually believe it. That's how brain-washing works. That's how advertising works. That's why prisoners and people who have been kidnapped for long enough often start to feel sympathy for, and often support, their captors. That's why we buy what we see on television.

The problem with our Positive Affirmations, though, was that they violated God's truth. We told ourselves what wonderful people we were, and that the messages about us being bad, evil, ugly people were all lies. We said that often enough, and we eventually believed it and demanded people treat us better, professed that we were indeed loveable, and proclaimed an inherent right to be loved. Some of the outcome of this routine, purely from a mental health perspective, was positive in that there was less misery and people did treat us better.

But it was not God's truth, and feeling better without God in our lives made our "last situation worse than our first" (Luke 11:24-26). Since we felt so good about ourselves — we were 'good people' — Jesus didn't have anything to offer us. We didn't need a Savior because we no longer had anything from which we felt like we needed to be saved.

But God wants us to learn what *He* wants us to know. If you've been hearing negative messages your whole life, then the same process that worked for us in the 70's will work for you now, but with God's truth at the core.

The purpose of memorizing Scripture, from a mental health perspective, is to allow the truth of God's word to penetrate your heart, and restore the damage that has been done by your past.

Memorized Scripture cleanses your mind. Let me repeat that: *Memorized Scripture cleanses the mind* (Ephesians 5:26).

Think of it as a mental scrub brush. It will give you a whole new clean, bright, and shiny way of thinking.

Remember: This is a critical component of mental health recovery! Do not skip this step.

Memorizing a pertinent verse and repeating it to yourself over and over again will drive a point into your heart that desperately needs to be driven. Much like a hammer hitting a nail will eventually drive it into a board, so will your mind and mouth repeating Scripture eventually drive it into your heart. As a matter of fact, the real transforming miracle happens best when you follow this guideline:

Memorize something you don't believe about yourself.

Intellectually, you know your selected verse is true because you know that *all* of God's word is true. Internally, though, it just doesn't seem to apply to you. Many of my clients have told me that they totally accept that God's promises are all true — for you and me and everyone else, but not really for them. The negative messages of their childhood have made it impossible for them to personalize them and incorporate them into their souls. The negative messages in their heads are simply too loud.

When you run across those verses, the ones that make you go, "Yeah, right," or "Is that so? When?", then those are the ones you need to memorize so well that they roll off your tongue without you even thinking about them. You must repeat them time after time after time as you go through your day. Write them on pieces of paper and tape them to the refrigerator, glue them to your steering wheel, write them on the inside of your forearm. Most of all, write them on your heart.

That's what memorizing verses and repeating them to yourself over and over and over again will do. It will write them on that stone tablet in your chest. Eventually, they'll be yours, they'll apply to you, and you will be transformed.

Trust me. It works.

This sounds crazy, I know, but there is a lot of Scriptural backing for it. You won't find the word "memorize" in your word search, but much of the first several Psalms is about learning and relying on Scripture, and Psalm 119 is even more so. You have to memorize it to do that. Much of the first three chapters of Romans are about the wisdom of God. The ancient Jews would often memorize complete books of the Bible, and many still do.

But carrying it around on a piece of paper and reading it over and over isn't quite the same thing as memorizing it. When you memorize it, you are forced to focus on each and every word. Nothing slips past you. You can't just gloss over any of it. You must hesitate on every phrase to memorize it. You're incorporating it into your heart in a way that just reading it, even repeatedly, can never quite achieve.

Other than falling in love with Jesus, I'd say memorizing Scripture is the second-most important step to using the Bible as a mental health book.

And actually, memorizing Scripture is one of the best ways to fall in love with Jesus. When you hear Him speaking words of love in your head all day long, how can you *not* fall in love with Him?

Memorizing The Chapter And Verse Reference

When I started to memorize Scripture, I did what I saw everyone else doing. I memorized exactly where in the Bible the verse I was reading and memorizing could be found. Chapter and verse. Galatians 2:20, Philippians 4:13, Ephesians 4:8-9. Chapter and verse, chapter and verse. As far as I was concerned, if I didn't know the complete chapter and verse reference, I didn't know where it was.

Since my aging memory could only capture and retain so many of those full references, though, my memorized verses became more and more limited, and eventually, I gave up. No use. I just can't do it.

Therapy with God

Well, I quickly realized that that wasn't the solution, either. I realized that if I'm going to show a verse to someone in the Bible, then if I know what chapter it's in, I can find the verse when I get there. That's especially true if I'm using my own Bible, because I probably have it underlined and I know where on the page it is. Even if I don't have my own Bible, I can still find it fast enough if I only know the chapter.

If I'm *not* going to show it to them in the Bible, then just having the verse memorized is good enough. Who was I trying to impress with the fancy chapter and verse references, anyway?

If you can memorize the chapter and verse and that's within your skill set, then by all means do so and you'll be better off for it. I just wanted to give the rest of us some comfort that memorizing Bible references isn't an all-or-nothing deal, and it's not an end in-and-of itself. There's a lot of value in memorizing just the chapter reference, or even just the Scripture verse itself, and it gives you a lot less to memorize. That meant a lot to me.

Memorize One Thing At A Time

Another mistake people tend to make is to try to memorize too much at once. The key is to *focus*. When a lion is on the hunt and there's a herd of gazelle in the field in front of her, she'll select a single gazelle and *focus* on that one gazelle. In reality, all of the rest of them are totally safe. She focuses on and chases that one animal until she gets it down. If she allowed herself to pick and choose and change her mind as she did the chase, she'd never catch anything. Without the focus, all is lost for her.

The same is true for memorizing Scripture. Focus on a single verse until you know you have it. Then focus on incorporating it into your spirit before you move on to the next verse. If that process takes a month, then so be it, as long as it isn't negligence that's making it take that long. Remember, focus is the key.

Rote Versus Spiritual Incorporation

There's a huge difference between memorizing Scripture so the words come out of your mouth in the proper order and incorporating that same verse into your spirit. Clearly, the latter is the goal.

You can tell when someone has memorized a verse simply by rote because there is no expression or passion in their voice when they recite it. They may as well be reading the grocery list.

When you memorize a verse, go back to "slow down, meditate, pray, apply." That's my mantra for Bible study of all kinds, and especially so with memorizing verses. Slow down, think about what it means, imagine yourself truly believing it down to the depth of your soul, and talk about it with Jesus. "Lord, you know I am really struggling with this verse and how it applies to me. Please open my eyes and my heart, and help me to truly believe it, and to believe that you mean it for me personally."

If you could truly believe that verse about yourself, would that get you a little emotionally spun up? If not, then you've chosen the wrong verse. If so, then let your voice reflect your feelings when you recite it to yourself out loud. Put your heart into it. Turn it into a prayer and an opportunity to visit with Jesus again.

> I heard a story once where a retired pastor was visiting another church. The elder pastor asked the young pastor, "Do you know the 23rd Psalm?" The young pastor said, "Yes sir, I do. Would you like me to recite it?" "Yes, son, that would be nice." After the younger pastor had recited the 23rd Psalm, he returned the question. "Do you know the 23rd Psalm, sir?" "Yes, I do, actually." The young pastor invited the elder pastor to the pulpit, and he accepted. After he had finished and returned to his seat, the younger pastor returned to the pulpit humbled, and said, "I know the 23rd Psalm. That gentleman knows the Lord."

Recite your verse as if you know the Lord who wrote it. Recite it not from your head, but from your spirit, your heart, your very soul.

Pray your memorized verse to God.

Context Of The Memorized Verse

Now, a caution regarding memorizing Scripture: Make sure the meaning you've given the verse you're memorizing is in context with the Bible's intended meaning. Don't memorize a single verse out of context and try to apply it to your life. Go back to "I can do all things through Christ who strengthens me" (Philippians 4:13). That's a great verse, but out of context, it implies I can leap tall buildings with a single bound while balancing my 3-year-old son on my lap through Christ who strengthens me.

Although Christ will give us strength to do whatever it is He calls us to do, that's not exactly what that verse means. If you read it in context, you realize that the Apostle Paul was talking about being able to be content with whatever life condition in which he finds himself. He can be content in riches and in poverty, in good health and in poor, in freedom or in bondage, whatever. He can *be content in all situations and circumstances* through Christ who strengthens him. That's what he's talking about. Make sure you understand the meaning of the verses you're memorizing, and that they're in context. Certainly, if you're operating in the will of God, then you can be confident that Christ will give you the strength, gifts, abilities, opportunities, support, etc., to succeed at that job. That's just not the context of that particular verse.

The Message To *You*

Finally, in memorizing Scripture, you need to be careful that it doesn't feed into the negative messages you already have to contend with. As an extreme example, if you see yourself as a terrible person and you memorize Paul saying, "Oh, wretched man that I am!" (Romans 7:24), well, you can see that that might not give you the peace you seek, and it probably won't undo the negative messages from your past.

Make sure that the messages you memorize, the ones that Christ is going to be whispering in your ear, are messages that you *don't* believe in your heart but want to and need to. They need to be messages that undo and reverse the negative messages from the past.

IX — OLD VERSUS NEW TESTAMENTS

Look For Jesus In Both

The biggest surprise to me when I was a new believer was that Jesus is in the Old Testament as much as He is. Oh, I'd heard about the prophesies, so I knew they were there, but little by little, the Old Testament started to unfold for me as a book entirely about Jesus, with the stories about the Jewish history being the subplots, much like a wonderful mystery story has subplots. Jesus, though, is the plot. He's the main story — the Hero.

"So what?" you ask. This is a mental health book. What's that got to do with mental health?

Well, pretty much everything. You see, as you become more and more aware, on a profoundly deep and personal level that the Bible was written — every single word — by the Creator of the Universe, the more confidence you'll have that what it says is absolutely and totally true, and absolutely and totally applies to you. We throw the terms "truth" and "word of God" around like we bandy about lemonade recipes. We often don't understand what they mean.

What it means is that the Bible is absolutely perfect. I can't emphasize that enough. Perfect. Not a single word is out of place. Not a single message has been garbled. Not a single commandment is misstated, overemphasized, inaccurate, inapplicable. Each and every statement made by God, the ultimate author and recorded by the human authors, is 100% perfect and 100% applies to you.

Further, it means that God is *really* in the details. Ever read Leviticus or Numbers? Wow, you talk about details. When you study them, though, you realize that all of those details point to Christ, and God was *meticulous* in their content. He's just as detail oriented and meticulous in your life.

If you *really* believed that was true, deeply, profoundly, way down deep inside, would it make a difference to your mental health? You bet it would.

It has to do with trust. Once you start to see Jesus and how you are to relate to Him everywhere in the Old Testament, the phrase "word of God" takes on entirely new meaning. It becomes something much greater than head-knowledge or just some Christian phrase. It becomes a part of the fabric of your being. You know that you know that you know that human beings could *never* have written this book. Never in a million years. The *only* explanation is that a profoundly Supreme Being wrote it — every word. No other explanation makes sense.

So if that's the case, then that same profoundly Supreme Being wrote the following:

> Philippians 4:5b-7 — The Lord is near. Be anxious for nothing, but in everything by prayer and supplication with thanksgiving let your requests be made known to God. And the peace of God, which surpasses all comprehension, will guard your hearts and your minds in Christ Jesus.

The Creator of the Universe has told you to be anxious for nothing because He is near. When you feel His nearness and achieve that freedom from anxiety, He promises that His peace will guard your hearts (e.g., feelings) and minds (e.g., thoughts) like a sentry guards a military post. Isn't that mental health?

Ok, let's say I've convinced you that, *if* the Old Testament really is about Jesus, then it does seem to give the Bible a lot more credibility. But the question is, How can I be sure that the Old Testament is about Jesus, and what exactly does that mean, anyway?

Well first of all, remember that until you read and read and read and read and read, you are just really going to have to take my word for it. But having said that, there are some things I can offer you.

Let me give you a simple example from Numbers 21:5-9. Please go read that section of Scripture now.

> God got angry at the complaining Israelites in the wilderness and sent poisonous serpents in amongst their camp. After thousands had died, the Israelites went to Moses and begged him to beseech God to save them from the serpents. God told Moses to put a bronze serpent on a standard (very tall pole) in the wilderness so that when the people were bitten by poisonous serpents they could just 'look' to the serpent and they would be saved from the effects of the poison. Other than look to the serpent, they didn't have to do anything to be freed from the effects of the poison. No medicine, no sucking the venom out, no praying or kneeling or dancing around or anything. Just 'look.'
>
> That seems pretty arbitrary, doesn't it? Why a serpent? Why just 'look?' Why not pray? Why not go down on your knees in worship or make a sacrifice or *something*? If I'd been writing Numbers on my own, I don't know what I'd have come up with, but I can tell you it wouldn't have been a serpent on a pole.

But God is in the details. Let's go back and look at the symbolism again. Serpents represent sin in the Old Testament. Remember the Garden of Eden? The sin is represented by the serpents that are killing the Israelites, as well as the serpent on the pole. The poison represents the effects of the sin on us personally. Poles and trees often represent the 'tree of Calvary,' or the cross.

But why would Jesus be represented by a serpent? The New Testament tells us that "Jesus became sin for us" (2 Corinthians 5:21), so the serpent on the pole is a perfect representation of Jesus on the cross. Jesus referred to this story Himself when He said, "As Moses lifted up the serpent in the wilderness, even so must the Son of Man be lifted up" (John 3:14). The idea of "looking" to the serpent is the idea that all we have to do is "look" to the savior, and we'll be saved from the sin that is killing us. No sacrifices, no falling on our faces, no being good people — just look.

So the whole point of this story is to graphically illustrate the concept of "salvation by grace" as it's represented in the New Testament. Salvation by grace is a free gift from God that saves us from our sin and gives us the promise of eternal life in heaven. We don't earn it, we *can't* earn it, it's a free gift if we only repent of our sin, look to God's Son on the cross, and trust Him. It's truly a *free* gift (Ephesians 2:8-9).

Pretty amazing, huh? What, on the surface seems strange and arbitrary, is in fact a perfect picture of the Gospel of Jesus Christ. Remember this story the next time you see your doctor's "snake on a pole" symbol for the medical profession.

> In another example, Joshua (Joshua 3:1), who's name in Hebrew is Yeshua (pronounced yesh-OO-uh), and who's name in Greek is — check this out — Jesus, lead the Israelites into the land of promise, the land flowing with milk and honey, just like our Lord Jesus will lead us into our Christian Promised Land if we will believe in Him and follow Him.
>
> Noah (Genesis Chapters 6-8), a picture of Jesus Christ, led His family into the ark and was spared from the judgment of God (a picture of salvation for us) because he believed in God's promise that he would be protected if he trusted God. Every detail of that story is symbolic of some element of Christ. The Hebrew verb translated as "pitch" (he was to *pitch* the ark inside and out with pitch — Genesis 6:14), is translated "atonement" in 71 out of 94 times that the same Hebrew word is used in the Old Testament. Literally, it means "covering." Christ's death was the 'atonement' for our sin, protecting us from the judgment of God if we trust Him and get on board, just as Noah's family was protected from the flood, in the ark, protected by the pitch. There was one door in the ark — there is one door, Jesus Christ, into salvation (John 4:6). The ark was made of gopher wood (Genesis 6:14), the wood of coffins in those days — we enter into

eternal life by dying to our own flesh and being "crucified with Christ" (Galatians 2:20).

The pictures go on and on and on. Every story, on some level or another, is about Jesus Christ or His character or our life in Him or something relating to Him. The Bible is truly a miracle from God.

As you study your Bible more and more, you'll see Him in there more and more. As you see Jesus more and more in the Old Testament, around every corner and under every rock, you'll become more and more convinced that there is *no way on earth* that 44 old gray-haired guys carrying shepherd staffs and walking around in robes and sandals over a 1500 year period of time could have pulled off this book. The more you study the Old Testament and come to believe that to your very core, the more you're going to trust that every single word of it was written by God to you, and you will become more and more motivated — driven, almost — to trust Him and love Him and be obedient to His commands. And then the more you fall in love with Him, and the more obedient to His commands you become, the more you will experience the peace and joy and contentment that God has for you.

That's His promise, and *that's* mental health.

Exaggeration And Emphasis

I'd like to take just a minute to address something that bothered me a great deal when I first started reading the Bible: It's *really* bloody! I wasn't sure what to do with all that blood, and what seemed like some pretty extreme judgments on God's part. I wasn't really trying to be critical of God, and I certainly didn't view myself as a better judge of what punishments should be meted out, but I really struggled with that at first. And all those sacrifices? What's with all *that* blood? The animals never did anything wrong, did they? Why did there have to be so much blood?

You probably know this already, but the answer, of course, lies with Jesus Christ.

First of all, regarding the sacrifices, each and every single one of them points directly to the cross. Every sacrifice is reflective of the sacrifice He made for us. Every detail points to some aspect of the death or sacrifice of Christ.[11] Through the sacrifices, God was teaching the Jews the concept of a substitutionary sacrifice to atone for sins, so that when God allowed Jesus to be the final substitutionary sacrifice to atone for all sins for all time, they'd recognize Him.

The life is in the blood (Genesis 9:4; Leviticus 17:11, 14; Deuteronomy 12:23). When the sacrificial animals of the Old Testament shed their blood, the Jewish owner was spared of the judgment of God, a death sentence of their own, for their sin. The problem was that they had to do it over and over. When our "Lamb of God" shed His blood, our judgment was diverted and our lives were spared, once and for all.

If you study and come to understand the sacrifices (Leviticus Chapters 1-7), you will gain a rich understanding of how God sees sin, how we are to dedicate ourselves to God, how we can find freedom from the emotional guilt of our own sin, the difference between unintentional sin and intentional sin, and a lot more. Don't see the study of the sacrifices as either boring or bloody. See them as the freedom from bondage you seek.

Ok, but what about all of the other killings? What about all of the wars and atrocities?

Think of it this way. I'd mentioned earlier that one way you can think about the Old Testament is that it's a video of the New Testament concepts. For the purposes of this discussion, think of that video as being an animated movie (please forgive what seems to be a disrespectful reference to Scripture, and stick with me as I make my point).

When animation developers really want children to notice something or make a big point, all of their character's movements are extremely colorful, loud, big, and exaggerated. They really want the little kids to notice, stay focused, and pay attention, so they really exaggerate and emphasize every movement of the characters.

The Old Testament is much like that. God wants us to really *get it* that sin is bad. The Amalekites (pronounced uh-MAL-luh-kytes), for instance, are a people in the Old Testament who are symbolic of the sin-filled life, the world system. God *really* wants us to *get it* in a big way that he really, really hates sin and the sin-filled world system, so He orders the Israelites to exterminate the entire population, including all of their women, children, and even their animals. Wipe out every single trace of them, never to reproduce again. Wow. That seems really harsh. But, out of His enormous love for us, God is making a point that He doesn't want us to miss.

In addition to that being an accurate history of what really happened (the miracle of the Bible), He is also trying to tell *us*, the New Testament believers, that He wants us out — completely and utterly out — of the world system to which we were in bondage before our liberation by Christ.

> The Apostle Paul says, "But may it never be that I would boast, except in the cross of our Lord Jesus Christ, through which the world has been crucified to me, and I to the world" (Galatians 6:14).

He wants us to exterminate any trace of the world system in our hearts and lives, so He uses the Amalekites to make the point in a very big way. When you read that story and make the connection, you're going to have a very different perspective of the movie you watched the other night, or the magazine you got at the check-out counter, that gossipy conversation you had with a friend, or that fast-food lunch you have every day that continues to pack on the pounds. God tells us that those things will hurt us — they are the Amalekites in our lives — and because He loves us and wants us to live wonderful, healthy, and God-filled lives, He wants them *completely* exterminated so they can never reproduce and plague us again.

God used the people and the history of the Old Testament to teach us, vividly and passionately, how He wants us to live. Every single story is about Jesus Christ, some aspect of His character, some lesson He wants us to learn about life or about ourselves, something. He did that because He loves us and wants us to live abundantly (John 10:10) here on earth, as well as eternally with Him. He is very much into the details, and there is much to be learned from a thorough study of the Old Testament.

In the end, as bloody as the Old Testament seems, it vividly reminds us that the life is in the blood, Jesus' blood, which protects us from ourselves and the enemy, and makes the atonement for our sin. The Old Testament stories show us how to live our lives and keep our eyes focused on Christ. The more you study the Old Testament and see Him there, the more in love with Him you will become.

X — CHATTING WITH JESUS

Prayer

I saved this technique until the end of the Techniques section because I want it to be indelibly imprinted and fresh when you get to the application section. There is nothing you can do to improve your internal life that is more important than your close and personal relationship with Christ. If you learn nothing else, learn this lesson.

The Apostle Paul said, "Pray without ceasing" (1 Thessalonians 5:17).

What?? How on earth do I do that? Oh sure, I pray when I get up and go to bed, I pray at meals, I pray when I need help. But what does he mean to "pray without ceasing?"

Wow, I had to give that a lot of thought, and frankly, I'm not quite there yet, but I'm getting better. Think about this:

> If you were handcuffed to someone 24 hours a day, much like you see in some of the westerns and adventure movies, the probability is pretty high that you'd talk to them quite a bit throughout the day. It wouldn't necessarily be a formal *conversation*, but just casual chit-chat all day long, on and off.

Well the reality is that you're a lot closer to Jesus than you would be if you were literally handcuffed to him. I decided that for me, that's what it's like to pray without ceasing. I 'chit-chat' with Jesus

Therapy with God

continually throughout the day. Anyone watching me might think I'm cracked, but that's what I do.

So how does that work out practically for me? Let me give you some specific examples of what I might say in this on-going dialogue:

- "Wow, Lord, what a beautiful blue sky today! What a fabulous artist You are. Thanks!"
- "Ok Lord, what'll it be today? A spot in the back of the parking lot, or are you going to bless me with one up front?"
- "Lord, I really need your strength right now to stay away from that restaurant. Protect me from myself, Lord."
- "Father, I know you don't owe me a thing, and You know I'll love you regardless, but I'd love to have… [fill in the blank]."
- "Father, wow, I'm not sure where that horrible thought came from, but I know it doesn't please You, and it sure doesn't glorify You. Please forgive me for my evil/selfish/hurtful thought, and help me make my thoughts obedient to you more quickly than I seem to be able to do."

I was having a conversation with a dear friend one day, lamenting about how I was struggling in my prayer life because I really didn't know how to pray. She said, "Then, don't pray." I said, "Huh? That doesn't make any sense." She said, "Yes it does. You're trying to pray in your own strength from your own mind. Just let the Holy Spirit pray through you." Ever since then, I have turned my prayers over to Him and I just let my mouth say the words He speaks into my heart. It completely revolutionized my prayer life and I found total peace and freedom with my prayers. It was at that point that I really started to connect with Jesus in a very special way.

Reach out and touch Him, be real and talk to Him throughout the day. He's right there. Chat with Him. Acknowledge Him. Put in requests to Him. Thank Him constantly. The whole purpose of prayer isn't to change His mind about what He wants for us — it's to change *our* minds about who He is and what we want. Prayer is, first and foremost, "reporting for duty."

The more you make your prayers about you, the more dissatisfied you will be. The more you make them about worshiping and praising Him and trying to discern *His* will, the more contented and satisfied you will become.

As we pray, we connect with Him. The closer we connect with Him, the more we can discern His will. The more we discern His will, the more we *want* His will to be done, and the more our prayers will reflect that. Our prayers are about connection with the Father, not putting the quarter in the vending machine.

I desperately want to continue to fall head-over-heels madly in love with Jesus Christ of Nazareth, and I want you to, also. He's an unbelievable man, and one with whom you can establish an unbelievable relationship. Chatting with Him and getting to know Him personally is a pivotal step toward growing and enhancing that love. This is not in lieu of the more formal morning and evening devotions and the like, and it's not to say we can't approach Him with formal requests. The Lord teaches us to do that in what we call "The Lord's prayer." Chatting is in addition to our formal prayer time. Both are critical components of your prayer life.

You do need to remember that He's still your Lord, so the chatting can never be so casual as to be irreverent or common. But to regard Him as the Lover of your soul and connect with Him minute by minute are the cornerstones of your love for Him. That love then becomes the cornerstone of your obedience to Him. And that obedience becomes the cornerstone of your joy.

Praying without ceasing, to me, is being constantly aware of His presence, in the room, with me right now, and then 'chatting' with Him as I would anyone who was constantly in my presence. To do otherwise would be rude, and to do so brings you that closeness to Him you seek.

Intermission Verse to Ponder: "There is an appointed time for everything. And there is a time for every event under heaven— A time to give birth and a time to die; A time to plant and a time to uproot what is planted. A time to kill and a time to heal; A time to tear down and a time to build up. A time to weep and a time to laugh; A time to mourn and a time to dance" (Ecclesiastes 3:1-4).

SECTION 4

****

APPLICATION

XI — THE SEVEN BIBLICAL FREEDOMS

What Robs Us Of Our Joy And Peace?

So now, let's get down to brass tacks. What's the real culprit here? What is it that actually robs us of our joy and peace? I'm going to discuss some very specific things that do that, and ask you to apply them to your own situation, carefully and one at a time, to see what fits. I don't claim to be an expert in your life. That's between you and God. These are the things that Scripture has pointed out are problems, and the degree to which these things are problems for you personally, you and God have to determine. But I will tell you this — the degree to which these things *are* problems to you personally is the degree to which your joy and peace will be shattered.

> Now's the time to pray, "Father, please open my heart to Your truth. Please open my eyes and let me see what's going on in my heart, and why I feel such pain. Your Bible tells me that, through my relationship with You and with the Holy Spirit, I already have peace and joy in my heart (Galatians 5:22), but I don't feel it. Help me understand what's going on in my heart, and why I'm blocking the fruit of the Spirit in my life. Reveal to me what You see in my heart. Amen."

The Seven Biblical Freedoms

I'm going to start off with what I call "Biblical Freedoms." I'm sure that there is a lot more than just seven, but I like the number seven, so I stopped there. You can look at your own life and see what else you might be able to come up with that fits this profile.

"Biblical Freedoms" are things which, if we hold on to them, keep us in bondage, rob us of mental health, and break God's heart as He watches us suffer. I've listed them as "Freedoms" as distinguished from the joy-robbers because in a very real sense, they're paradoxical. I'm telling you that you can be free of things that society has taught us are good things. They are actually part of what sets Christianity apart from so many other world religions that have rules. They have rules — we have freedoms. You wouldn't think that getting rid of them would bring you freedom — but it does.

I heard a great story that illustrates the problem with the Biblical Freedoms. Like so many great stories, you never know if it's true or just a parable, but it makes a great point so I offer it here. In Africa, people trap and eat monkeys. A very effective trap is to take a gourd of some sort, drill a hole in it about the size of a monkey's hand, put a nut inside the gourd, and tie the gourd securely to a tree. The monkey will come along, discover the gourd with the precious nut in it, and reach in and grab it. The problem the monkey then faces is that with his little hand wrapped around the nut, it will no longer fit through the hole, so can't get his hand back out and he's trapped. He fights and screams and pulls at the rope to get away, but in spite of the fact that it's going to kill him, he will not let go of the nut.

We are like that with things we love, regardless of how much they hurt us. Think about the following 'freedoms' as that nut in the trap. If you hold on to them, they will kill your joy, your spirit, and your witness. Release them, and you are free.

Study these freedoms, and you be the judge. Here's the full list to start with:

1. The freedom from expectations
2. The freedom of dying to self
3. The freedom from "Why?"

4. The freedom from self-esteem
5. The freedom of being a Godly spouse
6. The freedom of a gentle and quite spirit
7. The freedom of humility

1. The Freedom From Expectations.

One of the biggest thieves of peace and joy is expectations and rights. I have a *right* to be happy and healthy. I have a *right* to have a good husband/wife/job/whatever. I *expect* my life to be fulfilling and peaceful and comfortable, and when that doesn't happen, I get mad or frustrated or hurt or anxious or something.

Let me ask you a penetrating question:

What do you think John the Baptist's expectations were? (Matthew 14:3-12, Matthew 11:2-11)

John the Baptist had dedicated his entire life to preparing to preach Jesus' first coming, eating locusts and wild honey, dressed in luxurious camel hair (not!), sacrificing what might otherwise have been a life with a wife and family, and there he was in a dungeon for his efforts, under the threat of death. Furthermore, Jesus, who was performing miracle after miracle after miracle, was his *cousin* (Luke 1:36)! Didn't Jesus know he was in jail? Couldn't Jesus have rescued him? Where was He? "What's going on here," he must have thought.

> Finally, he couldn't take it any longer and sent his disciples to Jesus to ask Him whether or not He really was "The One" or if they should wait for another (Luke 7:20). What on earth was John thinking? Of *course* he knew that Jesus was the One. He saw the dove descending out of heaven. He heard the very voice of God proclaim Jesus as His Son (Gospel of John Chapter 1).

But John had expectations that weren't being fulfilled, and that colored everything else he knew to be true.

And Jesus said to John, "And blessed are you when you are not offended by Me" (Luke 7:23).

Expectations: the devils playground. "You deserve..." he whispers to us. "You have a right..." he declares. And because of our selfish, sinful, "It's about me" natural flesh, we choose to believe him.

Notice — it's a *choice*. We can choose to say, "Yeah, that's right!", or we can choose to say, "Get behind me, Satan!" (Matthew 16:23).

When our expectations aren't being met and our rights aren't being fulfilled, the result is bitterness, anger, resentment, cries of "it's not fair." We lose focus, we lose perspective, and we lose our fellowship with God. Rather than turn to God, we blame Him.

So what exactly are 'expectations?' The expectations I'm talking about here can be as simple as your son taking out the trash to as horrible as your spouse walking out on you. The intensity is very different, but the underlying principles are the same. The effects on your emotions and your life are very different, but the method of dealing with them is the same.

Before we get to the 'how' though, we need to understand something about the way we think. Imagine yourself just willing away all of the expectations of your life. Poof — they're gone. No more expectations or rights whatsoever. What do you see happening? What will change in your life if you could just miraculously stop having all rights and expectations?

If you're like most people, your fear is that if you stop having expectations, you will stop trying to have those expectations met, so they won't *get* met, and your situation will get even worse. We believe that the only thing that's getting us anywhere close to getting what we want is our expectations and our own efforts to get those expectations met. It feels like a rope we're holding on to as we hang over a cliff. If we let go of the rope, we'll fall to the ground far below and die.

Well, that makes sense from the world's perspective, but it's just not true in God's economy. It is a great paradox that if we give up our expectations and trust God, our lives will actually improve. God is there to catch us and set us free from our life on the rope.[12]

"But John's life sure didn't improve," you say. No? I understand that this is an extreme example, so please bear with me. But one minute John was in a dank, dark dungeon away from his family and friends and wallowing in the mud in misery, and the next minute he was filled with peace and joy and complete understanding in the arms of the Lord. "Of course!" he must have said. *"Now* I see what you had planned all along! Thank you, Lord, for not answering my prayer the way I wanted." John needed to decrease, and Jesus needed to increase (John 3:30). That was always John's mission: the ultimate fulfillment of his purpose in God.

Jesus knew what he was doing with John, and John's prayers weren't going to thwart Jesus' plans. Did John's anxiety and doubts and questions change his situation? How much better would John have felt, and how much better a witness might he have been to his disciples had he said to God, "I trust you Lord. I know You are in control here and I'm your servant. There's nothing I can do to change my circumstances, so I will trust that You are in complete control, and whatever happens will be Your will." Referring to being content in all circumstances, the Apostle Paul said, "I can do all things through Him who gives me strength" (Philippians 4:13). Is there peace in that? You bet.

God knew what He was doing in John's life, and He knows what He's doing in yours.

Read the story of Joseph in the book of Genesis (Genesis Chapters 37-50). Many terrible things happened to Joseph, but he never stopped trusting in and relying on God. As a result, God blessed him and used him to fulfill His amazing purpose. As it turned out, it was those 'terrible things' Joseph went through that were the very training ground for the profoundly critical job he had to do later on in his life. Beatings, being thrown in a pit to die, dragged off to Egypt to slavery and then imprisoned for many years for nothing he did wrong — these were all Joseph's training ground for his God-given purpose. As a result of Joseph's faithfulness and perseverance in trusting in God in spite of his terrible circumstances, plus his willingness to make the best of and learn from each situation, he rose to great power in Egypt and was able to save the people of Egypt, as well as the entire nation of Israel, from extermination.

If you and Jesus have never spent time together in the story of Joseph in the Old Testament, please do so. It's a great account. Not only does it show you how God's providential plans can work in your life, but it beautifully illustrates the peace that can come when you are released from the bondage of your rights and expectations.

Now read the book of Esther. One day Esther was a happy young woman who loved and trusted the Lord and was living with an uncle who cherished her. The next day she was captured by the king's thugs and brought into his harem to go through two years of polish and refinement at the hands of the king's eunuchs. After the two years, she, along with all of the other women who were captured, was forced to sleep with the king against her will with the hope of impressing him and becoming the new Queen of Persia. If she failed, she would be sentenced to a life in his harem, serving his 'needs.' If she succeeded, she would be a Queen, but with few more rights than if she was just one of the harem women.

What did Esther think about her situation? Did she wonder where God was? Scripture doesn't say, but what would you think if that was you?

Esther was chosen, and became Queen of all Persia. What she didn't know was that, as a result of that turn of events in her life, she would be in a position to save the nation of Israel from annihilation. Her uncle, who was grief-stricken at having lost her, heard that the King had been duped, and the people of Israel were to be completely exterminated at the hands of the Persians. Her uncle counseled her to intervene with the King, an act punishable by death. In response to her great fear, he said, "And who knows whether you have not attained royalty for such a time as this" (Esther 4:14). In spite of the threat of death, she warned the king, and Israel was saved. Had she not been taken hostage and put into service for the King, a terrible atrocity would have been committed.

God is still in control, even in your situation. It may not always seem like that to you, but He is. Find your freedom in that.

So how do you achieve that freedom? You give your rights and expectations to Him. When you feel yourself getting angry or frustrated or fearful because something you *expected* to happen didn't, do what you can, if you can, and then pray it away to God. Don't let it rob you of your joy. Hold on to your witness with all of your strength. Trust God and pray it right onto the foot of the cross.

Think of it this way. Take a moment and read 1 Peter 4:12-13. When your expectations are not being met, something in your life is happening that you don't like. Something is not getting done, you are feeling some sort of pain, you are enduring some sort of inconvenience, there is loss, possibly grief. When expectations aren't being met, it just feels bad.

But what if you *knew*, for instance, that through this situation, God was working on you to build up a specific character quality that He knows will be necessary down the road for something much harder and much greater?

As I discussed in the section on feelings, life is a series of boot-camps and battles. Very seldom do you have true R&R. God has a plan for your life, and it isn't for you to sit around in ease and comfort. There's a battle to be waged. He has work for you to do. If you're not in the middle of the battle, then you're probably in boot-camp. Boot-camp feels bad, but it's the very training you need to be able to handle the next battle.

Jesus, speaking of the new church, said, "...and the gates of hell shall not prevail against it" (Matthew 16:18). I think we sometimes think, in our self-focused perspective, that we're supposed to sit around waiting for the gates of hell to attack us and we'll win that battle through the power of Christ. Gates don't attack, folks. We attack the gates. The picture is that we're on an assault against the gates of hell. We're the aggressors, not the gates. There's a battle to be waged against the spiritual forces, and if we don't take the offensive, people are lost.

So what's that got to do with expectations? God wants you prepared for battle and engaging the enemy. You have some learning and training to do. One of the things soldiers learn in boot-camp is how to handle pain. They feel it, sure. The pain doesn't go away. But they learn different ways of dealing with it while staying focused. If they didn't have those painful boot-camp experiences, then when they got hurt in the real battle, they'd risk falling apart. Their own safety would be threatened, and they'd be no good to their comrades who might need them.

The same is true in the battle in which we find ourselves. If you let your son's trash incident rattle you, how are you going to be able to handle your spouse working late and missing dinner, or your daughter failing school? And those are just the tip of the iceberg of life.

It's all boot-camp. God cares far more for your character and for your preparation for battle than He does your comfort. God will either do or allow whatever He has to in your life to teach you how to fight the enemy.

So how is your son not taking out the trash training for fighting the enemy?

Two things: First, remember that the best weapon the enemy has against the church of Christ is to ruin our witness.

Dealing with your son's disobedience, first of all, is an opportunity for you to demonstrate grace and unconditional love. When your son doesn't take out the trash, he's not 'earning' your love. He's not doing what he is 'supposed' to do. When Jesus died on the cross, we weren't 'earning' His love, either. Although it is on an entirely different scale, it gives you a small taste of what Jesus might have been feeling when He loved us unconditionally "while we were yet sinners" (Romans 5:8). In a very simple and small way, we 'join' Him in that expression of grace and sacrificial love.

Second, we share in His sufferings, and for this we are to rejoice (1 Peter 4:13). If you are suffering for any reason whatsoever, whether great or small, it is an opportunity to share in the sufferings of Christ. Why?

Because people are watching. It's your witness. Your reaction to your pain can either glorify God or diminish Him in the eyes of those who are watching. A glorified God draws people in, and that's your job.

Bad times are wonderful opportunities to show the power of God in our lives. If we never have bad times, we never have that glorious opportunity. Nobody is impressed with someone who loves God when everything in their life is always wonderful. We talked about

Job earlier. It wasn't until Job's life fell apart that God was glorified through him. Job learned, in the end, to yield his rights to God.

The little things like the trash incident are opportunities to learn and grow in preparation for the big things that, when we handle them God's way, glorify God.

People watch Christians like they do no other group on the face of the planet. They lie in wait for us to fall, to look like hypocrites, to show that we don't really trust God the way we say we do, that we're no better off for our faith than they are without it. When the world sees us crumble under the pressures of life, they say,"Ah HAH! I *knew* it! I was right! Your so-called God isn't what you keep saying He is at all! He's just a fraud and a flimsy crutch, and you don't really buy what your sellin'."

Ok, so who's watching you react when your son doesn't take out the trash? God, the angels, the enemy, and your son. If you handle it well, it's an example for him, it's more training for you, it's a thrill for the angels, and it's a warning to the enemy. You're in boot-camp. Use the trash situation to learn patience and grace and as an opportunity to express unconditional love. Far more than that, though, with the little things, learn the skill of "turning it over to God." Then when the bigger stuff comes, where people really *do* watch you, when it really counts, you'll already know how to do it.

It's a skill you need to practice, and God is always giving you opportunities to do so.

Trust that whatever God is allowing in our lives now, no matter how great or small, it is training for battles to come. We are in a raging battle for the souls around us, folks. Every opportunity we can take to show God as being faithful to give us strength and be there when the big trials come is an opportunity to show them that our God is real.

To be ready for the big trials, you need to practice with the little ones. Learn how to turn them *all* over to God, you will sharpen the skill, and at the same time, find rest unto your souls (Matthew 11:28-30).

That's why the Apostles Paul, James, and Peter all proclaim in one resounding voice — rejoice, not in spite of, but *because* of, your trials.

Therapy with God

When your son doesn't take out the trash, let there be consequences, of course, because your job is to train him. No question that's true. When your boss is mean to you or takes credit for something you've done, or when your best friend tells other people an embarrassing secret about you, certainly learn the practical skills of discernment and boundaries and self-protection. Do what you can to accomplish what you can and stay as safe as you can. Always do what you can.

But at the same time say, "Lord, take this anger and anxiety about this situation from me. Let me give this 'right' to You as my advocate and my champion. Help me find peace in my soul by leaving this otherwise-frustrating situation at the foot of Your cross. Let me be a good witness to those who are hurting me." Even if there are practical consequences and reactions to a situation and steps you must take, find your *inner peace* through Him in all of these situations. Training with the little things that plague you will help prepare you for the bigger things to come.

Like the soldier on the battlefield, if you can be at peace, calm and focused, you will keep your wits about you better, allowing you better judgment as to how to *deal* with the situation at hand. Give your expectations and rights to God, see it as a learning experience in God's grand plan for your life, and as people are watching, they'll be drawn to the Lord who gives you strength.

Ok, now the pep-talk. Remember we're talking baby-steps here.

We are a nation built on people fighting for their rights. It's in our blood and our culture. It's in all of our favorite movies. This is a huge obstacle for us because it flies in the face of everything we hold to be true. We want to hold onto our rights with both hands.

But you've done that your whole life. Is it working? Does doing so truly bring you peace and joy? Does holding on to them solve the problem? Do you want to talk about unfair? Let's talk about Jesus. Jesus had done nothing wrong and yet He never fought for His rights. He just trusted God, His Father. He certainly asked for the "cup to be taken," and He cried out to Him. But in the end, He surrendered and trusted Him.

This is not an easy skill to learn. It's natural to want to hold on to our rights. Understand, though, that there are lots of things that are 'natural' in our temporal bodies, but that does not make them right, they do not necessarily glorify God, and it does not make them good for us. Paul said, "Who will set me free from the body of this death!" (Romans 7:24). We need to fight the 'natural' in our bodies. That's part of the battle we are waging, and to honor God, we *must* win.

Freedom from expectations requires that we understand that God is in control, He loves us far more than we love ourselves, He knows what's best for us and knows His plans for us (Jeremiah 29:4-14), and will turn all situations into good for us (Romans 8:28).

Think about it this way: The anxiety you have been experiencing and expressing trying to protect your rights hasn't caused the situations to change so far, so why should you expect it to do so in the future? By allowing your unmet expectations and rights to rob you of your joy, you have caught yourself in your own trap, and you have lost your witness.

Reflect on this definition of Joy: The deeply-rooted confidence that God is in control.[13]

Whatever you can give to Him leaves room for your peace and joy to flourish. Whatever you keep, robs you. The choice is yours.

2. The Freedom Of Dying To Self.

The next freedom we experience is the freedom of dying to our own flesh and selfishness. When we are in the world, we have this competitive "I gotta win" spirit, which means I have to look out for myself because everyone else is looking out for themselves. This spirit of competition creates anxiety, a sense of loss and pain when we 'lose,' and relationship problems when our motives become clear or interfere.

When we are about ourselves, we fall victim to the "He who dies with the most toys wins" mentality. As Christ followers, we are commanded to be about the other guy (Philippians 2:3; Galatians 6:2). Therefore, when we 'lose' so to speak, that means the other guy 'wins,' and in Christ's economy, we win as well. It's the ultimate win-win situation. In the world's economy, there are winners and losers, and we want to be the winners. In Christ's economy, the more we 'lose,' the more we win in His eyes.

> "For whoever wishes to save his life will lose it, but whoever loses his life for My sake and the Gospel's will save it" (Mark 8:35).

Think of it this way: If your son needed a kidney transplant, but to give it to him you needed to get a second job, you would do that without the second thought for the inconvenience to your time. When your child received the transplant and his life was spared, you would rejoice and be thankful that you had the opportunity to work to secure your child's safety. You would view it as a 'win-win' situation. You gave of yourself and your time selflessly to benefit your son. Having a son in need is 'bondage.' Having the freedom and opportunity to serve his needs was a huge blessing to you.

God views all of his children that way, and He wants us to view each other that way, as well. He sent Jesus to the cross to serve us. Jesus washed His disciple's feet as an illustration of service, and told us to do the same thing with others, regardless of who they are or how we feel about them.

Always remember that Jesus washed Judas's feet knowing he was about to betray Him.

The more we obediently serve others and put others' needs before our own, the more God sets us free from selfishness. We lose that "I gotta win" mentality, and that competitive anxiety fades into contentment.

Why does God want us to die to ourselves? For several reasons: First, because Jesus did and He wants us to emulate Jesus. Second, because the world system says, "Me, me, me," and He wants us to be different, to be set apart, so people notice that there is something different about our Lord. If we just tell people about Him but we look like everyone else, then what do we have to offer them that they don't already have? For us to draw them into a relationship with Christ, they have to see His reality in our lives and they have to experience His power through us and our lives.

Without the power of Christ, we could never pull off the "die to self" approach to life. Oh, we might be able to squeak it out for a season, but eventually we'd grow resentful and wonder why we're the ones who have to keep dying to *our* self. Why can't the other guy die to *his* self once in a while? We'd grow resentful, buckle, and probably even whiplash back into being more selfish than before. "I'm not going to let *that* happen ever again!" we say.

The only way we can make this a permanent way of life is with the presence and power of the Holy Spirit, and a deeply held commitment to Jesus. We have to have our needs fulfilled by Him and Him alone, and only *then* do we have any hope of making selflessness a way of life. Our consistent, unwavering selflessness, then, becomes the 'proof' that people need to believe that Christ is real, as they see that He's real to us, and as they see Him shining from us. They are drawn to Him through our selflessness, and as we become His witnesses, we experience a boundless joy that surpasses understanding. Paradoxically, dying to self is the ultimate self*ish*ness — there is no more fulfilling way of life.

The more we realize that it's not about us, the more we "die to self," the more peace, the more freedom, and the more mental health we experience. And people are always watching.

3. The Freedom From "Why?"

Wow — do we like the word "Why." I think it's one of our favorite words. We think children who constantly ask, "Why?" are cute, inquisitive, thinkers. Many of the worlds great innovations and philosophies were grounded in the question "Why?".

So why, then, do I offer you freedom *from* "Why?" Because all too often, our "Why?" becomes, "Why, God?"

What does that mean? It means you're questioning God's judgment, His provision, His love for you.

"Why are you allowing this pain in my life, God?" "If you're a loving God, why did you allow me to get fired." "Why did you allow my husband to leave?" "Why did you allow my mother to die?"

Please understand that all of these are terrible things. They hurt, and we hurt, and God understands our pain and our grief. But

Therapy with God

remember Job? In Chapter 1, we are privy to a conversation between God and Satan where Satan gets permission from God to wreck Job's life. Why did He give Satan that permission?

For His glory. Satan believed that once Job's life was wrecked, he would curse God to His face. Satan contended that the only reason Job loves God is because He put a hedge of protection around him and blessed the work of His hands. God doesn't care what Satan thinks, but He cares what we think, and He cares what the angels think. He used Satan to show us how a man who loves and fears God reacts to adversity.

So Satan destroyed everything in Job's life. He took his farm, his flocks, his crops, his herds, and finally, all ten of his children. Naturally, Job tore his clothes and grieved bitterly.

But he never cursed God. Instead, he said, "The Lord gave, and the Lord hath taken away. Blessed be the name of the Lord" (Job 1:21).

Then, for the next 27 chapters, Job had to endure his friends telling him that the reason God put him through this is because he is a sinner, and that there is some hidden sin in his life. Throughout that torture, God never spoke to Job to assure him that this was all in God's hands, and He had a purpose for Job's troubles that he could not divulge to him. This was to show that Job loved God, regardless of his circumstances.

Finally, after that interminable, torturous onslaught of blame and condemnation, Job buckled. Chapters 29-31 show Job lamenting what has happened to him, feeling like God has abandoned him, and finally, in the end of his tirade proclaiming his innocence, he asks God to answer Him, and give him and explanation as to what has happened. He never condemned God, He never rejected Him, but he asked God, "Why?" (Job 31:35).

Starting in Chapter 38, after another friend had taken his shot at Job, God did indeed respond to Job's question, "Why?" For the next four chapters, God answers Job. What was God's answer?

"Who do you think you are?!"

God said, "Did *you* place the stars in the sky? Did *you* stop the waters at the beach? Did *you* create the leviathans that roam the earth? What gives *you* the right to question Me, Job? What I do, I

Therapy with God

do for my own purposes, and if I choose to tell you, then that's my choice, but if I don't, then that is also my choice."

For four chapters, Job was rebuked by God to put him back into the proper place, the proper perspective. God wanted Job to remember that He is in control, and that to really, truly experience the peace and joy of God in any and all circumstances, Job needed to remember that.

When Job finally *saw* God through this trial, he retracted and repented in dust and ashes (Job 42:5-6). He took back his "Why."

Then God referred to Job as "My servant" *four times* in the next two verses. This was a term of great love and endearment. When Job retracted and repented, God restored him to a full relationship to Himself. Verse 9 says that the Lord "lifted up the face of Job," meaning He comforted Him and Job felt comforted by God.

God never answered Job's question. He simply demonstrated to him that the question had no place. Once Job understood that the ways of God were "too wonderful for me, which I did not know," he finally *saw* God, understood everything clearly, and he took it all back. At that point, as God had tried to do with Cain, Job's "countenance was lifted up."

Cain never got it; Job did. Cain refused to trust God; Job repented and honored God. Cain was condemned; Job was blessed.

These are perfect illustrations of what happens in our hearts when we make those same choices. If you insist on asking God, "Why," then you will never receive the blessing of peace and joy God has for you. Your own confusion, irritation with God, and frustration with your circumstances will condemn you to a life of anxiety, pain, and strained fellowship with God. You become Cain.

Now, before I close this section, I'd like to bring it home. Ok, so that makes sense regarding questioning God, but what about my normal every day circumstances that have nothing to do with God? What about things like, "Why can't my husband put the cap back on the toothpaste!?" or "Why can't my teenager see that the trash is falling out onto the floor and just take it outside?!" or "Why can't my boss leave me alone and just let me do my work?!"

Totally valid questions that deserve to be answered. But let me ask you, do you get answers? Do the situations ever change? When you've asked your teenager that question a thousand times, does he ever answer it to your satisfaction? Do things improve because you've asked that question again and again?

Or are you just robbing yourself, and possibly those around you, of peace?

Now again, your teenager needs to be disciplined and coached. I'm not taking that away from you. All I'm doing is trying to help you see that the question "Why" isn't helping you do that. It isn't *ever* going to get the cap back on the toothpaste, and it isn't going to change your boss's heart. All it does is rob you of your joy.

Remember this phrase? "It is what it is."

That's the big "why-stopper." It simply is what it is. Share with your husband your desires, teach and discipline your teenager, try to get along with your boss, but lose the "Why."

It simply is what it is.

Satan loves the question, "Why" because it puts him in the position of questioning God's authority in your life. Satan whispers "why" in your ear and sucks you into his way of thinking. You have a right to know why something is happening to you, don't you? Satan sure thinks so.

In the Gospel of John 12:5, John recorded the words of Judas Iscariot. It was the only time in the entire Gospel of John that Judas spoke. What was the first word out of Judas's mouth that day? "Why." Hmm.

God has a purpose for your life, and He has a purpose for this situation in your life. Just learn to trust Him. If you free yourself from the burden of having to know "Why" and just rest in the grace and provision of God, whether it feels good or bad at the time, whether it's about some great pain in your life or the cap on the toothpaste, then the peace of God will, by default, guard your heart.

4. The Freedom From Self-Esteem.

Self-esteem is a concept that was propagated during the 60's and 70's and has really taken root in our self-centered society. I won't go into it fully here because I cover it in detail in Chapter 13, "The Issue of Self-esteem." I wanted to include it here briefly, though, because it is certainly one of the Biblical Freedoms, and needs to be considered as such.

By way of introduction, self-esteem is far less about how we feel about ourselves than it is how we perceive that our primary care-givers felt about us, and how we feel about them. We are a reflection of them in our own eyes, so if we esteem them little, we will esteem ourselves little. If they esteemed us little, then we've 'inherited' their perception of us as our own.

I propose we give up the notion of 'self' esteem, and turn instead to 'God' esteem. If He regards you as valuable enough to Him to die for, then why would you think less of yourself than He does? Think about that. To have a poor self-esteem says essentially, "Christ's opinion of me isn't good enough. My parents' opinion of me is more important to me than Christ's." It also says that you think that God really does make junk. That's a lie straight from the pit of hell.

Ok, now, please don't be offended by that. I am totally aware that this is a new concept, and it won't go down particularly easy since our entire mental health community is all about self-esteem. It has become a part of our culture. I take exception to it, but for those of you who have suffered from it, take heart. And for the professional out there for whom this is a new idea, also take heart. I learned it from somebody else, too, and until I did, I was preaching self-esteem right along with the rest of you. What I offer here for all of us is not condemnation, but hope and freedom.

One thought: If you're not a believer in Jesus Christ, then regretfully, 'self-esteem' is all you have. We all need to have esteem. We need to believe that we matter; we need confidence in our ability to relate, to get things done, to achieve our purpose. The difference between those who have God and those who do not is simply the source of that esteem. What I'm proposing here is that if you're a believer in Christ, then you stop relying on yourself for that esteem like the world does, and turn instead to Him. That's where the freedom comes from.

When you hear yourself being down on yourself, say, "Get behind me, Satan!" and rebuke that evil voice in your head. Say instead, "God thought enough of me to die for me, God thinks I have value and purpose, God will give me the tools I need to fulfill that purpose, so I *refuse* to listen to you tell me I'm worth any less than that!"

I know that will be hard at first and you won't believe it. Do not give up, though. You keep saying that, actively reject those dysfunctional messages, and before you know it, it will have sunk into your heart.

Please understand that this short treatment of the issue probably isn't enough to shift your thinking on the idea of self-esteem. That's why I spent an entire chapter on it. Please don't make a judgment about this difficult concept until you've read that chapter.

5. The Freedom Of Being A Godly Spouse.

This section is intended for the marriage that has some of the normal strains of two people living together in the same house. It does not address the issue of abuse, either physical or emotional. Emotional abuse includes controlling behaviors, demeaning verbal assaults, financial control, isolation, and other behaviors meant to control the marriage. They usually leave the abused spouse feeling helpless, less-than, worthless, and often stupid. It will destroy your soul if left unchecked, and can be as dangerous to your well-being as physical abuse. If you are in danger by either physical or emotional abuse, then get professional help immediately, and if need be, seek safety. When you're in danger, there is nothing un-Biblical about separating for a season if needed to sort it out. I will say, however, that if you're at the place where you need to leave to seek safety from physical danger, you're probably past the point where you should have sought legal help. If this is your situation, *please* consult with your pastor, seek legal and physical protection, and get the help you need to stay safe. It may be the exact 'wake-up call' your spouse needs to get the help *they* need, as well.

So for everyone else who lives in a marriage that is strained and full of the difficulties of non-abusive marriage conflicts, this section is intended to set you free, not put more bondage on you. Even so, this is a tough concept, so please bear with me.

There are as many different marriage dynamics as there are marriages. This section does not pretend to solve all of the problems.

If you are in a difficult marriage, I always recommend marriage counseling. There are some wonderful ways of dealing with the conflicts and communication issues that a good Christian Marriage Therapist can teach you, and you will never regret it. This section simply introduces you to the concept of the Godly spouse as presented in Scripture so you can start with the foundation for marriage that God presents. The therapy can then refine this foundational beginning.

The conflict of being a Godly spouse goes back to the issue of 'winning and losing.' We're taught by Hollywood and society to look out for ourselves and make our marriages about us. When we are looking out for ourselves in our marriages, we perceive it as a competition. At first it's love and harmony and trying to impress each other, but it eventually becomes, "I have to look out for myself because he's only looking out for himself." It's "every man for himself."

God says that first and foremost, you are *His* child, and it is *His* responsibility to look out for you and provide for you during your stay on earth. To complain about your spouse says to God, "Your provision is not good enough for me. I have to fight for my own rights because I don't trust that You will provide what I need." The fact is that God will provide what we need, and we will learn a lot through the difficult processes of our lives. The problem is, He doesn't always provide what we *want*, and sometimes that cuts against our grain. We just need to be careful about the difference.

Being a Godly spouse means to give it all to God. Stop fighting, stop expecting, stop being frustrated and angry and always feeling like you're losing out. Understand that your spouse is God's gift to you, and even if they aren't what you'd like them to be, even if they aren't that wonderful Godly husband or wife God wants them to be, and even if you do not understand God's judgment, work with Him.

Understand that God is in control, and even if you feel like you married your spouse out of disobedience and rebellion toward God, God promises you that if your love Him and submit your life to Him now, He will use it and turn it to good (Romans 8:28), just as He did David's marriage to Bathsheba (2 Samuel Chapters 11 and 12). In spite of adultery and murder and disobedience to God, God allowed

David and Bathsheba to be tremendously successful as rulers, give birth to King Solomon, and be in the genealogy of our Lord. He is not punishing you with this marriage: He is asking you to lean on Him and grow within it. It may not always be easy, but Jesus has set a higher standard for Christians than for the world. Learn to lean on God for strength, love, acceptance, and provision, and you will find freedom, blessings, peace, and a better marriage as a result. That's a promise from God (1 Peter 3:1-2).

I know this is a tough one if you're in a difficult marriage. So again, please bear with me on this topic. I cover it in more detail in Chapter 20, "Topical Examples: New Testament," and hopefully it will make more sense to you there.

6. The Freedom Of A Gentle And Quiet Spirit (1 Peter 3:4).

Here we are again, addressing the competitive worldly perspective. A gentle and quiet spirit is "precious in the sight of God," and God promises us wives that if we have a husband who is not acting in a Godly way, when he sees our "chaste and respectful behavior" and "gentle and quiet spirit" he'll start to see us differently, he'll start to see the world differently, but most importantly, he'll start to see God differently. If you want to see God turn that man of yours into a Godly man, have the spirit that God wants you to have: gentle and quiet. And frankly, men, this applies to you, too. If you want to see your wife start to love and respect you the way God wants her to, know that the Scripture verses that apply to you also point to a gentle and quiet spirit. It goes both ways.

Ok, I can hear you now. "*Gentle and quiet!!??* I'd have to get a personality transplant!" No, that's not what this is saying. You don't have to become a demure little church mouse. God is telling you that it's the *spirit* that is the focus here. A gentle and quiet spirit belongs to a man or woman who understands, first of all, that their life is not about them. Their priorities are straight: God first, spouse second, children third, and everyone else a distant last. He understands the meaning of pride and how destructive it is. She understands the meaning of agape love and how critical it is, and where she gets her 'love tank' filled — from God. He understands that the definition isn't talking about the volume of his speech, unless he uses that volume to control and hurt people. It isn't talking about the strength of her personality, unless she uses that strength to get what she wants. Personal strength is perfectly compatible with a gentle and quiet spirit if it's being used to glorify and honor God through how she relates to her husband and others.

Truly wives, when you disagree with your husband, tell him so. If you think something should be handled differently, be honest with him. Communicate, state your desires, tell him how you feel, tell him what you want, tell him how he's hurt you. And then turn your pain, your desires, and your expectations over to him and to God.

Husbands, when your wife disagrees with you, listen to her and honor her as a partner in this life with you. Respect her opinion and enter into dialogue with her. It doesn't mean you necessarily have to yield to her opinion, but absolutely listen and think about what she is saying. Much of the yelling that goes on between two people is because one partner doesn't feel heard by the other. The voice inside of our heads tells us that if we're not being heard, speak louder — and louder — and louder. Listen to your partner. That's the respect God requires of all of us.

I address this whole issue in more depth in Chapter 20, "Topical Examples: New Testament," but for now I'd like to make a couple of observations. First of all, the King James Version says, "meek and quiet spirit." The word 'meek' means 'strength under control.' The very command acknowledges and honors our strength. God isn't asking us to be milk toasts and doormats. He is asking us to respect the positions our husbands have as those accountable to God for how the family functions, and help him make it a success. Secondly, husbands and wives both need to understand that no husband can be an effective leader of his family without her permission and support.

I need to repeat that with more emphasis:

No husband can be an effective leader of his family without his wife's permission and support.

Without her permission, it will just be an on-going battle and nothing will be accomplished. If she has to get her way, then either bitterness or anger will be the predominating atmosphere, or the husband will just give up and fold in on himself. If he's a tyrant or a demagogue, then she will rebel against feeling like she is being oppressed and 'under the rule of his thumb.' Honor God by honoring your spouse's God-given role in the family. Remember this: They are just an earthly stand-in for your heavenly Bridegroom.

When you give up the fight to 'win,' and you understand that it isn't about you and that your primary job is to honor and represent Jesus to your spouse, your children, and to the people who are watching, then your expectations will shift. Focus on Him and let Him fill your spirit with His. When that happens, you'll have that 'quiet spirit' naturally, and you'll experience the peace and joy that brings.

7. The Freedom Of Humility.

This is very similar to the concept of meekness, but has an added element. Humility, is that state of mind that says four things:

1. I am totally and utterly dependent on God for everything that I do and for everything that happens to me.
2. I will be absolutely obedient to God's will, regardless of the circumstances, regardless of the consequences, and regardless of how I feel or what I understand.
3. I am content with the provision of God, and trust that He will give to me what's best for me and what I need to serve Him when I need it.
4. I understand that I am a sinner, no better than anyone else on the face of the planet, because if any of us have been redeemed, it was through God's grace and mercy that that is so, not through anything we did or could have done. I see myself honestly and fearlessly, to the extent to which I am able, as God sees me.

Now, if you can embrace that in your innermost being, believe it to your core, and manifest it in your relationship with God and others, then you are truly humble.

Now let me talk for a minute to the rest of us. I don't know about you, but I know I'm a long way from that. I believe it totally, I seek it, I crave it, and I know that I know that I know that it's the ultimate destiny and heaven on earth, as well as a great source of joy and peace. I also know that it's the Final Frontier, waiting to be explored by the brave of heart and fearless.

In the book of Numbers, Moses is referred to as the most humble man on the planet (Numbers 12:3). That means he understood and embraced the above precepts. It didn't mean he was weak, or introverted, or namby-pamby, or had a low self-esteem or anything else we assign to the word 'humble.' It means he totally understood his relationship to God.

Now let me ask you a question: *Who wrote Numbers?*

That's right. Moses. Moses described *himself* as the most humble man on the face of the planet. What does that tell you about humility? What does that tell you about *false* humility?

False humility is more akin to self-deprecation than humility. It says, "Oh, I'm such a lowly person, I'm less than you, I'm a low-life, I'm *so* unworthy!" You'll *never* hear Moses saying those things.

Or it says, "Aw, shucks. I can't take credit for *that*. I have to give *all the Glory to God,*" while saying in our hearts, "Wow, I really was good."

David was a man after God's own heart. He was bold, he was brave, he was a great leader, but if you look at him from the perspective of the above list, he was also very humble. He *totally* depended on God. Except for the unfortunate incident with Bathsheba (2 Samuel Chapter 11), he was also totally obedient to God. And if you read Psalms, he totally understood his relative position in the world. He was the richest man on the face of the planet, and yet he said, "I am poor and needy" or "poor and sorrowful" five times in the Psalms he wrote, and inferred the same thing many more times as well.

How could he have so much and yet see himself as so poor? Because he was humble, he was "poor in spirit" (Matthew 5:3) as

Jesus said. He understood that all that wealth was at the mercy of God, he held onto it with a soft touch, and knew that as the Lord giveth, so at any time, the Lord could taketh away again. He never put his trust in his wealth, his family, his kingdom, his fame, his power, or anything else. He put his trust in God, and God alone.

And David had love for God and peace in his heart[14] in the midst of his trials.

So here's the entire list again. Reflect on it for a moment before you move on to the Seven Joy-robbers:

1. The freedom from expectations
2. The freedom of dying to self
3. The freedom from "Why?"
4. The freedom from self-esteem
5. The freedom of being a Godly spouse
6. The freedom of a gentle and quite spirit
7. The freedom of humility

XII — THE SEVEN JOY-ROBBERS

The Damage We Do To Ourselves

Now let's touch on the items that we all *know* are joy-robbers and disappointments to God. There's nothing paradoxical about them. These are items that we often know are wrong, but we deem them 'too hard,' or we fall into the trap that says, "Hey, I am who I am. This is the way God made me, so it must be okay."

As a Christian, you don't have that excuse. God says that you are a new creature in Christ, and that the old things have passed away and new things have come (2 Corinthians 5:17). Of course you struggle with sin — we all do. But Jesus said, "blessed are those who mourn, for they shall be comforted" (Matthew 5:4). The 'mourning' He was talking about was primarily mourning about our sin. If you're making excuses for it and accepting it as 'normal,' then you don't qualify for this blessing. He knows we sin, but He expects us to *mourn* about it, repent of it, ask His help in defeating it. Once we've done that, He wants us to allow Him to comfort us by forgiving us and then giving us the strength to be free from the bondage of it.

He also said, "Blessed are those who hunger and thirst after righteousness, for they shall be *filled*!" Don't you want to be comforted and filled by Jesus Christ? He isn't saying here that we *might* be filled — it's a *promise*!

Mourn and hunger and thirst after righteousness, and God will bless you and fill you. Sounds like mental health to me.

Now let's look at the list of joy-robbers.

1. Disobedience
2. Lust
3. Pride
4. Fear
5. Loneliness
6. Offense and Unforgiveness
7. Unconfessed Sin

1. Disobedience

Disobedience to the will of God is the single most destructive joy-robber that exists (Psalms 107:10, Romans 3:10-18, Jeremiah 7:23). Even when you disobey out of ignorance, the effects of the disobedience can wreck your life. What if you'd never read that it was a sin to hate your brother? So here you are, hating with all your heart. You have a very good reason — he betrayed you. Nobody would blame you for living in unforgiveness and bitterness. That's the world's way. "I will *never* forgive him!"

Does the fact that you are not aware that it is sin relieve you of the pain of it? Of course not. You're consumed by it. It controls your life. Whenever you think of him, hate and bitterness well up in your chest. If you ever actually saw him, you'd feel the rage all over again. Even though the betrayal happened years ago, he still owns you.

God has given us His Bible to help us live fruitful, glorious lives of freedom and peace and victory through Him. He has many, many commands and ways to handle different situations. He calls them "commands" rather than "suggestions" because He knows that if we are to experience that victorious abundant life and be effective witnesses for Him, they are not optional. He wants us to understand how critical they are, so He calls them commands.

Now, we all know the Ten Commandments, so we know we're not supposed to kill or steal or lie or commit adultery. Those are easy to understand. But what about loving one another with that sacrificial, unemotional agape love? What about rejoicing in trials or turning the other cheek? How about loving your spouse when he's a jerk or she's cold and detached? These are a lot harder.

I've had many women tell me that they feel like hypocrites when they do loving things for their husbands, including having intimate relations with them, when they don't really love them. Their thinking is, "But if I don't feel it, then doing something loving is a lie, right? Aren't I being a hypocrite when I pretend to love him when I don't?"

No, you're not. Regarding intimacy, remember that God says that husbands and wives have authority over each other's bodies, and that they are not to deprive one another (1 Corinthians 7:3-5). (This, of course, assumes there is no physical or emotional abuse occurring.) When you are not conducting yourself as a husband or wife, either sexually or just in your expressions of love, you are not only depriving your spouse, you are being disobedient to God. If your acts of love for your husband are not borne out of your love for him, make them gifts to God, instead. God loves our sacrifices if they come out of our love for Him, and our desire to be obedient to Him. It's the opposite of hypocrisy.

Regarding your love for your spouse, remember that the love you are commanded to have for others is agape love. It's not a feeling, but a decision of the will to act in a particular way. Act in a loving way toward them out of love and obedience to God, and your feelings for your spouse will follow. You will also start to feel them respond in like kind (1 Peter 3:1-4). Just do it. Alcoholics Anonymous calls it "fake it until you make it." It's virtually impossible without the Holy Spirit living inside of you, but with His power and your commitment to obedience, all things are possible.

Think of it this way. If you tell your son to clean his room, are you saying, "I want you to clean your room out of your love for me and desire to please me, but until you love me enough and feel like it and really want to, you don't have to."

Of course you're not saying that. You want him to clean his room, period. It would be wonderful if he did it out of his love for you and his desire to please you, but until his heart is there, obedience will have to suffice, and it's the minimum requirement.

God expects the same from us. He would love it if our hearts were there with Him in our obedience, and He wants us to delight in being obedient to Him, but until we grow in our faith and love for Him so that happens, obedience is the minimum requirement.

So why does God feel so strongly about our obedience to Him? Remember, He's our creator. He knows how we tick, He knows how we think, He knows what blesses us and gives us peace and joy and contentment. We know that if our son gets into a habit of keeping his room clean, he will live a more organized life, he will have more peace and less chaos in his heart, and he will get into habits and patterns that will serve him his entire life. Our commandment to him to clean his room is not arbitrary or punitive. It may feel like that to him, but we know it's not. We know that if he does it out of obedience, he will begin to see the good in it, and it will become his own. He will actually learn that to do what you tell him to do benefits him directly, and you'll have his heart. His 'faith' in your judgment will grow.

God knows the same thing about us. He knows that when we obey him out of pure obedience, we will eventually see the fruit of that obedience in our lives and then the 'wanting' will follow. It will no longer be out of simple obedience — it will be out of our love for Him. That's how our faith grows. That's how our love for Him grows. It starts with obedience and then, seeing how that obedience serves us — not just God, but us — our stone heart melts.

Just do it and your heart and your joy will follow.

So how do we find out what His commands are? By reading, meditating, praying, applying. That's why He wrote it all down for you. He wants you to know what it is He wants you to do. But you must read it and desire to be obedient to Him. Read, read, read. Meditate on what you're reading and how it applies to you and your life. Read about the Old Testament Israeli history and see how their obedience served them and their disobedience condemned them. Their stories are very motivational to learn and to obey. Listen to sermons on the radio, read good books that teach the commands of Christ[15].

Most of all, though, read your Bible. Devour it. Swim in it. Find out what God wants you to do, and know that it is the well-spring from whence your peace and joy flow.

Just do it. Just be obedient out of pure obedience, and your heart, your faith, your love for God, and your joy will follow.

2. Lust

I think we have a distorted perspective on what the word *lust* means. I'm going to resort to some Greek to try to clear up the misconceptions.

There are four different Greek words that the New Testament uses that translate into the word *lust*. They are, with their definitions:[16]

> Epithumeo (*ep-ee-thoo-may'-oh*) — verb: to turn upon a thing; to have a desire for, long for, to desire; to lust after, covet, of those who seek things forbidden. Also translated as desire or covet in the NT.
>
> Hedone (*hay'-dow-nay*) (from which we derive our word "hedonism") — noun: pleasure, desires for pleasure. Also translated as pleasure in the NT.
>
> Orexis (*or'-ex-is*) — noun: desire, longing, craving for; eager desire, lust, appetite; used both in a good and a bad sense, as well of natural and lawful and even of proper cravings (of appetite for food), also of corrupt and unlawful desires. Used only in Romans 1:27 to describe men lusting after other men.
>
> Pathos (*path'-os*) — noun: whatever befalls one, whether it be sad or joyous (spec. a calamity, mishap, evil, affliction); a feeling which the mind suffers, an affliction of the mind, emotion, passion (passionate deed; used by the Greeks in either a good or bad sense, in the NT in a bad sense, depraved passion, vile passions). Also translated as affection, or inordinate affection in the NT.

And so the 'lust' the Bible is talking about isn't just sexual lust, although it certainly includes that. It's really the lust you feel when you intensely want something you don't actually need. It could be something material like a new car, or it could be a particular person you want in your life. If you feel consumed with desire for it, it is lust. That is not to say you are not allowed to desire something you don't have and don't need, but if it transcends just 'desire' and crosses over into passion, then you may be dangerously close to lust.

The Book of James says, "Then when lust has conceived, it gives birth to sin; and when sin is accomplished, it brings forth death" (James 1:15).

The context here is that we are tempted to sin because of our lusts. When we give in to that sin, something in us dies. James says that when we want it badly enough, we become willing to compromise, or push the limits, or disregard good judgment to get it. We become willing to sin, and then the actual sin is not far behind.

The picture of birth is significant in the Bible. It infers a slowly developing process, over time, that takes on a life of it's own with a significant ending. Be careful. Even the smallest 'want' can grow into a flaming passion if it's not checked. It sneaks up on you. It can grow slowly, imperceptibly, but before you know it, it has you.

If you want something you don't have, check yourself. Is this inordinate affection? Does your heart burn when you think of having it? Do you want it more now than you did at first?

Lust can affect our relationship with God as the enemy convinces us that our want is a need. Lust says, "I don't have what I want. God isn't providing me with what I need. God doesn't want me to be happy. I don't trust God. He's holding out on me. If He really loved me, then He'd give this to me." We feel that God isn't paying attention, and our trust in Him fades. In the end, we just stop asking God for anything at all. Why bother.

But James goes on to warn us not to be deceived about God's provision in our lives. He assures us that every perfect gift is from above. The inference is that if we have it from God, then it's a perfect gift. If we don't have it, then it isn't a perfect gift for us, and God doesn't want us to have it. It may be that He doesn't want us to have it right now, or possibly not in the way we want it, or maybe not at all. The point is, though, that God is still on the throne. He loves us, and He protects us as much by what He holds back as He does by what He gives.

Our society says, "You deserve a break today," "You're worth it," "Have it your way," "Come to this hotel and we'll treat you the way you deserve to be treated." Our expectations are that other people will treat us in accordance with our wishes, and we'll get what we want when we want it. When our children act that way, we call them "spoiled." We are a nation who is spoiled.

Does that mean you shouldn't pray for what you want? Of course you should. Your Heavenly Father wants you to go to Him for everything. Pray to Him, and then trust Him. Trust in His provision and love, and be willing to wait for God's perfect timing, or be willing to hear, "No."

My parents used to call it "delayed gratification." Unless you can learn to wait, you'll be unhappy your whole life.

Wait for God. The writer of Psalms said, "...they who seek the Lord shall not be in want of any good thing" (Psalms 34:10). But who gets to decide what's "good?" You guessed it — God does.

Rest in that. If it's good for you in God's eyes, you'll have it. He does love you, and He does want what's best for you. That's where real trust comes in. The Israelites complained and whined in the wilderness. They didn't trust God, and they didn't believe Him. Because of that, an entire generation of them had to die in the wilderness (Numbers 14:23, Hebrews 3:8-19). They never made it into Canaan, the land God had promised their fathers. We look at the Israelites and say, "What's their problem?", but in fact, it's a perfect picture of us. We whine and complain when we don't get our way, but if we don't learn to trust God, we live in the wilderness. Do you sometimes feel like you're living your life in the wilderness? Check your lust.

When we trust Him to provide "all good things" to us, then we are already in our Promised Land.

3. Pride

Here it is. The devil's favorite weapon against us because it separates us from God and ruins our witness. Pride is what caused him to be thrown out of heaven (Ezekiel 28:13-19) and he wants us to suffer for it as well. Pride is what caused Adam and Eve to sin against God. They wanted to be "like God" (Genesis 3:5), as did Satan when he rebelled.

Our nature is to want to be our own God. That is why we take so long to come to the Lord in the first place, and it is a battle we fight our entire Christian lives.

Again, a look at the Greek definitions will help. There are three Greek words translated as *pride* (as well as a few other related words):

Huperephania (*hoop-er-ay-fan-ee'-ah*) — haughtiness, arrogance; the character of one who, with a swollen estimate of his own powers or merits, looks down on others and even treats them with insolence and contempt

Alazoneia (*al-ad-zon-i'-a*) — empty, braggart talk; an insolent and empty assurance, which trusts in its own power and resources and shamefully despises and violates divine laws and human rights; an impious and empty presumption which trusts in the stability of earthy things

Tuphoo (*toof-o'-o*) — to raise a smoke, to wrap in a mist; to make proud, puff up with pride, render insolent; to be puffed up with haughtiness or pride; to blind with pride or conceit, to render foolish or stupid; beclouded, besotted.

Wow. That's pretty condemning. The common theme, which runs through all of them, is self-sufficiency. But isn't that what we're supposed to do? "Rugged individualism," right? Self-sufficient. Pull ourselves up by our boot-straps.

Well, no. That's what society says, and that's the world's way. But that's not God's way. He says that reliance on ourselves and our own strength is an indicator that we don't trust Him. Then when our lives fall apart, we get depressed. We've 'failed.' We're embarrassed, we're shamed, we're angry. "I should have..." fill-in-the-blank.

Pride says, "I can do it on my own. I am my own god."

And beware, Christian. Pride can also take the form of, "God has something really special for me to do. He's set me apart from the rest of you to do something really profound for His Kingdom. That's because He sees something in me that you all don't have. I have a very important destiny. God is using me in a powerful way. I am very special."

Wow, that one is subtle. We all want to do something profoundly important for God. But until we can handle it in a Godly way, we have to keep growing and maturing. God won't allow us to use His gifts to hurt people with our pride. That's not what they're for. He'll wait until we're ready.

Pride also says, "I can do it. Why can't you? What's your problem?" Pride eventually says, "I'm better than you." That's sin. It hurts relationships, it makes us judgmental, it often makes us bitter and angry, and it drives us away from God.

It's a mental health issue.

But watch this. This may surprise you. Pride also says, "I'm not as good as you," "I'm not worthy," "Nobody would like me if they really knew me," "I'm not smart," "I'm not pretty," "I'm not talented."

So why are those things pride? Because it's still all about me. Pride says, "I *should* be all of those things and I'm not." I *should* be self-sufficient and I'm not. My focus is still on me. It's all about me.

This is the deal. You're worthy to the extent God says you're worthy. Not a shred more or less, and it's not about you — it's about Him.

You're smart to the extent God needs you to be smart to do what He wants you to do. Not a shred more or less, and it's not about you — it's about Him and His Kingdom.

What society calls "low self-esteem" is still about us. We've made it a 'me' thing that is just as sinful and prideful and just as destructive as being 'better than.'

If you think you have low self-esteem, then the work you need to do is this:

"God, I've made it about me, and it's really about You. My desire is to be content with the intelligence, looks, personality, etc., that you have given me. My desire is to take the negative messages I've received from the significant people in my life and crush them under the messages that You give me. Your Bible tells me that I'm a child of the living God, a Prince or Princess, a friend of Christ, and an inheritor of the riches of God. Please help me learn to trust You and Your precious words to me. Please help me to stop making it about me, and start making it all about You."

So if I get rid of the pride, what takes its place?

Humility. What is humility? What is it not? Humility is not self-deprecation or low self-esteem. Humility is not letting people walk on you or being a door-mat. Humility is not the fear of saying, "no." Humility is about strength. Humility is about willful submission. Humility is about your relationship with God.

As a refresher, humility says:

1. I am totally and utterly dependent on God for everything that I do and for everything that happens to me.
2. I will be absolutely obedient to God's will, regardless of the circumstances, regardless of the consequences, regardless of what I understand, and regardless of how I feel.
3. I am content with the provision of God, and trust that He will give to me what's best for me, and what I need to serve Him when I need it.
4. I understand that I am a sinner, no better than anyone else on the face of the planet, because if any of us have been redeemed, it was through God's grace and mercy that that is so, and not through anything we did or even could have done.

When we are humble, we aren't above serving others for their benefit — not ours. When we are humble, we know that our expectations are subjugated to God's expectations for us. When we are humble, our relationships become about honoring God, not about getting what we want from them. When we are humble, we seek God's direction often and follow it when we get it. Since we know that God's direction will always enhance our lives (even if it doesn't feel like it at the time), we diligently seek Him and purpose in our hearts to be obedient to Him.

God knows us better than we know ourselves. If we can achieve humility and learn to trust Him and follow Him, Scripture teaches us that He will lead us into the Promised Land of peace and joy and purpose.

4. Fear

Fear is a real joy-robber, isn't it? What exactly is fear?

Again, the Greeks have several different words for our word *fear*. You can look them up in bible.crosswalk.com, but in essence, they are 1) quaking fear related to danger that prevents you from doing something without a great deal of courage, 2) reverential fear that causes you to show respect and honor and obedience, and 3) timidity, fearfulness, and cowardice.

Clearly, the second definition is appropriate as it pertains to God and to our God-given authorities. Definition one may be appropriate, depending on the circumstances, but God expects you to listen to Him as to whether or not you are to press forward, and then if you get His go-ahead, trust that He will be there with you to give you strength and skill.

The third type of fear, called Deilia (*di-lee'-ah*) in the Greek, is never appropriate (2 Timothy 1:7). It says, "God, you're not really there for me, and I can't trust you to help me through this." It says, "I don't know what I'm doing and I might fail, so I'm not going to try." It says, "I'm not good enough, I'm not smart enough, it won't work anyway, and it's never going to work out the way I want or need it to."

Oops. There it is again, "It's all about me." I don't mean to be harsh with this, but unless this message sinks in to the core of your being, none of this will make any sense to you, and neither will it have any effect.

Couple the "I" and "me" with a lack of trust in God, and you have either pride or fear or both.

"So what do I do about that? The practical reality is that I truly am fearful, and you admonishing me about it isn't going to make it go away."

The first step is to *not* beat yourself up over it. But you do want to acknowledge to yourself that it is not okay, and that it robs you of peace. That will motivate you to get the help you need.

The second step is to pray.

> "Lord, I need your help. I'm fearful and I know that it is not pleasing to you, it grieves your Holy Spirit, it hurts me, and it's a poor witness for others. Please help me grow in my faith so I can learn to trust you more. Help me learn to know, way down deep inside, that you are there for me and that I can rely on your provision and protection in my life. Help me know that you're in control, and I don't have to be. Guide me as to what it is you want me to do in this situation, and give me the wisdom and strength to accomplish my part. Then give me the faith to turn it over to you."

The Alcoholics Anonymous Serenity Prayer, repeated here as a refresher, is perfect:

> God grant me the serenity to accept the things I cannot change, the courage to change the things I can, and the wisdom to know the difference.

And to that I would add, "And the faith to turn it all over to You."

There are simply things over which you have absolutely no control. If you have some ability to effect change, and your efforts fall within the will of God, then by all means, do so. Remember that your life on earth is a partnership with God, and you definitely need to do your part. But once you've done that, and you know in your heart that there's nothing left to do, then God says that's the time to just surrender it to Him.

The Apostle Paul said, "Be anxious for nothing" (Philippians 4:6). That's easy to say, but a whole lot harder to do. But go to your Bible and look at that verse. Remember that Paul didn't put in the chapter and verse numbers. It was just a long series of sentences as a single letter. We tend to separate it in our minds in accordance with the verse numbers, but that's not what Paul did. So look at that verse. What's the sentence — not the verse — but the sentence immediately preceding his "Be anxious for nothing?"

"The Lord is near."

So what was Paul saying? He was saying the Lord is near, and as a result of that, you have the freedom of being anxious for nothing. When you feel yourself being fearful, pray. The Lord is near. He can hear you. He can intervene. He is your protector, provider, your comforter, your friend. He's there for you. The Lord is near, so be anxious for nothing. Let that penetrate your heart.

So whenever you feel yourself feeling fearful again, remember to just pray and pray and pray the Serenity Prayer. God is faithful even when we're not. Cry out to Him and trust Him, and He will give you peace.

Regarding faith, I will address how to increase your faith in Chapter 15, "If Only I Had More Faith," so let's table that question for now.

Also, remember that anxiety, panic attacks, and fear may be symptoms of physiological issues going on. If you are suffering, please get help. You can probably benefit from Biblically-based therapy, and may even need medication for a season. Don't pass up the gifts God gave us in the form of therapists and medications if you feel you might need them.

5. Offense and Unforgiveness

Wow, forgiveness is such a huge issue. Let's start with a definition of what it is, and what it isn't.

Imagine you've gone to your Uncle and borrowed $5,000 as a down-payment for a car. You diligently pay him the agreed-upon monthly payment for two years, at which time he comes to you and says, "I've decided to completely forgive the rest of the loan." What that means is that you don't owe him another dime. He has wiped the slate clean. It doesn't mean you've paid it: It means it no longer has to be paid. He paid it himself, so to speak.

That's the long and the short of forgiveness. It's just a conscious decision to release someone from the debt they owe you for the offense against you.

What debt is that? Just this: When someone offends us, we want them to *pay*! We want them to suffer like they've made us suffer, and we want them to understand the pain they've inflicted upon us by experiencing their own.

Forgiveness is very simply saying, "I give up my right to see you suffer and to pay me back for what you've done to me." That's it. That's the whole thing.

We get that definition from God. When we come to the Lord and ask His forgiveness of our sins and give our lives to Him, it doesn't matter what we've done, He immediately 'forgives' the entire list of offenses. We no longer have to pay Him back or suffer for what we've done. It's over. That's the same forgiveness He asks us to give others. The Lord's prayer says, "Forgive us our debts as we also have forgiven our debtors" (Matthew 6:12). The word "as" in that verse means "in the same way." How do you forgive others who have offended you? If you've ever prayed that prayer, you have asked God to forgive you in the same way. Is that what you really want? I'd say that for most of us, the answer would be a resounding, "No!"

Now let's discuss what forgiveness isn't. People use the phrase "forgive and forget" as if they're a matched set, inseparable. They're not. Forgiveness is a decision, but forgetting is an entirely different thing. We also lump reconciliation in with forgiveness, and they're not the same thing, either. Let me explain.

Forgetting is a much tougher task than forgiveness, as hard as *that* is. God has forgotten our sins as far as the east is from the west (Psalms 103:12). He expects us to work toward that, but since we're not God, it takes us a bit longer. The big trick is this: Once you've forgiven someone for an offense and the memory returns, you *gently* say to the memory, "Not now," and push it out of your mind. Every time it comes into your mind, you gently and lovingly push it out again. I heard someone once say you "live in forgiveness." That doesn't mean it doesn't come to your mind, but when it does, you don't harbor it, you don't meditate on it, you don't 'live' it.

The second trick is never to talk about it. When we're still in that 'offended' place, we tend to bring it up more often. We bring it up to our friends, our counselors, our family, and we bring it up to the person who offended us. That's the worst. When you bring it up to the person who offended you, you're saying, "I *said* that I forgive you, but I really haven't. I still want you to suffer. I still want you to feel guilty. I still want you to *pay!*" Whenever you start to feel the words coming out of your mouth, say to them, "No, not now. I'm not going to speak you now. I'm not going to let you out of my mouth now." Speaking them starts to bring them back into clearer focus in your mind. What you're trying to do is exterminate the memory through dissolution and slow extermination. You want the memories to *dissolve*, becoming fuzzier and fuzzier in your head until they are totally gone.

Over time, the more you do this, the less and less the memory will return. You'll never have amnesia with it, but if it doesn't live in your present-day mind continually, and you steadfastly refuse to talk about it, then you've succeeded in 'forgetting' it.

If you struggle with this, then this is a perfect time to go back to your memorized Scripture. Choose something you've memorized that is fairly long — hopefully 6-10 verses or more. Whenever you feel that thought, anger, memory, or whatever, pop into your head, then quickly start reciting your verses. Repeat them however many times you need to to drive that evil monster out of your head. Take every thought captive to the obedience of Christ (2 Corinthians 10:5) by doing what Christ did in the wilderness — quote Scripture.

Be patient with yourself as you go through this process. This is one of the toughest challenges Christians have to face, but it is also the one that glorifies God most beautifully to those who are watching. "Father, forgive them..." were some of His final words before He died.

Reconciliation is something else altogether. This one is very tough. God is certainly a God of reconciliation, and that is His heart. The problem is that some people just aren't safe to be around. I use David as my example. When King Saul threw the spear at Him, David ran. And he stayed gone. He never stopped his respect for Saul, he never stopped honoring him as King, he never spoke ill of him, he never stopped loving him, but he stayed away.

If someone is just unsafe for you, either because they're physically threatening or they are emotionally toxic for you, then I'd say you have Biblical backing for staying away, at least for a season.

However, if you're staying away out of a vengeful attitude of punishment, then you haven't forgiven them yet, and you have more work to do. You and God have to determine where your heart is and how reconciliation plays into your forgiveness and your relationship with them. Pray, and seek His guidance on that.

Now let me assure you, though, that even if you reconcile with someone, that doesn't necessarily mean you have to be their lunch buddy. God never asks you to phileo love someone, just agape love them. Reconciliation is that agape, self-sacrificial form of love that says you can be in the same room with them (providing they're safe for you), and be cordial to them. It doesn't require you to be best friends.

Also, remember that, although it's very true that God wants you to reconcile, the Apostle Paul said, "If possible, so far as it depends on you, be at peace with all men" (Romans 12:18). What that says is, do everything you can, humble yourself if you need to, be willing to 'die to your self' if that's what it requires, but understand that there may be limitations on the result. If they refuse to reconcile and you *know* that you've done everything you can, then you've satisfied God's requirement. They will have to stand before God for their part in the poor result. You talk to the Lord about your part, and just make sure you can stand confidently before Him when your turn comes.

So now let's deal with the offense itself. We are a people who love to 'take up' an offense. Why is that?

In addition to just making us feel 'better than' in a lot of ways, my experience in therapy is essentially this: If you offend me and I forgive you, I run the risk of you offending me again because you haven't paid a price for your first offense. If I don't forgive you, then I punish you by my unforgiveness, and since you're suffering, you're not as likely to do it again, and I'm safer.

Sounds pretty logical, right? The problem, though, is that the offender rarely knows he's being punished. Isn't that true?

Reflect on the following statement for a bit:

Unforgiveness is like feeding yourself rat poison while you're waiting for the rat to die.

Now let's take a moment and look at a little Greek. The Greek word for the word "offense" in the Bible is "skandalon." The definition is, among other descriptions describing "offense," 'The movable stick or trigger of a trap?' We were talking about being offended, right? Did we take a u-turn somewhere? Nope. Watch this: What the Greek word wants you to know is that if you are offended, if you have taken up an offense, you're trapped in a trap — like a rat. And not only that, but you're the one who sprung the trap. The person who offended you is as free as a bird while you're trapped in this cage of anger, resentment, and joylessness. And by allowing yourself the option of feeling offended, you put yourself there.

In our culture, if someone offends us, we are told that we have a right to be angry and resentful and unforgiving. Well, that may be true, you may have that right, but you're still the one trapped.

So who is suffering, you or the rat? You know the answer. It's you. You've 'taken up an offense' and it's eating you alive, poisoning *you* from the inside out.

God says we are to forgive "seventy times seven" (Matthew 18:22) if we are offended. "But that's if they've repented and asked for forgiveness, right?"

Really? Is that the standard Jesus set? "Father, forgive them for they know not what they do" (Luke 23:34). "They" were casting lots for his clothes at the time. "They" were spitting on Him, mocking

Therapy with God

Him, and calling Him names. "They" had just beaten Him without mercy and plucked out his beard. Real repentant, they were. And what about us? Had we asked for forgiveness when He put Himself on the cross? Hardly.

So why did God do it? Very simply, for Himself. For His name's sake (Psalm 23:3).

No question, it's a very tough thing to do. But God knows it's not for the other guy — it's for you. If you're offended, then you're hurting, your relationships are hurting, and your witness is hurting.

It's a very serious mental health issue. Many people spend decades in this place of unforgiveness, and not only does their mental health suffer, very often their physical health does as well.

And there is also the issue of revenge. Remember this when you want to take your own revenge: God says He wants to be our avenger and protector, but if we take action ourselves, He will back out (Romans 12:19). If somebody has a price to pay, would you rather he pay the price you can impose on him or the one God chooses? Of course, you'd *say* the one God chooses, but is that how you live your life? Do you really turn the offense over to God for action? Most of us do not. We hold onto it with both hands and tell God, "Get him!" Will He? Not if we don't let it go first.

Where does that come from? Again, a lack of trust that God *will* take care of it for us; a lack of trust that He'll defend and avenge us.

Let me give you an illustration of how this works. Have you ever been bullied in school? Yes? That's because you didn't have a big, tough brother or friend as your protector. If you had, the bullies wouldn't have messed with you. Bullies are cowards and won't pick on someone who can fight back.

I also heard about a television show once about bears. A little bear cub was being threatened by a cougar. The little bear let out this meager, cub-sized growl and the cougar took off. What you didn't see until the camera backed out was that the Momma bear was standing straight up, right behind her cub.

Satan is a bully, folks. He'll use other people and circumstances in your life to destroy your witness because he knows that's what brings other people to the Lord.[17] He will tell you that you have a right to be angry and bitter. He will convince you that your rage and vengeance are perfectly justified. Your witness is one of the most powerful weapons you have against Satan, and he will do whatever he can to destroy it.

But you have a Big Brother standing behind you. Let him fight the fight for you. Don't take it on yourself. Let it go. It's robbing you of your witness and your mental health.

God commands us to love and pray for our enemies (Romans 12:14; Matthew 5:44). Pray for them fervently — not that they'll 'get it' and change their ways and ask you for forgiveness. This is praying for yourself. Pray God's blessings on their lives. Pray they come to salvation. I know, you won't feel it at first, and possibly not for a good while, but pray it anyway. Ask God to help transform your heart so you *do* mean it as you pray. God knows your heart. He knows you don't mean it, but He also knows if you *want* to mean it or not, and He will honor that request.

This is the single most critical step toward forgiveness. *Don't skip this step.* If you pray for them, three very important things will happen:

1. Your heart will be softened and your stress will go down.
2. Your witness will be strong in the sight of others.
3. Your enemy will have "burning coals heaped upon his head" (Romans 12:20), which means he will be convicted of the sin he committed against you and God, and come to repentance through that conviction.

His conviction is up to God, though. You can't look for it, wait for it, or make your actions in any way dependent upon it. Give it all to God.

Taking up an offense, and the resultant unforgiveness, is one of the biggest threats to mental health there is. I've seen people spend decades mired in their anger and unforgiveness, affecting everything they do for most of their adult lives. Society tells us we have a right. That may be so, but do we do ourselves right? Do we do God right?

God knows it hurts us. He commands we let it go because He loves us and wants us to have His peace.

You'll know you've truly forgiven them from your heart when you hear that something good has happened to them, and your first reaction is, "I'm happy for him." Until that happens, keep praying for them. Don't give up. It's just too important.

6. Loneliness

I used to hear the question asked, "If you were stranded on a desert island and you could take just one thing with you, what would that be?" I never understood the people who said, "The Bible." What?? A book? Are they nuts? How about food, or knives or something practical? How about a satellite phone!? What's a *book* going to do?

Wow, that seems like an eternity ago. I now know *exactly* why they would choose the Bible. Because loneliness is so deeply and profoundly oppressive that it wouldn't matter how many practical utensils you had: The loneliness would eventually kill you.

If you've ever seen the movie, *Cast Away* with Tom Hanks, you saw that his physical provision was fine. He had plenty to eat and drink, he'd created a shelter for himself that kept him safe and comfortable from the elements. But it wasn't enough. He needed Wilson. He 'created' a companion from a volleyball. He talked to Wilson, he conferred with him, he ran ideas past him when he wasn't sure what to do or how handle a problem. And when Wilson floated away in the waves, he fell apart. He knew what God knows — if nothing else is, the loneliness is fatal.

Do you feel lonely? Does your life feel like a desert island sometimes? Jesus wants you to know that you're not alone. Not in any sense of the word.

Does that sound like Christian pabulum? Probably. But it's true nonetheless. If you're a born-again Christian, then you have the Holy Spirit living inside of you. You're truly *never* alone. In Chapter 6, "How I Read the Bible," I talked about having Jesus sit on the couch next to me as I study my Bible in the morning. The fact is, I have Him sitting next to me, or riding in the car with me, or having dinner

Therapy with God

with me, or even going to the movies with me, all the time. I talk to Him that way, I feel His presence, and I'm truly never alone.

It takes some practice and some getting used to, but He's there for you just the same way He's here for me. Just start talking to Him like He is, and pretty soon you'll feel Him there.

Now, I know. Sometimes you just need Jesus with skin on. Well, I have good news for you for that, too. As a born-again Christian, you have a huge family just waiting for you to visit. They get together every Sunday morning, and very often on Wednesday evenings as well. Furthermore, they need you. There's so much family business to be done that they never have enough hands. Get involved.

The truth is, since you have the Spirit of God living in you, you love other Christians. You can't help yourself. You just do. Oh, that's not to say that that your personality will necessarily mesh well with everyone else's. I understand that's true. But there are so many people and so many opportunities to serve that I know you can find something to do that will get you involved with people in an area where you can serve God and have a ball doing it.

If you do that, two very important things will happen: First, you'll get closer to God, and second, you'll take the focus off of yourself.

If you're lonely and nothing is wrong with you physically, then the likelihood is that you're still all about you. Get out of yourself and get involved, and I guarantee you won't be lonely any more. If you're physically incapable of getting involved, then you present the perfect opportunity for someone from your church to minister to you. Bless them by calling and telling the people in the church office that you're lonely and could use some company. Someone is just waiting for the chance to pray for you and be there for you. But in the meantime, remember that Jesus is your best companion anyway, and you don't have to wait for Him to get there. Just start talking.

7. Unconfessed Sin

I saved this for last in the list of Joy-robbers because next to disobedience, it is the one that will rob you faster, more deeply, and more insidiously that any of the other thieves, and I want it fresh in your mind as we move out of this section.

What did Adam and Eve do when they ate the forbidden fruit? They hid (Genesis 3:8). They hid from God because they were ashamed. They knew they were naked and they were ashamed for the first time since creation.

But what happened then? When God questioned them about what they had done, did they confess it? Did they repent? Did they ask for forgiveness? No. They did none of those things. They blame shifted and made excuses

Jewish tradition says that once they were ejected from the Garden of Eden, they spent many, many years in a deep state of depression living in caves. Scripture doesn't address that specifically, but from my own experience with working with clients, I have seen the deep pain that unconfessed sin causes, and the deeply restorative power of true confession and repentance. I believe they would have stayed depressed until they repented and confessed, and their relationship with God was restored. Scripture doesn't address whether that ever happened, but it wasn't until their grandson Enosh was born that "men began to call upon the name of the LORD" (Genesis 4:26).

King David addressed this same issue in Psalm 32.

Please go read Psalms 32 now. David wrote that after his adulterous/murderous affair with Bathsheba. When he had tried to hide his sin from God, his "body wasted away," he felt like God's hand was "heavy upon" him, and his "vitality was drained away." But when he confessed it — even though God knew all along what he had done — his peace was restored, he rejoiced in the Lord again, and he was again shouting for joy.

When we have unconfessed sin in our lives, we hide from God, our bones ache, our vitality is drained away. We can even become physically ill. David described it aptly as his body wasting away. So true.

Let's look at Pharaoh for an example of what not to do in confessing your sin. God hit him with a total of ten plagues at which point he released the Israelites. But the first nine plagues, although not enough to inspire Him to set the slaves free, caused some great pain and devastation in the land. Listen to Pharaoh's attempts at 'confession' to get God off of his back:

After the 7th plague, the hail, thunder, and fire from heaven, Pharaoh said,

> "I have sinned this time; the Lord is the righteous one, and I and my people are the wicked ones" (Exodus 9:27)

"...this time?" What about all of the other times? And what's with "...I and my people..." Nope — sorry Pharaoh, you did this one yourself. You can't blame the people, too. This is yours alone.

The problem with this type of confession and repentance is that the motive is all wrong. Pharaoh just wanted relief from the plagues. It was never his intention to develop a relationship with God. Look at how Moses responds to his confession:

> "...as for you and your servants, I know that you do not yet fear the Lord God" (Exodus 9:30).

So confession to God is related to fear of God. Do you fear God? That's a very important question.

Moses knew that Pharaoh's 'confession' had nothing to do with his love for or fear of God. It was just to get God off of his back. And what happened then?

> "But when Pharaoh saw that the rain and the hail and the thunder had ceased, he sinned again and hardened his heart, he and his servants" (Exodus 9:34).

There it is. When our confession is from a hardened heart seeking only relief from consequences, then we can expect the cycle to repeat itself.

So God brought the locusts. What was Pharaoh's reaction? He 'confessed' again.

> "I have sinned against the Lord your God and against you. Now therefore, please forgive my sin only this once, and make supplication to the Lord your God, that He would only remove this death from me."

He started out okay here, but then he gave himself away. His motive was not to establish or restore a relationship with God: It was solely for the purpose of relief from the pain. He described God as *"your* God." And what did he mean by "only this once?" He was minimizing his sin, trying to convince Moses and God that he's not really a bad guy after all — not really. After all, he's only sinned once, right? God can forgive *that*, can't He? It was never his intention to subject himself under the authority of God. He wasn't *agreeing* with God about his sin: He was simply trying to get God off of his back again.

But again, once the plague was lifted, Pharaoh refused to let the people go.

Pharaoh's so-called confessions were filled with blame-shifting, pride, minimization, and self-serving motives. Don't shift the blame to others in your confessions: Point the arrow of blame at your own heart. Confess it as *your* sin and humble yourself before a loving, grace-filled, longsuffering God.

If you have unconfessed sin, then get on your knees before God and just tell Him. You can confess it to another human being if you'd like, and Scripture encourages us to do that (James 5:16), but the most important thing is to confess it to God — face to face. Tell Him everything you can remember about your sin. Go into the deepest darkest closet of your motives, your actions, your inappropriate pleasures in the sin you committed. Confess it all, submit yourself to His judgment, trust in His grace, and get rid of it.

If you don't know of any unconfessed sin but can feel a strange distance from God that you can't explain to yourself, then get on your knees and ask God to reveal any unconfessed sin you have to you. There are times when we either hide from our own sin because it was so far in the past that we've forgotten or blocked it, or we may not be aware it was sin until something we read in Scripture brings it to our attention. I was quite shocked the first time I learned that complaining was a sin. I'd never thought of it that way, and I had some confessing to do. Gossiping is another of those insidious sins, as well. Sin we don't know is sin, as well as sin we have forgotten, is still sin, and it still separates us from God.

Dig deep. Be open to any promptings you receive from the Holy Spirit. Be fearless in your internal search for your sin — past or present — and God will be faithful in revealing to you what's keeping you distant from Him. Connect with Him again through your confession, repentance, and deep, penetrating prayer.

Purpose in your heart to agree with God: Sin is sin. Confess it, get rid of it, cleanse your heart of it, and rejoice once more in your relationship with God — face to face.

Fill-in-the-blank

Well, there's the list. But there's no doubt that I've missed your specific, personal issue. Maybe your spouse is distant or an obsessive pack-rat and you feel overwhelmed. Maybe your kids are out of control. Maybe you're just depressed and don't know why.

Whatever it is, if you dissect it into its component parts and discuss it with your therapist, I'd bet that you would find most of what you're dealing with in the above list in some form or another.

Whatever your unique situation is, try to view it through the lens of the Freedoms and Joy-robbers, and ask God to help you. See if the answers don't come.

XIII — THE ISSUE OF SELF ESTEEM

What Is Self-Esteem, And Why Do I Care?

As I said in the section on Biblical Freedoms, self-esteem is far less about how we feel about ourselves than about how we perceive that our primary caregivers felt about us, and how we feel about them. We are a reflection of them in our own eyes, so if we esteem them little, we will esteem ourselves little. If they esteemed us little, then we've 'inherited' their perception of us as our own.

The issue of self-esteem has loomed large in our social consciousness for many decades, but that was not always the case. Several decades ago we had the birth of the self-esteem movement, and became mired in the 'inner child' work that we were promised would help us reconnect with the pain of our past and give us a chance to undo the damage. We spent time with groups of like-minded people with stuffed animals on our laps, trying to re-feel what it was like to be us as children, so we could deal with the pain and grow out of it.

If you've never done it, it sounds a little crazy. But like the 'positive affirmations,' it actually worked. We felt the pain, redefined the meaning we'd given it, and felt better about ourselves. We embraced our inner child, comforted it, and grew up.

That's all well and good, but the truth is that again, it drew us farther away from God by making us less dependent on a relationship with Him. Feeling good about ourselves is not God's purpose for our lives. Not that it's a bad thing, it's just not terribly relevant. We need to rethink how self-esteem fits into God's bigger picture.

First of all (and you know where I'm going with this), what's the first word in the term 'self-esteem?'

Self, of course. Self-esteem is, in the end, all about me. How do I feel about myself? How do others see me? What happened to me when I was a child? How is it affecting me now?

Now, let me stop here. Please let me assure you that I'm not trying to criticize people who see themselves as having a low self-esteem. I know it's real, and it hurts. Our focus on it is natural given where we've all come from and how we've been bombarded by the media. I've certainly been there, so I hurt for you. Society has screamed at us that our success in life is directly connected to our self-esteem and so it's natural that it would matter to us very much. But it's bondage, and you don't need it.

What I'm trying to do here is liberate you from that bondage. I'm trying to set you free from society's standards of success and failure and human value. I'm trying to give you an entirely different perspective. When I'm done, I pray you'll see the entire issue of self-esteem the way I do — as a vicious lie straight from the pit of hell.

Satan wants to distract us from the real issues — faith and trust in God, focusing on Him and His eternity, and focusing on other people in accordance with God's will for our lives. As long as I have a 'low self-esteem,' I have a reason for my troubles, I can blame others for it, and I can sit at the Pool of Bethesda for 38 years (John 5:1-18). I want more for you than that. You deserve better.

So what does God have to say about self-esteem? Virtually nothing. There's not a single mention in the Bible about self-esteem except as it concerns how we treat other people. Treat others as you want them to treat you (Luke 6:31), and love your neighbor as yourself (Luke 10:27). The inference with both of these is that God already expects that you love yourself. That's not on the table. What's at issue is whether or not you treat others the way you'd like to be treated.

"Ok, sold. But how can I just flip the light-switch and turn off years of feeling bad about myself and suddenly feel *good* about myself?" Well clearly, you can't.

Before we can eliminate low self-esteem as a problem, we need to honor it as real.

Poor self-esteem usually happens when some primary caregiver, or even a long-term spouse, makes you feel like you're not worthy, smart, loved, loveable, whatever. If a primary caregiver, particularly one or both parents, mistreats you or neglects you, it hurts deeply. It's natural for us to expect our own parents to treat us well, and when they don't, it makes us feel like we don't deserve to be treated well by anybody. As children, we tend not to put the blame on them because they're our parents and we have the childhood illusion that they are perfect. By the time we realize they are not perfect, it is too late. The deep, negative lessons have already been gouged into the stone tablets in our minds and that is what we grow up with. A friend of mine called the people who sent you those negative messages, 'the chorus.' The chorus is constantly screaming those negative messages in our heads, and it's those messages from the chorus that create in us a low self-esteem.

The negative messages from the chorus come up at the most inappropriate and inconvenient times. You may be trying to get up the courage to call someone you've just met from church to ask them out to lunch, and you hear the chorus say to you "Why would they want to have lunch with *you*?" and you put the phone down. Or you're considering applying for a new position at your work, but you hear the chorus say, "You know they wouldn't want you for that position. Why bother? You know you're just going to be rejected and hurt," and you put the application in the trash. Or your husband or wife treats you like they hate you or they're cheating on you or something, and you hear yourself saying "Why not? That's what I deserve. At least they're staying. If I boot them out, I'll spend the rest of my life alone because nobody else would love me the way they do, even if it's not perfect."

Do any of those sound familiar? That's the chorus. Just remember that ultimately, the chorus is Satan.

See yourself in a room with a huge black line running down the middle of it on the floor. You're on one side of the line, alone, and the chorus is on the other side, screaming at you. See Satan standing amongst them, screaming with the loudest voice. You can't shut them up and you can't get rid of them. The only hope you have is to out-shout them and hope they eventually go away. But there's too many of them, and they shout louder than you, and you're the one who eventually gives up and you join them. It's just easier buying into what they're selling.

That's low self-esteem.

So What Do I Do Now?

So what do you do about your low self-esteem? First of all, acknowledge that it isn't God's way, and it breaks His heart. Acknowledge that it's the worst form of bondage. God wants to help you out of it, so turn to Him for that help.

Read the following verses and let them touch your heart. This is where memorization, covered in Chapter 8, "Memorizing Scripture," is essential.

> Romans 8:16 — The Spirit Himself testifies with our spirit that **we are children of God**, and if children, heirs also, heirs of God and fellow heirs with Christ, if indeed we suffer with Him so that we may also be glorified with Him
>
> 1 Peter 1:3 — Blessed be the God and Father of our Lord Jesus Christ, who according to His great mercy has caused us to be born again to a living hope through the resurrection of Jesus Christ from the dead **to obtain an inheritance** which is imperishable and undefiled and will not fade away, reserved in heaven for you.

Who gets the inheritance? The children. You are a child of God and He has an inheritance waiting for you.

1 Timothy 1:17 — Now to the **King** eternal, immortal, invisible, the only God, be honor and glory forever and ever. Amen

This same King is your Father in heaven. You're royalty! You're a prince or princess!

2 Thessalonians 1:5 This is a plain indication of God's righteous judgment so that **you will be considered worthy** of the kingdom of God, for which indeed you are suffering.

The suffering that you believe is hurting you or ruining your life is the *very* thing that God looks at so that you will be considered worthy of the kingdom of God. If you ever suffer, then God says you're **worthy** of the kingdom of God. It doesn't matter if your parents or your friends or your coworkers or even your spouse think you're worthy or not — *God* does, and He's the One who counts.

2 Corinthians 2:2-3 You are our letter, written in our hearts, known and read by all men; being manifested that you are a letter of Christ, cared for by us, written not with ink but with the Spirit of the living God, not on tablets of stone but on tablets of human hearts.

The Apostle Paul told the people of Corinth, and God is telling us, that we are human epistles, we are letters carried to the whole world proclaiming the gospel of Jesus Christ. Remember that "You may be the only Bible some people ever read." You have a profoundly critical purpose.

2 Corinthians 6:16 — ...For we are the temple of the living God; just as God said, "I will dwell in them and walk among them; and I will be their God and they shall be my people."

1 Peter 2:5 — you also, as living stones, are being built up as a spiritual house for a holy priesthood, to offer up spiritual sacrifices acceptable to God through Jesus Christ.

Not only are you a child of God, a prince or princess, and an epistle spreading the love and grace of God, but you are also part of the **temple** of God, a living stone in his spiritual house, and a member of a holy priesthood!

When the Israelites were building the temple in Jerusalem, they would chisel the stones away from Jerusalem and transport them to the building site, already chiseled to exactly the size and shape they needed to be to perfectly fit into the wall, exactly where they were supposed to go. Each stone has a specific place in the wall it was individually designed to fit into, and each stone is specifically chiseled to fit perfectly in contact with the stones below it, above it, and on each side of it. There was no concrete used to build the temple. The stones were designed to fit so well together that once they were placed one on the other, you couldn't slide a credit card between them.

God sees you that way. The chiseling process that God is putting you through here on earth is to make you into exactly the living stone He needs you to be to fit exactly where He needs you to fit in the Kingdom of God. Each person plays a critical role. If you're not taking your place in God's living temple, then there's a hole and a weakness. True, the temple might not collapse if one stone is missing, but there's a weakness nonetheless. There's a spot He's reserved just for you, and only you can fill it.

Now you have a choice to make. Do you believe that, or not? It's your choice, but your freedom depends on the choice you make.

God loves you, died to save you, adopted you as His child, lives **inside** of you, and has a plan for your life! Take *that* low self-esteem!

With God living in you, there's no room left in there for low self-esteem. Evict it. Memorize something from the above list or anything else you choose and repeat it over and over and over in your head. Scream it at the chorus, and let Jesus whisper it in your ear.

The final word on self-esteem is this. The more you focus on yourself, your history, and the chorus in your head, the more you give way to the devil and give him a foothold in your life. He loves it, it ruins your witness, and he will delight in making you miserable.

If you focus your attention on eternity, keep seeking things above and not things of this world, make Jesus the Lord and Lover of your life, and obey His commandments out of your *love for Him*, then your low self-esteem will fall by the wayside as a non-issue.

Focus on God, read His word, love Him, receive His love, serve the saints,[18] and God will esteem you. And that's all the esteem you'll ever need.

XIV — BIBLE-BASED THERAPY

The Seven Pillars Of Change

Ok, here it is. Finally. Here's the 'how to' portion of the book. These are lessons I've gleaned from Scripture as I've studied, as I've worked with clients, and as I've tried and failed and succeeded in applying them to my own life. These are the lessons that have transformed lives and performed miracles before my very eyes in my office. This is where you surrender yourself to God and fall in love with Jesus, step by step. That's true, penetrating, and lasting mental health.

This section presents what I believe to be the cornerstones of mental health therapy God's way. As I continue in my practice and in my research, I'm sure I will be able to add to this list, and I'm sure it will be evolving my entire life. But there is no question in my mind that if you embrace these changes in your life, if you study them and practice them and melt them into your heart, you will realize the joy, the peace, and the abundant Christian life you seek. Before you study these therapies, pray that God would open your heart to the truths that are presented here, and that He would coach you through your study and application of these principles.

Now, I'm a professional therapist, so it would be disingenuous for me to say there's no place for a professional therapist in this process. There certainly is. As is the case with all change, it comes slowly and needs to be dealt with in baby steps. As you go through the process of learning these techniques, a professional therapist can help you continue to make progress, can hold you accountable to the process, and can keep you stable while you learn how to lean on Christ. If you don't already know how to lean on Him and you feel like you need help quickly, please get professional help. Your therapist would delight in helping you learn how to lean on Christ, so you can lean on her as you learn to lean on Him. You be the judge, but don't hesitate to get professional help if you think it might help.

Fruit of the Spirit

I wanted to start off this section with the Fruit of the Spirit because I believe that the Fruit of the Spirit holds the key to good mental health. Many people who suffer have a block, an obstacle, that no matter how much therapy they go through, they are stuck in their misery. For some inexplicable reason, they hold on to their misery with both hands. They are either afraid to progress because of the unknowns, they are afraid of the terrifying drop back into misery if they find peace for a time, or they feel like they just don't deserve to feel good. The bottom line is that they have a motivation problem. They *want* to 'want' to get well, but they can't make themselves actually *want* it. The obstacles are just too big. This section addresses that motivation problem.

In Galatians 5:22, the Apostle Paul describes the fruit of the spirit as "love, joy, peace, patience, kindness, goodness, faithfulness, gentleness, self-control."

When I first became a Christian, I was thrilled to see that list because I believed that if I could just *do* those things, then I'd be a 'Godly woman,' and who doesn't want that?

It didn't take me very long to realize that achieving that goal was an absolutely impossible task — if you regard it as a task. As I was looking over that list one day in longing resignation, I heard God speak into my heart and say, "Child, that's *My* fruit, not yours."

Right! The *fruit of the Spirit!* It's *His* fruit, not mine. He gave me this fruit when He gave me His Holy Spirit. I have it now. I don't have to work to get it. It's already mine!

Wow. That's amazing. I already have love. I already have joy - bottomless, unspeakable joy. It came part-and-parcel with the Holy

Spirit. I can't refuse it and I can't reject it and I can't lose it. They're all mine, right now.

But I had a problem: If I have them already, why don't I feel them?

To answer that question, we need to dig a little deeper. Remember that you live in a spiritual battle. Our lives are not about us - they're about winning the spiritual battle for Jesus. That's our job. He has commissioned us to 'be My witnesses' (Acts 1:8) to all the earth, and that means to go out, bring people to Him, make disciples, baptize them, and teach them to obey Christ (Matthew 28:19-20).

So let me ask you a question. If you're depressed, anxious, negative, guilty, angry, etc., how many disciples do you think you would win for the Lord? What kind of a witness do you think you would be? Would someone want to be discipled by you?

Think of it this way. If you were a soldier in the Army and your General said to you, "Soldier, I want you to take that hill. Here's a rifle you can use to defeat the enemy." Unbeknownst to your General, your Lieutenant said, "Yes, I agree with the General, you need to go take that hill, but the rifle really isn't the best weapon in this circumstance. Here, use this air rifle instead. It'll work much better." You pick up the air rifle, it's much lighter than the rifle the General gave you, and it just feels right, natural. So you give in to the Lieutenant and select the air rifle. What you don't know, though, is that the Lieutenant is actually a plant from the enemy, and his job is to make you powerless against them.

How effective do you think you would be in taking the hill? Would you succeed? How would your decision to give up the General's weapon in favor of the Lieutenant's weapon serve your General, whom you love and to whom you have trusted and dedicated your whole life? Your tragic decision to give in to the Lieutenant's pressure has doomed you to failure. By taking the Lieutenant's suggestion, you have essentially told your General that in spite of your love and loyalty, you don't care what he says, and you don't care about pleasing him.

That's a perfect picture for us. Depression, anger, negativity, you know the list - those are all the weapons Satan's Lieutenants want you to use. They are his game plan. When you use them in your spiritual battle - otherwise known as your life - then you are playing right into his hands and you will lose the battle.

So what's the solution, then. What are the real offensive weapons our General has given us to use in this spiritual battle?

The weapon your Lord has provided you for your attack on the gates of hell (Matthew 16:18) is the Fruit of the Spirit: Love, joy, peace, patience, kindness, goodness, faithfulness, gentleness, and self-control. You got it all when you received the Holy Spirit. When you open fire on the enemy, you get all of the power all at once.

This is the weapon that will defeat the enemy, and it is the Lord's greatest weapon against the enemy's schemes. Jesus gave it to you the moment He commissioned you for service. It came, part-and-parcel with your Holy Spirit that indwells you. You just need to unleash it's supernatural power in your life, and the enemy can't win.

So why can't I unleash the Fruit of the Spirit? What's the block?

You already know. See this as a prison cell. Each bar of the cell has a name, and the names are 'depression,' 'anger,' 'fear,' 'negativity,' etc. Behind the bars are the Fruit of the Spirit. You have them in you, but you have them behind the bars of the weapons the enemy has provided you for battle. You have them locked away and incapable of helping you. You have the key, but you won't use it to set them free in your life.

Why is that? Why do we keep the Fruit of the Spirit locked up behind bars? In my experience, the answer generally lies with the messages we've received from childhood. We talk about this later in the book, but in general, if you receive the subtle message that you don't deserve to be happy because 1) you're not worthy of it, or 2) everyone else in your family is miserable, so you'd be betraying them to be happy, or 3) everyone else is miserable and you let their misery rub off on you. In any event, on those brief moments when you accidentally allow true joy in your life, you stop yourself, immediately reverting back to the negative aspects of your life before the joy takes root. The bottom line is, you're not going to allow anyone to take away your misery, and you hold on to it with both hands. I've seen that over and over and over in therapy with clients. They hold the key, but they can't find whatever it takes for them to use it. Achieving their own joy isn't enough.

Well, let me shatter that into dust and give you the motivation you need to get well. Reflect on this truth:

Your joy isn't about you. It's about Christ.

You are in a spiritual battle, and the Fruit of the Spirit is the weapon He has provided for you to successfully fight that battle. He has given you the weapons of love and joy and peace, etc., to vanquish the enemy. You are *obligated* to be joy-filled. That's your job.

How is love a weapon? How can peace defeat the enemy? When others see you being joyful and peaceful and loving in spite of your circumstances, what will they say? When they see you being patient with someone who is intolerable to everyone else, or when they see you being kind and loving to the unlovable, what will be their reaction? Won't they say, "I want that"? Of course they will. You will draw them in and rescue them from the enemy's grasp. They will see the reality of your Lord in your life, and they will want Him in theirs. Satan loses and the angels in heaven rejoice.

When you keep the Fruit of the Spirit behind those bars of misery, then you're giving in to Satan's pressure to use the weapons he's given you, the depression, unforgiveness, pain, etc., and you will fail in your commission from Jesus. By allowing His weapons to stay behind the bars, you are telling Jesus that His great commission just isn't that important to you.

I understand that your depression and anger and addictions are real, and that you can't just 'flip a switch' and turn them all off. But I have seen many, many people holding on to their misery in their misguided perspective that they don't deserve to be happy. They allow their guilt to keep them in bondage. That's one of the enemy's prime weapons, and that's the perspective we need to destroy.

The reality is that it isn't about whether you deserve to experience that fruit or not: You are obligated to. That's your job. You are a soldier in Christ's army, and to be an effective soldier you *must* use the weapons He has provided, the Fruit of the Spirit. To do that, you *must* put the depression and misery behind those bars.

It's just not about you or your joy or your misery or anything else. It's about Christ's battle, and you are on the front lines. To fight to win, you must unleash the power of the Fruit of the Spirit.

So now that we've established the 'why,' let's talk about 'how.'

By way of introduction, here's the whole list:

1) Perspective Therapy
2) Pray Therapy
3) Worship Therapy
4) Thank Therapy
5) Do Therapy
6) Speck-and-log Therapy
7) Laugh Therapy

As you read, just remember that there's nothing magic about these therapies. They're not just different ways of thinking. They require work. They require action on your part. You must actually do these things for them to change your life. You must incorporate them into your day, every day. Therapy is work. It's not just sitting in a therapist's office week after week telling him your problems and getting it out. You have to go away and work the program. You have to incorporate changes into your life.

If you made it this far in the book, though, I know you're ready to work.

So let's get started…

1) Perspective Therapy

Perspective is very simply the way you look at a situation. If you're looking at a single card from a deck of cards, you can look at it several different ways and see a different picture, but you're still looking at the same single playing card. In one perspective, it's a rectangle two inches by three inches with a colorful background. Flip it over and it's the same size with numbers and small icon-like pictures of clubs, hearts, spades, or diamonds. Flip it on its side and it's a very different size with either no real color at all, light brown, or gold. Turn it at angles and the possibilities are endless. And that is just a simple playing card.

Your life situation is exactly the same, only a lot more complex. You can look at it as bad luck. You can look at it as punishment from God. You can look at it as being in the wrong place at the wrong time, a function of your poor decisions, somebody else's negligence or malice, or just your destiny. The way you choose to look at it will drive whether or not your circumstance buries you or strengthens you. Which would you prefer?

Clearly, everyone wants to be strengthened by their circumstances, but some people aren't. Some people allow their circumstances to ruin their lives. They simply see them as too overwhelming to face. They crumble, they hide their faces, they become depressed, they isolate. They blame, they make excuses, they wallow in it and it becomes who they are (John 5:1-16). They are defined by it.

Why do some people do that and others don't? Why are some people strengthened while others are buried? It's the chorus. It's Satan and his minions and the people in their heads telling them they're incapable of handling this situation and there's no way out. Their personal, inner strength has been crushed by the chorus, so they give up and give in. The chorus wins.

So how do you turn that around? How can you ensure that you will come out of this stronger and more able to face the next challenge?

By reorienting your perspective to be in alignment with God's. By learning to see your circumstance the way God sees it.

I hear you: That's a lot easier said than done. True enough. Remember though, you must fight the chorus. You must fight your natural tendency to give in. Perspective Therapy is one of the weapons you use. Learn it and use it. Fight the fight. Do not give up.

You'll never be able to shout louder than the chorus in your head. Without help, your situation will bury you. Without support, you'll crumble and start to believe them. The solution, then, is to get someone to join you who can drown them out. You need Christ on your side of the line.

I heard a great story once of two men who were out in the woods together. They were relaxing by a creek with their bare feet in the water. All of a sudden, a bear appeared. One of them grabbed his hiking shoes and started to lace them quickly onto his feet. His partner said, "What are you doing?!! You can't outrun a bear!" The man said, "I don't need to outrun the bear. I only need to outrun you."

Christ doesn't need to out-shout the chorus. He just needs to be the loudest voice in your ears. For that, He can whisper if He's standing close enough. He just needs to whisper in your ear the truths of His heart into yours.

At first, you won't believe Him, and you may even snarl at Him for lying to you. Eventually, though, as He continues to repeat the same loving words over and over again, you'll start to listen, and eventually you will say, *"Yeah — that's right! Get behind me, Satan!"* Satan and his chorus will start to see you growing stronger and stronger, and they'll eventually give up. Little by little, you will exterminate them from your head.

As you hear the loving words of Jesus in your head, you'll slowly refocus your attention from earth to eternity. You will embrace the reality that your citizenship is in heaven (Philippians 3:20), not earth. As you hear His still small voice in your head, you'll start keeping your eyes on things above (Colossians 3:2). You will start to see things of this world as temporal, and things of God's world — things that are important to Him — as eternal (2 Corinthians 4:16-18). How other people view you will pale in comparison to how *He* views you, and it will warm your heart. How you view your situation will evaporate in comparison to how He views it and you will find your peace in the storm.

As He whispers in your ear, over and over, day by day, you will watch your whole perspective shift. You will *choose* to see this current situation through His eyes. You will *choose* to see it as a strength-building time of your life, and you will thereby gain strength. People will see you growing stronger, not in spite of your circumstance, but because of it. You will be Jesus' witness through this trial, and they will want to know what you know.

How does He whisper in your ear? Of course, through prayer and through Scripture. As you read and talk with Jesus through your readings, as you chat with Him throughout your day, you will hear His voice whispering in your ear. You will feel His presence in your life and in your heart moment by moment. Soon the chorus will be gone, and your circumstance, although still there, will be transformed. You will have a completely different perspective about it. You will see it through the eyes of God.

So how do you hear Jesus' words in your head and in your heart? By now, you know where I'm going with this: Slow down, meditate, pray, apply — and most of all — *memorize*.

When you memorize Scripture on which you've spent time meditating, and hear God's glorious voice in your head over and over again throughout the day, you will come to believe them, and your perspective will shift to be in alignment with God's. Like the hammer hitting the nail, little by little, the new words, thoughts, and perspective will penetrate your heart and drive out the old messages and destructive, negative perspective. Just as the negative messages repeated over and over penetrated your soul, so will the words of God. It takes time, but it works. Work the program every day.

Slow down, meditate, pray, and apply, and watch your circumstance and your life transform.

2) Pray Therapy

All Christians pray at some point or another, even if it's just at dinnertime. Then there's the formal prayer in our morning devotions, the evening prayer before we go to bed, and the intercessory prayer we offer to the Lord on behalf of others in need. We might even throw up what I've heard called a 'flare-prayer' in times of immediate need throughout the day. None of those things are what I'm talking about here. I'm talking about deeply penetrating, meaningful, heart-changing conversation with the Lord on an on-going basis.

Pray Therapy is sort of akin to Talk Therapy, but with a twist. The phrase Talk Therapy usually conjures up a picture of sitting in a therapist's office once a week talking through your problems so they can help you out of your current bondage. Certainly there's nothing wrong with an hour a week, and people's lives have been rescued through that process. But imagine for a moment you could talk to your therapist whenever you wanted, whenever a thought popped into your head, whenever a challenge showed its ugly head. Imagine you could just speak, and they'd be there. Is there a possibility you'd get better faster? Do you think you'd see more change in your life?

This is where I'd like to teach you to use Jesus Christ as your therapist.

There are three critical components of Pray Therapy.

1) Meditation and Memorization of Scripture
2) Being handcuffed to Jesus
3) Being real

Let's start with being handcuffed to Him. We talked about this before, but it bears repeating. How do you see Jesus? Do you see Him as a distant God somewhere 'up there?' Oh, you can talk to Him whenever you want, much like you can call your Grandmother on the phone whenever you want, and you know she'll be there, or you can visit your neighbor when the mood strikes you. But your Grandmother and your neighbor don't live with you. You have to have a 'thought' to call them to speak to them. But what if Grandma were handcuffed to you all day? If that were so, do you think you'd talk to her more throughout the day? I'd say so. As a matter of fact, to *not* talk to her throughout the day would be rude, right? Certainly, you'd be thinking of her constantly. How could you not? She's right there in your face, handcuffed to your wrist.

As a born-again believer, you are a lot closer to Jesus Christ than you would be even if you were literally hand-cuffed to Him. He lives in your heart. He's right there every moment of every day. Unlike Grandma, He can hear your thoughts and knows your innermost heart. When you learn to see Him that way — right there — then learning to talk to Him constantly and leaning on Him for strength becomes a much more natural way of relating to Him. And it will help you fall in love with Him, too.

When you memorize and recite Scripture with Jesus in the room, handcuffed to you, when you speak to Him from the real you, from the inner-most pain and troubles of your heart, then you're slowly, little by little, erasing those negative messages of the past that hold you in bondage and incapacitate you. Speak it out loud and *see* Him whispering in your ear through your memorized Scripture. Every time you say your verse, every time you speak your heart to him out loud, see Christ whispering in your ear, and visually *see* the chorus fading away until you can't see them at all. The Word of God is sharper than any two-edged sword (Hebrews 4:12), and that sword will cut that chorus right out of your head.

God said it — words have power over life and death (Proverbs 18:21). We typically think of that verse in the context of how we treat other people, especially our children. But they have just as much power when we use them on ourselves.

When you say, *"Boy, am I stupid!"* often enough, you start to be crushed by the weight of your own stupidity. When you say, "my own *parents* didn't love me — how can anyone else?!" often enough, you start to expect people not to love you, and you fall victim to the self-seeking manipulators and charmers of the world who will convince you that they're the best you're ever going to get.

Learn to believe about yourself what God believes about you. Speak to Him constantly and memorize Scripture that proves to you that the others are liars. Pray it all to Jesus as much as you can. Hear Him repeating it back to you with His love and His seal. Talk to Him. Tell Him your fears and doubts. Hear Him gently respond with His assurance that what He says about you in Scripture is all true, and it applies to you.

Read your Bible with the anticipation that He is going to coach you through it today. Expect Him to reveal to you some clue about your problem, some way of seeing it differently, some approach to resolving it. It's all there. All of the answers are there. Look for His peace there.

Remember that the enemy wants you to doubt the validity of God's word. In the 2003 movie, *Luther* with Joseph Fiennes, he addressed that very issue. He said that if the devil tells you that you're a sinner and that you don't deserve God's forgiveness, tell him (paraphrased), "I admit that I'm a sinner and that I don't deserve eternity in heaven. *What of it*? My sins have been covered by the blood of Christ. He paid my way."

What of it? That's right. What of it? I heard someone on the radio say, "If Satan reminds you of your past, remind him of his future." Scripture is there to remind you of your future, too, and to remind you that you have a God who sacrificed everything for you and wants you to experience His abundance on earth as well as in heaven.

If you're a believer in the Lord Jesus Christ, all of that applies to you. Memorize and pray to God a hundred times a day something you *do* believe in your head because you know that all of Scripture is true, but that you *need* to believe in your heart. Drown out the screaming negative messages with Jesus Christ's gentle whisper. And talk to Him throughout the day.

3) Worship Therapy

What Worship Is

So here I am telling you that to worship God is therapeutic. Let's start off with a definition.

As I researched this question, I came across various definitions, some from people describing what they called 'Biblical Worship,' and others were coming from the more general dictionary sources. From all of these, I've come up with an amalgamation that, for me, describes what true worship is.

The words I found in the various definitions were:

1. adoration
2. submission / obedience
3. humility
4. service
5. dependence
6. homage / bowing / kneeling / prostration
7. devotion / commitment / focus
8. prayer / praise / song / dance

Therapy with God

That's a lot, but I believe they describe the essence of worship. Adoration, humility, obedience, homage. Some of the items on this list are actions, and some of them are inner states of being. They are both required for it to be true worship.

You know you worship something when it is the most important thing in your life. You focus all of your attention, energy, and time on it, you would die for it, and you live for it. It defines who you are, and drives what you do.

God created us to be a people who worship. We can't help ourselves. It's just who we are. And God wants us to worship Him. It's not for Him, it's for us. Worship is for us? Yes, it is. You mean God doesn't have a self-image problem? No, He doesn't. He has given us Himself to worship for many reasons. The reason we will focus on in this book is that it enhances our relationship with Him and our experience of life. Let me explain.

Why Worship Is Therapeutic

So why is Worship the next step in our therapy? First of all, because He is so deeply and profoundly worthy of it. "True enough, but how does that improve my mental health?" you ask.

In the book of Isaiah (Isaiah 6:1-8), Isaiah is having a vision of God, high and lifted up, sitting on His throne and His robe and smoke are filling the Temple. Angels are flying around the throne passionately crying, "Holy, Holy, Holy..." Isaiah is having a fantastic vision of God, seeing Him in His true Majesty.

Isaiah had just spent five chapters saying to the Israelites, "Woe is you, woe is you, woe is you. You are a stiff-necked, adulterous generation and God will show you His wrath."

But now that He's seen God, and for the first time really 'gets it,' he turns the focus on himself and says, "Woe is me, for I am undone; because I am a man of unclean lips and I dwell in the midst of a people of unclean lips." Why does he feel that way? He tells us — "for mine eyes have seen the King." He goes from "Woe is you" to "Woe is me" for one reason and one reason only — he finally saw God.

Have you seen God yet? Do you understand His unspeakable majesty? Do you really understand His glory? Do you understand how worthy He really is of your worship?

If you don't feel that to the core of your being, then spend more time reading, reflecting, meditating on the wonder of our God and see yourself in comparison with Him. When you see Him, high and lifted up next to you, you'll really, really understand the word 'grace' as it applies to His decision to save you. This is not the same thing as beating yourself up with low self-esteem. This is you understanding the wonder and beauty and majesty of our God and *receiving* how great He is and how much He loves you.

Now think about the universe, the world around you, the air you breathe. The Jews have a song they sing during Passover that essentially says, "If You never give me anything ever again, what you've given me so far is more than enough." Do you believe that? If you don't, then you need to rethink your position, and you need to worship God more than anyone. Once you do, once you feel His majesty to the depths of your soul, once you really understand who He is, then you will be able to receive the greatness of His free gift of salvation and experience a joy-filled, open relationship with Him. You will be well on your way to falling in love with Him and experiencing the greatest joy there is.

To learn to truly worship Him, and Him alone, from that private place way down deep inside, is the pathway to that inner revelation, peace, freedom, and joy.

We Love To Worship

Second, we need to worship God because we are a people who love to worship[19]. We *love* it! When we go to a fabulous movie or a football game where our team wins or we see a fabulous Renoir, or even hear a particularly moving sermon, what's the first thing we want to do? We want to talk about it, we want to call someone and tell them about it. We try to tell the author/originator of the object of our admiration how thrilled we are and thank them. To do so makes *us* happy. Do you want to feel a little lift? The next time you have a good experience at a restaurant, track down the manager and tell them what a wonderful job the server did. Then feel your feet not touch the floor as you leave the restaurant.

God, as our Creator, made us a people who love to worship. We *will* worship something. As a society, we worship intelligence, money, power, stuff, golf, football, famous people, our spouses, our children, our pastors, our ministries. The problem with all of those things, though, is that they're transient — artificial and temporary, they fail us, and they replace God in our hearts. Their usefulness in making us truly contented and satisfied with ourselves is fleeting and paltry, but as we worship them, we allow ourselves to become dependent on them. We put 'all of our eggs in their baskets,' so to speak. They become our slave masters.

What do you think about when you wake up in the morning? What do you focus your attention and energy on all day long? What would the time you spend show to be of importance to you? What do you consider to be worth dying for? Whatever your answers to those questions are may be the object of your worship.

This is not to say that if you have a full-time job, or if you're a full-time mom, or whatever else takes up your day that it is necessarily an object of worship. It is not to say that if you love your spouse or your children and would die for them, that it's necessarily worship. What I'm saying is, if that's all you think about, if they're the complete focus of your affection and your life, and especially if they define who you are and you couldn't live without them, then that may be worship, and it or they may be holding you in bondage. They may be your slave masters.

Is your husband or wife your slave master? Your children? Your career? Your money? Your reputation? Your life plans? Ask yourself these penetrating questions: What or who owns you? What drives your life? What would destroy you if you lost it? What do you fear losing the most?

When we worship our money and then lose it, our world falls apart. When we worship our intelligence and then fail at something, we are crushed and fall into despair. When we worship our spouse and they leave us or die, they take our identity with them. When we worship our children and then they're gone, we die inside. Penetrating pain and grief are normal in all of these circumstances, and God wants to be there with us and hold us as we grieve. Grief is not an indicator of worship, but spiritual destruction is. People describe it as "there is no one there inside of me any more. The person that used to be me is gone, dead." Many of our deepest fears come from the possibility that we might experience that inner destruction some day when we lose our object of worship, or when it fails us in some profound way. Our own fear of that loss and inner destruction then becomes a link in the chain that holds us in bondage.

Jesus represents total freedom from the bondage of earthly worship. If you worship Jesus and you lose your money, then you'll trust that He will see you through and provide what you need. You hold on to it with a gentler grasp. If God takes it away, so be it. It's all His anyway. If you worship Jesus and you lose your spouse, you still see Jesus as your true life partner, and although it will hurt intensely and you will grieve for a season, you'll still have your identity and your hope which springs, not from your spouse, but from Him. Or the worst loss a parent can experience, if you experience the loss of your child, you will grieve desperately and your life will never be the same, but you will live inside nonetheless. Your inner world will be intact. You will hold on to God with both hands and grow stronger through your ever-deepening reliance on and faith in Him.

God commands us to worship Him and Him alone because He knows that, when we do, we are set free from all of the things that hold us in bondage. His commandment for us to worship Him is an act of supreme love. If we can learn to truly worship God from our innermost being, then we no longer need to worship the things that keep us locked up and hold us captive

Worshipping God is the greatest gift you can give yourself. The transformation in your heart takes time, but trust in Him and His promises. Worship Him alone to be truly and absolutely free.

We Become What We Worship

The third big reason to worship God is because it makes us want to be more like Him. We are a people who become what we worship (Psalm 115:4-8).

I remember when one of the Harry Potter books had just come out a few years ago. There was a picture in the newspaper of four kids with the new book in their hands. Two of them had their faces pointing upward, screaming, and two of them had the Harry Potter glasses on, beaming from ear to ear. It was a perfect picture of worship. Absolute abandonment to joy and 'becoming' like Harry. When I was growing up and loved Rock and Roll, we all wanted to become our favorite singers. We dressed like them, we talked like them, and we acted like them. We wanted to *be* them. I always had a dream I'd be the fourth member of Peter, Paul, and Mary.

We become what we worship. God wants us to become like His Son, and we want that, too. To be like His Son means, among many other things, to have the very greatest of mental health possible. The closer we get to achieving that supreme goal, the closer we get to the ultimate in mental health. Worship Him to become like Him.

Swim in it. Drink it in and feel His warmth on your face. Close your eyes. *Feel* Him loving you and love Him back with all your heart. Pick up the gift of love and salvation He has placed on the table in front of you. Pick it up, unwrap it, hold it to your chest, and say, "Thank you, Jesus."

Then worship Him. Worship Him with your thoughts, your time in His word, your song, your words of praise. Delight in Him through worship, lift your hands, and have a ball! You don't have to be in church or listening to music to worship Him. Just speak. If you don't know what to say, read the Psalms, particularly the ones that David wrote. Even in His darkest hours, he worshipped God with his whole heart and his beautiful words. The more you focus on loving and worshipping God, especially when you feel sad, the faster you're going to see the remarkable restorative and resurrection power of our Lord. Worship Him and become like Him.

When Isaiah said, "Woe is me" (Isaiah 6:1-8), the angel touched him with the coal of forgiveness, and God said, "I have a job I need done. Is there anyone who can help me?" Isaiah said, "Here am I; send me."

Once Isaiah saw God and could therefore see himself realistically and humbly, he opened the door to God's forgiveness. Once he got it, once he'd been forgiven, once he saw himself next to a righteous, holy, perfect God and mourned for his sinfulness (Matthew 5:4), God could use him. He was finally in the right place — the place of humility, subjection, and total dependence on God — a place that produces worship with total abandon.

Why do we Worship? Because God is worthy, because it positions us to be fully used by God, because it makes us more *like* God, because it brings us immense joy. Worship Him with all your heart, openly, without reservation, out loud, and feel yourself heal.

4) Thank Therapy

I got this term off of the Internet and I love it. "Thank Therapy."[20] Just think about it. Doesn't that sound like great therapy?

Just like God is worthy of our worship, He is certainly worthy of our thanks. Sometimes, though, we don't feel like thanking Him, or we just don't think of it.

The problem is that we often buy into the concepts of coincidence, luck, and skill. If you believe in these things, then it's just too easy to credit the good things in your life to them. When you get a green light, it's coincidence. When you get a good parking spot, it's luck. When you get that promotion at work, it's because you were in the right place at the right time, or worse, you're just that good.

I heard a story once where a man was sliding rapidly down a very high roof. If he falls off, he'll surely die. As he was sliding, he cried out, "God, if you save me, I'll dedicate the rest of my life to serving you." At that moment, his belt caught a nail and stopped his fall. He said, "Never mind, God. The nail caught me."

We look at that example and say, "What's the matter with him? Can't he see that God made that happen?" What about us? What about you? How often does God have a close and intimate interaction in your life and you just miss it?

The therapeutic part of Thank Therapy is to shatter that delusional thinking that the good things in your life are about coincidence, luck, and skill. Certainly, God expects good planning and skillful execution on your part, but to disavow God's role in your success and good fortune is to bite the hand that feeds you.

Therapy with God

Thank Him for the good fortune you have. Thank Him for the intelligence He gave you. Thank Him for the opportunities He presented at just the right time. Thank Him for the promotion. Thank Him for the right spouse. Thank Him for the sunshine and beautiful blue sky. Thank Him for the green light when you're in a hurry.

The green light? Ok, so you don't necessarily believe that God is in every single little detail of your life like green lights and such. You may be right. But if that's true, then how do you explain Him saying, "Are not two sparrows sold for a cent? And yet not one of them will fall to the ground apart from your Father. But the very hairs of your head are all numbered. So do not fear; you are more valuable than many sparrows" (Matthew 10:29-31).

All of the hairs of my head are numbered? If this is true, and I believe it is because Jesus says it is, then why is it that we find it so hard to imagine Him being in the green light?

And what if He *isn't* in the green light but you thank Him anyway? First of all, what harm does that do, but second of all, wouldn't you think it would draw you closer to Him regardless? Thanking Him for everything, even the littlest things, will make you more aware of His presence, moment by moment. I know you believe in that. Anything you can do to bring Him into your consciousness throughout the day, do it. It won't hurt, and you have much to gain. If you get into the habit of doing that, you'll never stop. It's absolutely wonderful.

So thank Him for all of the good things that happen in your life, even the littlest things, even the green light.

But let's shift gears for a bit. What about the red light? Can you thank Him for that? What about the rain that ruined your picnic? Can you thank Him for that, too? What about the job promotion they gave to your coworker? Can you thank Him for that?

Before I explain how to do those things, let me explain to you why you want to, and how it affects your mental health.

If you get into a pattern of thanking Him for *everything* just like Paul said (Philippians 4:6, 1Thessalonians 5:16-18), you start to really see His hand in your life, you start to trust Him more and more, and you start to feel more peace, comfort, and hope.

Contentment and trusting God doesn't say, "I know you'll work out my life so I'm comfortable and happy." It says, "I know you're going to work out my life so it glorifies You, and regardless of how it feels to me, if it serves Your divine and perfect will, if it fits into your big plan, if it helps me fit into your eternal temple better, I'm privileged to be a part of it and it brings me inner peace and joy."

Think about this definition of joy again:

Joy is the deeply-rooted confidence that God is in control.[21]

If you could really incorporate that into your heart, would you feel more joy? Would you have more peace? More contentment? Would your anxiety go down? Would you feel more purpose in your life?

Doesn't that sound like mental health?

The more you thank Him, the more and more *aware* you become that He is present and that He's in control. The mental health aspect of Thank Therapy is to make you more and more aware that He's there, and He's intimately involved in your life. He's always been there — you just need to become more *aware* of Him. You need to *receive* his closeness. Draw close to Him and He will draw close to you (James 4:8). Who draws first? You do. You draw first because when you draw close to Him, that's when you realize that He was there all along.

Now, exactly how do we do that? We get into the habit of thanking Him constantly, and by thanking Him for things you'd never think of thanking Him for.

Let's just start with something easy. Let's start with that red light. You're in a hurry, you're late, and you get stopped by a red light. Your immediate reaction is to beat on the steering wheel and cry, "Oh, man! Lord, *please* make this light hurry up and turn green. I am late!" Let me ask you a question. Does having a fit change the light? Probably not.

Try this instead: Spare the steering wheel and say, "Lord, thank you for the red light. I was probably in too much of a hurry, I was probably distracted and not driving as safely as I should have been, and your red light slowed me down enough to help me stay focused and safe. So thank you, Lord, for protecting me by giving me the red light."

I know, I know. That sounds *so* stupid. "I could *never* do that!" No? I didn't think so, either. I'm a classic type-A personality. If the microwave doesn't boil the water in 60 seconds, I want to throw it through the window. So this was *definitely* out of my box. But in spite of the fact that I didn't want to, I didn't feel it, and I *sure* didn't mean it, I learned to thank Him anyway. Once you see the power of it, then it gets easier, but in the mean time, you just have to force yourself. It's just a habit you need to change — that's all.

As my words changed, so did my heart. So will yours.

Try this one: "Thank you Lord for the parking space in the back of the parking lot. I need the exercise, and you are probably reserving the spot up front for someone who can't walk as well as I can. Thank you Lord for thinking highly enough about me to allow me the privilege of making that anonymous sacrifice."

I know. It seems strange, but please just trust me and give it a try.

If all of this is still too different, if it's just too big of a leap to start off thanking him for the negative experiences, or if you are not into the habit of thanking Him for the good things yet, start with a silly little one to kick off the process: "Lord, thank you for the color green. It really blesses me. I really like green. It reminds me of trees and being in the woods. So Lord, thanks for green." Get into the habit of thanking Him for *everything*. Get into the habit of looking around to find things to thank Him for. That's the idea.

Here are a few others to kick it off:

- ➢ "Lord, thanks that the computer started up today."
- ➢ "Lord, thanks for the pound I lost this week."
- ➢ "Lord, thanks that the timer worked and the coffee is hot."
- ➢ "Lord, thanks for my friend calling me just when I needed to talk to her."
- ➢ "Lord, thank you that you protected me from getting sick today."

Therapy with God

Did you ever think of that one? Thanking Him for *not* getting sick today? Cancer starts with a single cell that eventually transforms from a perfectly healthy cell into one that is now cancerous. That single cell then splits and becomes two cells, which then split to become four, then eight, then sixteen and so on. Before you know it, you have a lump. Now imagine that that single cell has appeared in your body, and God, without you having a clue, reaches into your body and squashes that single cell between His divine fingers and says, "No. Not now." Totally without your knowledge, you are spared the experience of cancer. Have you ever thanked Him for what you never got?

Learn to thank Him for the good things you do have and the bad things you never had, and you will start to really experience His closeness in your life.

Then start to thank Him for the tougher ones. This is where the Perspective Therapy, the decision to choose a different way of thinking, can really be useful:

> "Lord, thanks for the traffic jam that allowed me to spend more time in the car with You before getting to work."
> "Lord, thanks for the problem at work today. I don't fully understand what's going on, but I trust You. I know You will work it out for good (Romans 8:28), and I thank You for the work You're doing in me through this (James 1:2-4). I know I'm going to grow, draw closer to You, and become more like You as a result."
> "Lord, thank You for the problem in my marriage. It's very tough on all of us right now, and we'll be glad when we're through it. But the suffering You're allowing us to go through now helps us better understand the suffering You went through for us (1 Peter 4:12-13). Please help us draw even closer to You as we learn to lean on You through this trial, and please help us learn what you want us to learn and glorify You in the process. Thank You for being with us through this. I trust You."

It bears repeating: Learn to thank Him for *everything*! Getting into the habit of thanking Him for the good stuff is just training ground for helping you learn how to thank Him for the bad stuff. If you haven't said, "Thank You, Lord" twenty or thirty or fifty times in a day, you've missed something, and you've missed the best opportunity you have to grow closer to Him.

Here's a few quotes from the Bible:

Eph 5:20 — always giving thanks for all things in the name of our Lord Jesus Christ to God, even the Father

Col 3:17 — Whatever you do in word or deed, do all in the name of the Lord Jesus, giving thanks through Him to God the Father.

James 1:2-4 — Consider it all joy, my brethren, when you encounter various trials, knowing that the testing of your faith produces endurance. And let endurance have its perfect result, so that you may be perfect and complete, lacking in nothing.

Phil 4:4-7 — Rejoice in the Lord always; again I will say, rejoice! Let your gentle spirit be known to all men. The Lord is near. Be anxious for nothing, but in everything by prayer and supplication with thanksgiving, let your requests be made known to God. And the peace of God, which surpasses all comprehension, will guard your hearts and your minds, in Christ Jesus.

"Endurance," "perfect result," "lacking in nothing," "The peace of God which surpasses all comprehension..." Does that sound like mental health? I'd say so. The common theme in each of these passages is to thank Him for everything. See the tough times, not as 'bad' times, but as 'growing' times meant to help you develop your character and grow closer to Him. Thank Him for caring enough about your character to give you those opportunities.

As Paul and James and Peter all said, learn to thank Him for everything.

Thankfulness And Complaining

So what kills the thankful heart and your dependence on God? More than anything else, complaining. It's instant death to thankfulness.

Just like saying, "Lord, Thank You," is a mind-set and a habit, so is complaining. Complaining says, "God, I don't like the way you're running my life. I don't like your decision-making skills. I can't see how this is going to turn out for my good at all. I don't trust You." Complaining, as the Israelites found in the wilderness, is sin.

The more you hear yourself complain out loud, the more you believe it, and the more you'll say it again. Words have meaning. Words have power. The spoken word has the power of life and death (Proverbs 18:21). When you speak the complaint out loud, you feed your bitter heart. When you complain, something in you dies.

I heard a story about an Indian Chief who was talking to a young boy. He told the boy, "You have two wolves living in you — a good wolf, and a bad wolf. When the good wolf is strong, you will be doing the right things, making yourself happy, and making your parents proud of you. But when the bad wolf is strong, you will go down the wrong path." The boy said, "Well which wolf will be the strongest in me?" The Chief responded, "The one you feed."

If you want to turn your bitter, angry heart into a heart of peace and contentment, starve the bitterness by refusing to complain — ever, about anything — and bury it permanently with thankfulness.

When the Israelites spent 40 years in the wilderness before God would allow them into the land promised to their fathers, they complained and complained and complained. God was extremely long-suffering with them, and time after time after time, He ignored that their requests came in the form of a complaint and granted their requests. Eventually, however, He'd had enough and started to crank up the heat on them. Many of them died for their complaints, and an entire generation was prevented from going into Canaan because of their unbelief (Hebrews 3:15-19), which manifested itself as fear and complaining.

That event is a perfect illustration of us, and how our own behavior and thought-life are keeping us out of our 'Promised Land.' God had to allow those who did not trust Him or *believe* Him to die in the wilderness because they would never have been able to partner with Him and be obedient to Him to defeat the enemy.

If we want to defeat our enemies, we need to *partner* with God. To do that, we need to *believe* Him, believe *in* Him, and be obedient to Him. We need to trust Him, even in the bad times. When we don't, we cheat ourselves out of His Promised Land, the land flowing with that spiritual and supernatural milk and honey.

Complaining is a sin, and there's no other way to describe it honestly. Why? Because it says that you think you make a better god than God does. That's what Satan thought that got him cast out of heaven (Isaiah 14:12-14; Ezekiel 28:12-19), and Adam and Eve ate the forbidden fruit to be 'like God.' If God isn't God in your life, then it's idol-worship, and that's sin.

Remember the Apostle Paul's words:

"For momentary, light affliction is producing for us an eternal weight of glory far beyond all comparison, **while we look not at things which are seen**, but at things which are not seen; for the things which are seen are temporal, and the things which are not seen are eternal" (2 Corinthians 4:17-18)

That says, "as long as I keep my eyes on heaven and on the eternal issues, I'll experience God's glory beyond all comparison and my circumstance will pale in comparison."

Really meditate on that verse and apply it to your life. It will transform your hurting, complaining heart into a thankful heart after God's own heart.

If there's something in your life that needs to change and you have some influence, then by all means, partner with God and do what you can to change it. However, if there's something over which you have no influence whatsoever, then pray that God will give you

Therapy with God

the serenity to turn it over to Him and then trust Him to deal with it. It is what it is.

Repeat that phrase over and over in your head: It is what it is. It is what it is. It simply is what it is.

Then pray to God for his help and intervention, thank Him for the lesson you're going to learn because of it, and draw closer to Him to help you through it.

I once heard this wonderful story about Enterprise, Alabama. In the late 1800's, the primary means of survival was cotton. The entire farming community depended on it. It was their life-blood. Then one year, the boll weevil moved it and decimated their crops, all of them.

The elders of the community got together to figure out what to do next and how to survive. The first thing they did, though, was to thank God for whatever He was going to do in their community through this disaster. Then they got down to planning. Someone brought up peanuts. They trusted God and all agreed. The crops began to grow, but the market for peanuts wasn't what the market for cotton had been, so there were still hardships.

Unbeknownst to them, there was this young man several states away named George Washington Carver. His prayer to God was that he be allowed to know everything there was to know about the universe. "Let me go to college to study astronomy, Lord" was his heartfelt prayer. Try as he might, he was never able to get into a college for astronomy. So he modified his request. "Lord, if I can't know everything there is to know about the universe, then let me know everything there is to know about the earth. Let me go to college and study geology." But again, it was not meant to be.

So in his frustration, his final prayer was, "Ok then Lord, I can't learn everything there is to know about the universe, and I can't learn everything there is to know about the earth, how about the peanut? Just the peanut. Can you teach me everything there is to know about the peanut?"

The rest is history. He began to think about the peanut, and out of that thought process came peanut butter, peanut brittle, peanut oil, and many, many other inventions credited to him. His only problem was that he didn't have a source of peanuts.

Enter Enterprise and their peanut crops. Enterprise, Alabama and George Washington Carver trusted God. God knew what He was doing all along. They came together and a testimony to God was born. To this day, there is a statue in the center of Enterprise that says, "Thank God for the boll weevil."

The elders in Enterprise could have complained and fallen into fear, but they chose to trust God instead. They thanked Him and praised Him as their first order of business.

Pray about your problems, sure. Cry out to God about your situation, absolutely. If the Israelites had cried out to God rather than grumble amongst themselves and to Moses, God wouldn't have had a problem with it. David did that over and over and over. "My God, my God, why hast Thou forsaken me?!" (Psalm 22:1) Jesus quoted that verse while He was dying on the cross. It was in the midst of Jesus crying out to God about His abject isolation from God that God did His most glorious work. Right after speaking those words from Psalm 22, right after crying out to God, the work was finished and our salvation was assured.

But prayer to God, crying out to Him, is a very different thing from complaining. Turn off the complaining, stop telling Him what to do, learn to cry out to Him instead, and turn on the thanking. Get right with God, and the peace of God that surpasses understanding will fill your mind and your heart (Ephesians 4:7, Philippians 4:7).

5) Do Therapy

If you want to be blessed — *do* in the name of Jesus. Do whatever you can to serve someone else and serve God.

In the following verse, God is talking about fasting, that sacrificial act of depriving yourself for the purpose of and service to the Lord. That's the 'it' that the first line refers to.

Isaiah 58:7-8 — Is it [fasting] not to divide your bread with the hungry and bring the homeless poor into the house; When you see the naked, to cover him; and not to hide yourself from your own flesh? Then your light will break out like the dawn, *and your recovery will speedily spring forth*; [Italics mine].

God says if you serve others, your recovery *will* speedily spring forth. It doesn't say it *might*, it says it *will*. That's a promise from God.

In Chapter 11, "The Seven Biblical Freedoms," I talked about Cain (Genesis 4:2-7), Adam and Eve's son who killed his brother, Abel. God was unhappy with Cain's sacrifice, and Cain became very angry at his brother for having a better sacrifice than he did. God said to Cain, "Why are you angry, and why has your countenance fallen?" God is asking why Cain is angry and depressed, but I notice that God did not engage in talk therapy with Cain. He didn't even give Cain an opportunity to respond. He knew Cain was in trouble and if he didn't make a major adjustment fast, he'd end up really blowing it. God simply said, "If you *do better*, will not your countenance be lifted up?" *Do* better. That's God's prescription for a fallen countenance.

God didn't say, "Let's work on your self-esteem." He didn't ask him why he gave such a poor sacrifice. He didn't try to engage in conversation with him at all. He didn't have the luxury of the time to engage. He just said, "Do better, and you'll feel better. Don't, and you're sunk."

By *do better*, I'm talking about getting up off the couch and out of the house and getting involved in the work God is doing.[22] Hands-on stuff. You need to find something that lifts you up as well as other people, and involves other Christian brothers and sisters. Don't go it alone. I'm not talking about setting up a one-woman or one-man ministry where you're the lone ranger. You need to strap yourself to others who are working so you can support one another, lift each other up, encourage one another, fill in when one of you isn't able to make it, etc. The family of God needs you desperately. The joy you receive will be from the people you help, the people you're working with, and the Lord, directly into your spirit.

Check this out:

Isaiah 58:10 — And if you give yourself to the hungry and satisfy the desire of the afflicted, then your light will rise in darkness *and your gloom will become like midday.* [Italics mine]

Wow — I don't know about you, but I sure want any gloom I ever experience to be like the midday — the bright and shining sun. God says if we give of ourselves, then that *will be* the case. He doesn't say it *might* be — He says it will be. That's a promise from God.

"But what can I do? What do *I* have to give?" you might say. Actually, you have at least five things from which to choose:

1. Time
2. Talent
3. Treasure
4. Temple
5. Testimony

Let's go over each of them in detail to see where you fit in.

Time

As therapy for mental health issues, there are very few things you can give to the Lord's service that will make you *feel* better than your time. Giving of your time will give you a sense of true purpose, it will get you intimately involved with other believers, it will give you opportunities to witness for Christ, and it will help people who need help. It is simply one of the great laws of the universe that there are never enough committed volunteers, and getting involved will make you feel better. This is classic *Do* Therapy.

When Elijah was running from Jezebel because she'd threatened to have him killed (1 Kings Chapter 19), he was deeply depressed to the point of suicide. God spoke to him and as a first step toward recovery, He said, "Arise, eat." Get up Elijah and take care of your physical needs.

Therapy with God

He did so, but then went and hid in a cave. Arising and eating wasn't quite enough to get him going.

This time, God did do a little talk therapy with Elijah: He gave him a chance to vent. Elijah told God how he felt and what was going on in his life right now. After a few major meteorological and geologic phenomena and some additional venting by Elijah, God said," Go…" God knew that Elijah's cave-dwelling was toxic, and the venting wasn't enough to get him out of the depression. God said, "Go…" and gave Elijah a commission to serve. In serving God, Elijah was introduced to Elisha, who "ministered to him" (1 Kings 19:21). You don't hear about Elijah's depression again.

God knew what Elijah needed. He needed to arise, eat, get out of the cave, vent, go, serve, and fellowship with someone of like-mindedness who could minister to him.

That's God's prescription of mental health. If you give of your time, God has promised that He will deal with your depression, and your gloom will be like the mid-day sun.

Now, I know that the practical reality is that we don't always *have* time to give. We have jobs and kids and spouses and lawn to mow and horses to shoe. I know that's true, and I'm totally sympathetic to that. But if you're reading this book because you're suffering from some sort of mental health issue, then this section is for you. If you truly understood how important this step is in dealing squarely with your mental health issue, I believe you'd find a way. This is not another *should,* though. Don't let this turn into a guilt thing. This is an *opportunity* to be ministered to by God Himself by serving God.

Take the kids with you and teach them how to serve. You and your spouse get involved in something together. Get up earlier, turn off the TV more often, economize, ask for help, whatever it takes, even if it's only an hour a month. Don't let your life's 'busy-ness' rob you of God's perfect mental health therapy.

God said, "Go," so go.

Talent

The second gift you have to give to God is a gift He gave to you first: your talent. Talent is related to Spiritual Gifts, so refer to that section as you consider your talents.

Psalm 37:4 says, "Delight yourself in the Lord, and He will give you the desires of your heart."

What does that mean? It's what the computer industry calls an "If-Then" statement. **If** you do something, **then** God promises He'll do something in response to it. The 'then' is conditional upon the 'if.'

If you delight yourself in the Lord, then He'll give you the desires of your heart. When I first became a Christian and read that verse, I thought, "Way cool! God has *promised* me that I get what I want if I just delight myself in Him!" Well, that thought lasted about a microsecond when I realized, "Wait a minute. That doesn't make any sense at all. What if I desire a Lamborghini? I don't see too many Christians driving around in Lamborghinis, so what's up?"

Then I heard a sermon that changed the emphasis of the way I was reading it. God will give me the *desires* of my heart. In other words, the very desires I have were planted in my heart by God, if I am yielded to His will. If I'm truly delighted in Him, I'll only desire a Lamborghini if it glorifies Him, serves His purposes on earth, and brings people into the Light of Christ. So far, God has not felt that that is the case, so I have no desire to have a Lamborghini.

If it doesn't honor, glorify, and serve Him, I just don't want it. (Side note: That's the *perfect* remedy for dissatisfaction and coveting. Make it all about Him.)

So how does all of this apply to talents, and how does it apply to mental health?

First of all, one of the desires God will place in your heart is a desire to do what He wants you to do. If He wants you to teach Sunday School, He'll put a desire in your heart to teach, to learn Scripture, and to want to help people know the Bible better. In giving you that desire, He will also give you the intelligence to learn deeper concepts and the ability to convey those concepts to others in an understandable way. He will give you a personality well suited to standing or sitting in front of a group of people or a single person, conveying to them what you've learned. Because we all love to do what we do well, you will then *desire* to teach Sunday School. God has given you that *desire*, and then he's given you that talent to carry it out.

If He wants you to feed the poor, He'll give you a heart that aches when you see poor people who are hungry. As a result of that aching, you'll *desire* to serve food to the hungry poor. He has given you that desire and the talents to go along with carrying it out successfully.

We are never so fulfilled as when we are accomplishing the purpose for which we were intended.[23] God is most glorified in us when we are most satisfied in Him.[24] The sources of those two quotes are different, but the idea is the same. We all have some grand purpose in God's world, and when we are accomplishing that purpose with the talents and gifts and desires He's given us, we are gloriously fulfilled and satisfied.

Jesus said, "I have come so they may have life, and have it more abundantly" (John 10:10). So what does Jesus mean by "abundantly," and what does that have to do with doing and giving?

Memorize this definition:

**Abundance is:
where you maximize your God-given potential
to accomplish your God-given purpose
so that your blessings overflow
to the benefit of others."[25]**

Close your eyes and swim in that for a minute.

Does that sound like mental health? The key words are potential, purpose, and overflow. God gives you the potential and the purpose, and you have to put it into overflow. Put those words into action in your life, and you will feel that abundance that Jesus promises.

Treasure

Matthew 6:21 — "For where your treasure is, there your heart will be also."

Acts 20:35 — "It is more blessed to give than to receive."

There are three main Christian concepts that deal with Treasure: the treasure itself, giving, and the blessing you receive when you give. We need to address all three for any of them to make sense. Initially, it may seem that this has little to do with mental health, but in fact, it is a very serious mental health issue.

Many people in the Christian community have the wrong perspective when they hear or use the word 'treasure.' Their hearts are more bent toward the worldly definition, which then distorts what they believe about giving and blessing. This has caused a great deal of bondage, self-recrimination, and even depression as their distorted Christian perspective draws them farther and farther away from God. In this section, I try to make some clear distinctions between the way the world sees these issues, and the way God does. When you understand the difference, you will be empowered to make Godly decisions about your own giving, and to filter the worldly messages out of what you hear. Worldly giving is bondage, Godly giving is freedom.

- **Treasure**

So what exactly is 'treasure?' This is the definition on http://bible.crosswalk.com:

1. the place in which good and precious things are collected and laid up
   a. a casket, coffer, or other receptacle, in which valuables are kept
   b. a treasury
   c. storehouse, repository, magazine
2. the things laid up in a treasury, collected treasures

Treasure means either the place in which precious things are kept, or the precious things themselves. Giving your 'treasure' means giving something you see as precious. Giving whatever you happen to have lying around, or giving money you don't need, doesn't qualify. If it isn't a sacrifice, if it isn't precious to you, then it isn't a 'treasure.'

As a real-world example, many people give away tons of old clothes. They go through their closets and bring out stuff they haven't worn in the past year, throw it all in a bag and take it to the local charity. That's a wonderful thing to do and we should certainly do that because many people benefit from it. Just remember that if it's stuff you don't need and wouldn't use anyway, it doesn't qualify as 'treasure.' On the other hand, say you take the time to sort through it and carefully wash and fold each item because you want them to be nice and fresh and welcoming to their new owners. If your time is precious to you and you gave this time as a 'gift' to the recipient and as a sacrifice to Jesus, then this could qualify as 'treasure.'

> King David gives us a visual example. He had been instructed by a prophet to build an altar to God and offer a sacrifice on it. He went to buy a threshing floor so as to comply, and the gentleman who owned the threshing floor knew King David and offered to give it to him free of charge. King David refused, saying, "**I will not offer burnt offerings to the Lord my God which cost me nothing**" (2 Samuel 24:24). God was pleased with David's sacrifice and prayer, and a "great plague was held back from Israel" (v 25).

'Treasure' has to be something of value to you. The degree to which something is valuable to you is the degree to which you are giving something of value to Jesus, because that is the degree to which you are clearing away the clutter in your heart and making room for Him.

- **Giving**

So, what about the 'giving' part? What does God have to say about the giving itself? Plenty. Let's review just a few verses:

Luke 14:11-14 — Jesus said, "'For everyone who exalts himself will be humbled, and he who humbles himself will be exalted.' And He also went on to say to the one who had invited Him, 'When you give a luncheon or a dinner, do not invite your friends or your brothers or your relatives or rich neighbors, otherwise **they may also invite you in return and that will be your repayment**. But when you give a reception, invite the poor, the crippled, the lame, the blind, and you will be blessed, **since they do not have the means to repay you; for you will be repaid at the resurrection of the righteous.**'"

Matthew 6:3-4 "But when you give to the poor, do not let your left hand know what your right hand is doing, so that your giving will be in secret; and **your Father who sees what is done in secret will reward you.**"

Luke 11:41 "But give that which is within as charity, and then all things are clean for you." This means that if you give a gift from your heart (that which is within), something of material value to you, then you are in a right relationship with God regarding your stuff versus your love for Him, and you will be 'clean,' or pure, on the inside as well as the outside (all things)."

So according to Jesus, a 'Godly gift', so to speak, is one that is:

1. of great personal value,
2. done with no expectation of anything in return,
3. performed in secret, and
4. given from the heart.

Ok, so a gift of no personal sacrifice with strings attached is clearly not a gift at all. Given. But what does that have to do with mental health?

When you give with an expectation of getting something back, it's no longer a gift — it's an investment for some kind of return, or a purchase of some kind of product. In addition to not satisfying Jesus' criteria as a 'gift,' there is a great risk in this kind of giving; you open yourself up to being dissatisfied with the other guys' part of the deal. What if you didn't get the reaction you had expected, even the simplest appreciation or thanks? How would your 'giving' make you feel then?

> Test your heart: Have you ever let anyone in front of you in traffic and had them not wave at you in thanks? What was your internal reaction to that?

Now let's crank up the heat a little: What if the person from whom you expected this reaction was God? What if *God* didn't live up to His part of the bargain? Might you feel cheated by God? Betrayed, maybe? "But they promised that if I give 'to God' (through them), God would bless me. They even had Scripture to back it up. Am I out of line expecting that He'll come through?"

Be very careful here. If your heart is wrong and He doesn't 'come through,' your disappointment can make you pull away from Him. You start to question God and feel let down by Him. You come to see Him as a God that *doesn't* provide or live up to His promises. Or you blame yourself as not being a good enough Christian. Your thoughts spiral downward. You don't understand. You're hurt. You feel anger, loneliness, fear, coveting, then the guilt and shame. You could spiral right into rejecting God altogether, seeing him as irrelevant in your life. You either see Him as unfaithful, or you turn the arrow on yourself and believe that you can never live up to His standard of 'righteousness', so why bother trying. Satan has won. I've seen this in therapy with my clients, and it's an extremely serious, life-changing mental health issue.

"Wow - that's pretty harsh, and pretty frightening! So, what do we do?" As always, look to Jesus for the answer:

John 15:13 — "Greater love has no one than this, that one lay down his life for his friends."

Jesus showed us the greatest love, and the greatest gift there is. He set the standard. He gave the greatest gift through the greatest love.

So how did Jesus' death define for us the perfect, Holy gift? Let's check it against the above Scriptures: First, He gave a treasure of great, unspeakable value - His very life. Second, He did it with no expectation of any personal return. His death was for our salvation - not His. Third, it was done in secret. Oh sure, plenty of people saw Him die, but how many of them realized He did it voluntarily - for them? Not even the disciples understood until after the resurrection. And fourth, it was from the heart. He did it out of His unfathomable love for God, and for us.

- **Blessing**

So if we're not to expect anything in return, then what does it mean to be 'blessed?'

Great question. Scripture absolutely promises that when you give, you will be blessed far more than you gave. But what does it mean by 'bless?'

After doing some research in my reference books and on the internet, I found what I believe to be a God-driven definition of the word blessing (quoting Rick Calvert) as translated from the Greek word 'makarioi':

> In the Bible the biblical use of the word '*makarioi*' took on a spiritual significance where one is "blessed" or "happy" if he exemplifies the quality of God by seeking His approval founded in righteousness. One's blessedness therefore, rests ultimately on his love to God and his personal communion with the Father in heaven. In the New Testament this word is probably more correctly translated "blessed" because the definition of "happy" is connected with luck, *hap* from the verb "happen." Happiness can come from without, and can

be dependent on circumstances; whereas, blessedness spews forth from the soul of man. It is fed by an inward fountain of joy, which no outward circumstances can seriously affect. Blessedness is therefore higher than happiness for it consists of standing in a right relation to God, and so realizing the true purpose of man's being. In the *Sermon on the Mount* Jesus taught that one can only be "blessed" if he humbles himself before God with a pure heart, having sorrow for sin, a meekness of character, and seeking God's approval by hungering and thirsting after righteousness. **According to Christ, the blessed life can be enjoyed even by those who are unhappy or suffering, a paradox which the carnal man cannot understand.** *[Bold mine]* This was a foreign concept to the Greeks, who taught the blessed life was only possible for a select few and disqualified any who were ever a slave, diseased, poor, or died at a tender age, but, Jesus taught blessedness with God is possible for all humanity no matter your circumstances or station in life.[26] (Rick Calvert, http://www.studylight.org/col/ds/)

So, we can see that being 'blessed' is,

- Having the favor of God,
- Having a fullness in God,
- Being a partaker in God's nature through faith in Christ,
- Having God's kingdom within your heart,
- Living in the world yet being independent of the world,
- Getting satisfaction from God and not from favorable circumstances.

To summarize, a blessing in this context could be defined as, "deep, inner contentment, peace, complete satisfaction, and the knowledge that God's presence is abiding in you." A 'blessing' is very simply the 'fullness in God.' There's no mention of material or earthly gain of any kind in this list. As a matter of fact, the last two items eliminate that possibility completely.

The blessings that Jesus promises when we give according to that Godly standard are internal and Spiritual. The Apostle Paul said:

2 Corinthians 9:7 — "Each one must do just as he has purposed in his heart, not grudgingly or under compulsion, for God loves a cheerful giver."

The word "cheerful" literally means, "hilarious" in the Greek. God loves a hilarious giver. One of my favorite church experiences was a few years ago at First Baptist Church of Glenarden in Maryland. My husband and I were visiting that Sunday. When Pastor Jenkins said, "Ok, it's time for the tithes and offerings," the congregation of hundreds erupted in applause and cheered. I was stunned, and my heart sang. They tell me they do that every week. Now, that's a heart given over to God, and hilarious giving in action.

"But before, you said that 'Godly giving' was anonymous. Does that mean that whenever I give, I have to give anonymously to get the blessings?" Scripture tells us that God sees our hearts and our motives (Jeremiah 17:9-10, Psalms 44:21). Are we giving for our own glory, fame, popularity? Are we trying to impress people? Are we doing it with expectations - even gratitude or recognition? Or are we doing it as a cheerful giver with a pure heart and no expectation of a return of any kind? God will know, and it will certainly matter to Him. It just makes sense that you will be given credit for your gift to the extent that your giving is pure.

However, Jesus' said something we need to reflect on:

Matthew 6:2 — "So when you give to the poor, do not sound a trumpet before you, as the hypocrites do in the synagogues and in the streets, so that they may be honored by men. Truly I say to you, they have their reward in full."

So, is He saying that if our giving is not 'in secret' that God will give us no credit at all? I can't answer that with certainty, but one thing is very clear based on the above verse: If you *do* receive a reward on earth, regardless of how small it is, you can be guaranteed it will negatively affect your reward in heaven to some degree or another. If you want to maximize your blessing to God and your reward in heaven, make your gifts anonymous - just a secret between you and Jesus - as often as you can, with no expectation of any kind. If anonymity is not possible, then just remember to deflect the 'thanks' to God. As I said in the section called "Freedom from Expectations," if you can eliminate the expectations from your giving, then you are totally free to enjoy the very act of giving itself.

Do you feel the freedom and the joy in that? Doesn't that feel like mental health?

- **Prosperity preaching and 'give to get'**

"So then why do we hear so many Christian messages that tell us if we give, we'll be 'blessed' by God financially? They tell us that we will be repaid by God 'a hundred-fold,' and that 'We can't out-give God.' Why are they trying to convince us that we'll receive material and financial blessings if all of this is true?" Some people call that "Prosperity Preaching." I call it, "give to get."

Christians have always known that when you give to God, He will bless you for your act of love. I believe that at some point, this positive message of 'give to God and be blessed by God' was hijacked by Satan and turned bad. It became a trap for good Christian people to fall into and become imprisoned by Satan's lie.

I can't read their hearts as to why some of them say what they do, but I do believe that most pastors are wonderful, Godly people. I trust that they believe they are providing Godly teachings that are appropriate, sanctioned, and uplifting for their congregations. I'm sure they work very hard to be good shepherds, and I'm confident that if they believed they had a flaw in their teachings, a hole in their fence enabling their sheep to go astray, they would take the steps to fix the hole.

But the message of prosperity is still being spread. Why is that? I don't know, but it is possible that they have simply bought into the lie and haven't thought it all the way through. Or it could be that they mean the word 'blessing' to mean exactly what this section is saying it means, but they don't realize that the colloquial use of the term is distorting the way their message is being heard. For them, they would just need to clarify what they mean by the word 'blessing,' and their problem would be solved.

One of the problems I have witnessed, though, is that even when the "give to get" message is just a subtle part of an otherwise wonderful sermon, its infiltration can be enough to shift our God-filled Spirits over towards a competing material worldly desire: God called it 'coveting.' The seed is planted that there is something material we can get out of this deal. An otherwise great worship experience can lay the fodder which Satan uses to attack the Holy Spirit in us and chip away at our relationship with God. Without any malice on the part of the preacher, it can lead us astray. We need to be very discerning with what we hear, regardless of the source.

I also believe that tragically, there are far too many preachers looking out for their own interests and are trying to line their own pockets. What seems to come across with some of them is a belief that unless you have some material motivation for giving, you simply won't give. You need to be under compulsion. The common misuse of the words 'treasure,' 'gift,' and 'blessing' seem to be pervasive within the highly available public Christian media, and these new definitions are forming roots in our tender souls. It is Satan's message, and it is being preached from the pulpit. They capitalize on their belief that you want to be wealthy so badly that you will be willing to 'play the lottery' with God in the hope that He will 'bless' you materially. They're the ones getting wealthy - on your back.

> Disclaimer: If you believe this section in any way disagrees with or violates the teachings you hear from your pastor, or if it confuses you in any way, please take it to him, and humbly ask him about it. I am not a shepherd - I am a sheep like you. Have him explain to you where he disagrees, so you'll know. As always, I want to prayerfully point you to your pastor, to Jesus, and to your Bible. [See my permission to copy at the end of this section.]

So the issue here is what we have learned to value as our treasure, true wealth, and long-term prosperity. Satan seldom lies outright - he just takes a truth and twists it a little. So with that in mind, what does Jesus say about all of that? Let His words set you free from this bondage:

Luke 8:11-15 — Jesus said, "The seed which fell among the thorns, these are the ones who have heard, and as they go on their way they are choked with worries and riches and pleasures of this life, and bring no fruit to maturity" (v 14).

> –We would certainly all agree that worries can choke the fruit out of us, but look at the other two: <u>riches and pleasures</u>. These are things the world tells us are good things. These are the things we spend our entire lives searching for and working for. And if you listen to some preachers, these are the things that God will give you if you give generously to them. So we're supposed to give to get the very things God says will choke the fruit out of us? Does that make sense? Not to me.

Matthew 6:19-21 — Jesus also said, "Do not store up for yourselves treasures on earth, where moth and rust destroy, and where thieves break in and steal. But store up for yourselves treasures in heaven, where neither moth nor rust destroys, and where thieves do not break in or steal. For where your treasure is, there your heart will be also."

> –So again He is telling us not to focus on what we have on earth, but rather on what we're putting away for eternity.

Matthew 19:26 — Jesus said, "…it is easier for a camel to go through the eye of a needle, than for a rich man to enter the kingdom of God" (v 24).

> –This is not to say it is impossible for a rich man to enter the kingdom of God because nothing is impossible with God (v 26). The point here is that people are prone to love their wealth above all things, and once they have

it, they tend to hold on to it with both hands. In this verse, Jesus had just invited a rich man to sell all his possessions and give to the poor and come, follow Him. He could not, and "...he went away grieving; for he was one who owned much property" (v 22). God won't force us to give it up, and many just won't. That's why it is so hard for them to enter the Kingdom of God. Their wealth becomes for them a snare and a stumbling block. Interesting that Jesus didn't say, "Sell your possessions and bring all your money and come, follow me." Hmm...

Matthew 25:34-40 — Jesus said if you give to the poor, you visit the sick, you invite in the stranger, "to the extent that you did it to one of these brothers of Mine, even the least of them, you did it to Me."

–If you give to others in need, you are giving to Him. Giving is the key — not getting. I agree that you have to receive it before you can give it, but the focus is still on the giving, not the receiving. That's not the message of the 'give to get' sermons

Luke 12:16-21 — And He told them a parable, saying, "The land of a rich man was very productive. And he began reasoning to himself, saying, `What shall I do, since I have no place to store my crops?' Then he said, `This is what I will do: I will tear down my barns and build larger ones, and there I will store all my grain and my goods. And I will say to my soul, 'Soul, you have many goods laid up for many years to come; take your ease, eat, drink and be merry.' But God said to him, `You fool! This very night your soul is required of you; and now who will own what you have prepared?' So is the man who stores up treasure for himself, and is not rich toward God.

– What good did all of his wealth do? His priorities were all wrong, and it was all a waste. His wealth became a stumbling block that distracted Him from things of God. We need to be very careful we do not stumble with our wealth.

Ecclesiastes 2:4-11 — All that my eyes desired I did not refuse them. I did not withhold my heart from any pleasure, for my heart was pleased because of all my labor and this was my reward for all my labor. Thus I considered all my activities which my hands had done and the labor which I had exerted, and behold **all was vanity and striving after wind** [bold mine] and there was no profit under the sun.

– If God meant the word 'blessing' to mean material wealth as a source of satisfaction and happiness, even in the Old Testament, then why did He inspire Solomon to write Ecclesiastes and call all his wealth "vanity of vanities," which means "a total and absolute waste." In the end of his diatribe about his wasted life, King Solomon said, "The conclusion, when all has been heard, is: fear God and keep His commandments..." (Ecclesiastes 12:13). After all his wealth and misery, he finally got it right in the end.

None of that sounds like 'give to get' to me at all. I see the focus in all of these passages as eternal rather than temporal, internal rather than external. I believe that many of the sermons we hear are perverting the use of the word 'blessing' and we need to be very, very careful not to let ourselves fall into that trap. When you hear them preach, just stay very cautious when they start talking about money. Be very discerning, and keep in mind how Jesus described the words 'gift,' 'treasure,' and 'blessing' in the passages above. If you choose to give to them, give it as a true gift, and understand with eyes wide open that any blessings you can expect from God are internal and eternal.

So what's wrong with God wanting to give to us materially? Can't He do that if He wants to? Of course He can, and He does.

Jesus isn't anti-wealth, or anti-poverty for that matter. One's financial position only seems to matter to Him to the extent that it helps or hinders a person's ability to give their life and their heart to Him, or to the extent that it affects a believer's witness. Some Christians are able to successfully enslave their entrusted wealth and have it serve God's purposes beautifully. For others, though, our quest for daily wealth is a minefield into which we need to tread very carefully. Pride is a serious problem for our sinful flesh as it is, and if the prosperity message is correct, that puts those who have more wealth than others in grave danger of becoming prideful. "We have more than they do, that must mean we're more favored by God than they are. We must be better Christians than they are, and are in the will of God better than them." The risks are enormous. He is not opposed to wealth, but He is opposed to what it can do to us. God loves us all equally with that agape, unconditional love, and **will provide what we need to accomplish His purpose** when we are ready to serve Him. Having wealth, or not having it, is perfectly congruent with being a wonderful, loving Christian. It just doesn't happen to be the blessings we get for giving. They are simply two separate and distinct issues.

I heard it once said, "Money makes a wonderful slave, but a tyrant of a slave-master."

As a wrap-up of the "Treasure, Gift, Blessing" discussion, let me include these simple charts for your convenience. Spend some time looking over them and see how they square with your view of treasure, your understanding of blessing, and your perspective and patterns of giving.

A Summary of Treasure / Blessings / Giving	
To The World	**To God**
Treasure	
Deem self of highest value, treasure things of the world: power, prestige, money, jewels, coins, stuff; talent, having it your way.	Cherish God above all, treasure all things Christian: Holy Spirit, Holy Scriptures, fellowship with Jesus and believers, bringing people to Christ.
Blessing Received	
Material / good fortune: happiness, temporal, insatiable desire, world's approval.	God's fullness: joy, contentment, satisfaction, God alone.
Giving	
About me: with an implied demand, seeking gratitude, boasting comes from surplus, for important people.	About God: without expectation, anonymous, sacrificial, for the least among us.

The following chart shows the different motives for giving. As you anticipate giving in the future, reflect on this list and prayerfully ask God to purify your heart.

RIGHTEOUSNESS IN GIVING

1. Self-seeking —-   Giving to get a worldly payback
2. Exchange — —   Give Expecting a Return Gift or Favor
3. Gracious — —-   Gift Expecting Only Gratitude
4. Blessing to God -   Give in Secret / Anonymously
5. Jesus' Sacrificial- Give in Secret, Sacrificial, Lay Down Your Life for Friends and Enemies

- **Treasure Therapy**

Ok, then, let's bring this all home. This section is about "Treasure Therapy," so to speak. With all of the above, how do I turn my 'Treasure' into a form of mental health therapy for myself?

Try this: The next time you go to a sandwich shop, look around, and see who is eating alone. Tell the server you want to pay for their lunch, but you don't want them to know who did it. This is just a secret between you and Jesus. See if your feet don't leave the ground when you walk out of the restaurant.

Or answer one of those radio solicitations that ask you to give them your credit card number and they'll send 100 Bibles to Africa.

Or give anonymously to one of the ministries in your church. Don't even tell the pastoral staff. Have a good laugh about it with Jesus, and feel your heart sing.

Give to your church fundraisers, give to the local nursing home, or give to the high school football team, it doesn't matter. Remember that what you're giving isn't necessarily just money, although that is certainly on the list of things to give. Give whatever is precious to you: money, personal possessions, time, whatever. Give it away so it doesn't take the place of Christ in your heart. Hold on to it with a very light grip. Always be ready to give if the Lord should ask you to do so.

A client of mine told me a story I would like to share with you. She had been having a very difficult day with normal life issues. Christmas was only a couple of weeks away, and she was feeling depressed, alone, and overwhelmed. A woman she was familiar with at work asked her if she knew where she might be able to get some help for Christmas because she could not afford to buy all of her children Christmas presents. This client decided that she hadn't been able to contribute to her church's benevolence fund that year, so instead, she wrote the woman a check, covering her needs for Christmas. She said her heart was instantly transformed, and she felt lighter than air. She said the feeling had not abated as of our conversation many days later.

Give hilariously, knowing that your rewards will be straight from Jesus directly into the treasure-chest in your heart. With those blessings from God, you can then overflow them onto others and change their lives. Share your faith in God. Share your love for Him and give other people the gift of your peace and your contentment with the life God has given you regardless of your circumstances. Overflow your love for Him onto others and give them your peace. Watch your inner peace and glow draw people to you, and thus to God, and watch His Kingdom grow before your very eyes. Feel your heart sing, and feel yourself drawing into the presence of God.

Release yourself from the bondage of expecting some financial or material gain from your giving. Let your giving build your character and the place for God in your heart; tell the devil to take a hike. Give from your heart with the intention of blessing God, and you can be assured that the blessings of God's fullness and approval will come back to you, just as He promised, a 'hundredfold.' You truly can't out-give God. Feel the freedom and the joy in that.

And consider this for a moment: When you think the word 'treasure,' teach yourself not to think of 'material' possession, anyway. The real treasure is Jesus Christ, Himself. When we are filled with Him, we can then offer Him to the world. He is the ultimate fulfillment of our desires for more treasure and more blessings. If you treasure Him above all else, then you will be filled and completely satisfied in Him, you will feel the full blessings He wants to give to you, and you will have abundant treasure to share with others as well.

> The 'blessings' of giving do not come from external material and financial returns that you get as a payback for giving. The true blessings are the inner change in your heart from the mere satisfaction of showing Him your love, and from receiving from Him His salvation, His favor, His love returned, and His Kingdom into your heart. These blessings are yours, regardless of your financial circumstance.

If you have fallen victim to the prosperity preaching and the 'give to get' message, then set yourself free and pray this prayer from your heart:

> "Father, please forgive me for expecting You to 'repay' me for my gifts. Your Son's sacrifice on the cross is all the gift from You I will ever need. Help me undo the messages that I have heard, and help me be one who gives from my heart sacrificially and joyfully as unto You, Lord, and cleanse my heart of all expectation of a return, except for those things that come from You directly: your fullness and peace on earth, and your eternal rewards at the resurrection."

Jesus wants to set you free.

Reflect on this final point: The bigger a part God has in your life, the more you think about Him, pray to Him, worship Him, give to Him, and love and obey Him, then the more you will have His presence permeate through you, and the bigger the place will be that He will be occupying in your heart. As others see His light in you, and experience His love through your sacrificial gifts to them, they will want what you have, and you will have an opportunity to lead them into the Kingdom of God. This is truly what God meant by, "laying up treasures in heaven."

The more you give with the heart of God, the more God will fill your heart.

Now go with God, and bless and be blessed.

[*Therapy with God* Copyright 2008 © susan henderson mchenry. http://www.TherapyWithGod.com. The *'Treasures'* section of this chapter may be reproduced in whole only (not in part) under the following provisions: **1)** This copyright statement must be included, and **2)** the *'Treasure'* content may not be changed in any way.]

Temple

Peter said that we are all stones in the living temple of God (2 Peter 2:4-5). Paul said that our body is the temple of the Holy Spirit (1 Corinthians 6:19).

So when you talk about giving of your temple, you're talking about giving of your body. God has asked us to love Him with all our "heart, mind, soul, and strength" (Luke 10:27). The 'strength' portion of that can, among other things, refer to using our physical bodies to serve the body of Christ. You can do this by taking your body to help move the chairs out of the sanctuary, mow the lawn at the church, serve the poor in the soup kitchen, take a meal to someone in the hospital or grieving. Use your imagination as to how God would like you to use your 'temple' in His service. Pray to Him about it. Search your heart to see what 'desire' He's planted there.

Giving of your temple is closely related to giving of your time, in that it takes time to give of your temple. The difference is that giving of your time could mean stuffing envelopes or church bulletins, answering the phones when the secretary has to be out, or sitting in a hospital room visiting someone who's in need. Giving of your body implies physical work. It takes time, but it takes arms, legs, your back and your strength as well.

I heard a story about a man who was in a church service, and he had just dedicated his life to the Lord. When the offering plate came by, he asked the usher to lower it, which he did. Then he asked him to lower it more, and more, and more, until the offering plate was on the floor next to the pew. At his point, the man stepped into the offering plate. He wanted to give his whole temple.

Giving your body, your temple of the Holy Spirit, allows you to love and worship God with your strength, it allows you to fellowship with other believers who are giving of their temples, and it gives you the extreme satisfaction of purpose within the body of Christ. If you have your physical faculties, the church needs you.

Testimony

Your testimony is the story of how God has worked in your life. It includes how you initially came to know Him as a new believer, but also how He has worked in your life since then, and even before then. When you share your testimony with others, they learn to see Christ as an ever-present Lord who directs your steps. They can see the glimmer in your eye as you talk about Him. They can feel the love in your heart for Him, and the light and power that comes out of your pores. Sharing your testimony is about spreading the Gospel of Christ.

Talk about Jesus as much as you can and share your story with anyone who will listen. Remember, you are the only Bible many people will ever read. Use that power generously.

St. Francis of Assisi said, "Preach the Gospel at all times, and if necessary, use words." Sometimes your best testimony is the way you live your life and carry yourself. Use words when you feel prompted to do so, but live your life in the light and the glory of the gospel message at all times. The most damage that can be done to the purposes of Christ in the eyes of the non-believing world is when a Christian openly and overtly sins. They don't understand that we're all just sinners like they are, and that we sin because of that. What they see is a sanctimonious, self-righteous holier-than-thou Jesus-freak who doesn't really buy what he's selling. They see a hypocrite.

Live your life like the world is watching, because in every sense of the word, they are. The unbelieving world is in an ever-ready stance to pounce on us with the slightest transgression with proclamations of "hypocrite!" They say, "See? I *knew* it! Those Christians are all the same! Just a bunch of hypocrites who claim they're better than everyone else and try to shove that junk down my throat."

Mahatma Gandhi said, "I like your Christ, I do not like your Christians. Your Christians are so unlike your Christ." So painfully true way too often.

So let's address the 'sanctimonious, self-righteous' part. If you think you're better than anyone else, then you need to know that God doesn't see you that way. When you see a brother sin, say to yourself, "There but by the grace of God go I" (1 Corinthians 10:12), and then gently and humbly come along-side him to wash his feet, offer your help in his difficult time of transgression, and lift him up. You may have to gently confront him with the truth of God's word, but remember to do so with humility. Share your testimony with him when you have struggled. The purpose isn't to make him feel 'less than.' He probably feels enough of that already. The purpose is to restore him back to obedience to God and restore His face-to-face relationship with Christ.

So what's all this got to do with mental health?

Two things: Obedience and purpose. First of all, if you're living your life to glorify God, then you're being obedient to Christ and serving God, and by definition, your life will improve in dramatic ways you can't even imagine if you're not already doing it. Your life is your testimony. Second of all, we *all* have as our Great Commission, our most universal and profound purpose on earth, to be witnesses and spread the Gospel message (Matthew 28:19-20). When you do that, you will feel the most miraculous and penetrating sense of joy and peace imaginable.

If you've never shared the Gospel message or brought anyone to the Lord, I *highly* recommend it for God, for them, and for your mental health. Your feet won't touch the ground for a week.

If you struggle with how to spread the gospel message and share your testimony, talk to your pastor. If there's one desire God has placed in all of our hearts, it's to spread His Gospel message. Your pastor will help you learn how and will give you opportunities to practice what you learn. You will never regret taking that step.

So "Do Therapy," including the five gifts listed above, is all about giving of yourself to the service of God's people — those who know Him now, and those who are still lost. Connect with God through Doing, and you will bring God's blessings and peace into your heart in ways you cannot envision.

6) Speck-and-Log Therapy

Jesus said, "Why do you look at the speck that is in your brother's eye, but do not notice the log that is in your own eye?" (Matthew 7:3).

Wow, don't we do that, though? Jesus knows us so well, doesn't He?

It's about judging others with a different standard of measure from the one with which we judge ourselves. Jesus says not to do that. But more than that, He's telling us we need to put ourselves through that sieve before we impose it on others. He wants us to make sure our own house is clean before we inspect someone else's.

So the red flag is this: If you feel yourself angry at someone else, disgusted with something they've done, or critical of some way they've treated someone or handled something, then let that be a red flag to you that *you* just might have a log in your eye.

God says that if we judge others, we ourselves are condemned because we do the very things we condemn others of doing (Romans 2:1). I have seen the same thing in my own practice with clients. I have had many occasions where a spouse will accuse another of cheating on them when, in fact, it's the accusing spouse who's cheating. I have had people bitterly complaining to me that their son or daughter or spouse never stops complaining. I have had angry people getting angry at their spouse for their poor temper.

God says we see the specks and ignore the log. We know it's true. But the question is, Why?

Again, in my experience in the mental health field, it isn't exactly because we're trying to deflect the attention from ourselves. You might think so, but it actually goes a little deeper than that.

It says, "On some level, I know I do that. I need to think of myself as okay and justified for doing it, so I need to believe it's a normal thing to do. If I do it and you don't, then that makes you a better person than me. Since I can't handle that, I have to see it in you with the slightest provocation. That makes me okay in my own eyes."

And then it says, "But I also know it's wrong. If I'm quiet about you doing it, then society will know that I accept it or approve of it, and they'll suspect that I do it, too. I can't have that. So I have to draw attention to the fact that you do it, showing them that I certainly don't do that, so don't look at me." So in the end, it's because we're trying to deflect attention from ourselves, *plus* feel better about ourselves as well and convince those around us we're fine.

Believe it or not, none of these thoughts are intentional. They're subliminal and internal. Once someone brings them to your attention, though, if you're being totally honest with yourself, it rings true. That's when you can stop yourself, find your connection with Christ, find your humility, and say, "Yep. There but by the grace of God go I."

> First Corinthians 10:12 — The Apostle Paul said, "Therefore let him who thinks he stands take heed that he does not fall." Take heed if you think you're above 'that' sin. Take heed if you think you could never do 'that.' Paul says to take heed. If you think you're in safe waters, take heed.
>
> And King Solomon says, "Pride goes before destruction, and a haughty spirit before stumbling" (Proverbs 16:18). The King James Version puts it, "and a haughty spirit before a fall."

God is very clear that our own pride is one of our own worst enemies, and is a great predictor of a fall. Your judgmental spirit is your signal to yourself that you have a pride problem.

Speck-and-Log therapy is when you consciously check yourself when you notice yourself judging someone else. Take note when you feel yourself feeing angry or disgusted at something someone does or has done. Does it really have anything to do with you, or is it just none of your business? Are you over-reacting to it? Do you have all of the facts? Have you given them the benefit of the doubt?

Have you asked them their side of the story? Have you considered the concept of grace? Let your negative feelings be a red flag to you that something in your own life might be amiss.

Are you judging them for something you, yourself, do? It's a "log in the eye" question. Jesus knows us better than we do, and He would never have said that to us if we didn't need to hear it.

When you notice yourself being critical and judgmental of someone else, take a minute to pray about that and ask Jesus to reveal to you where that might be a problem in your own life. It's about humility. Use your judgmental attitude as a barometer, a diagnostic tool if you will, to look inside of yourself and see what's there. The sin you find might be nothing more than just a complaining and judgmental spirit, or it may be some hidden, secret sin that plagues you and needs to be eradicated from your life. In either case, it will rob you of joy and of fellowship with God.

So let your own judgmental attitude, submitted to the Holy Spirit for His loving evaluation, be your best teacher that you have a problem inside.

The other question about judging people is thinking we are above *that* sin. We acknowledge that we're *sinners* in the global sense of the word, but we don't do *that*!

God says to be careful when you have that attitude. He says, "Let him who thinks he stands take heed that he does not fall" (1 Corinthians 10:12). That's a warning from God. Be careful. As soon as you see yourself as 'better than' the next guy because you don't do *that*, you risk God's loving and humbling hand to show you otherwise, or you simply fall into it on your own because you're not paying attention.

Solomon told us that pride, thinking you're 'better than' or 'above that' precedes destruction (Proverbs 16:18). Is that a prediction of the inevitable, or is that a warning that God won't allow our holier-than-thou attitude to continue? Who knows, and who cares. The fact is that it'll happen. You can bank on it.

So another red flag: If you feel yourself looking down your nose at somebody, God is telling you there's some kind of destruction in your future.

So then, what *do* I do if I see my brother sinning? Do I just ignore it so as not to 'judge' him? Do I pretend it's not a problem? Of course not.

Galatians 6:1 — The Apostle Paul said, "Brethren, even if anyone is caught in any trespass, you who are spiritual, restore such a one in a spirit of gentleness; each one looking to yourself, so that you too will not be tempted. Bear one another's burdens and thereby fulfill the law of Christ. If anyone thinks he is something when he is nothing, he deceives himself."

Paul isn't saying to ignore it, far from that. But he's also not saying to condemn him and beat him up and gossip about him. He says, "Restore him in a spirit of gentleness."

Let's look to Jesus for how to handle that. The foot-washing event is a wonderful example of what to do. Jesus was drawing a distinction between the sin nature — the full-body wash symbolizing salvation — and the actual sinning we do in our day-to-day lives. They didn't need their entire body washed — just their feet for the daily sin that plagues us.

Did the disciples wash their own feet? No. Jesus did it. Did He condemn them, publicly humiliate them, or talk about their dirty feet behind their back with his small group? No. He grabbed a bowl of water, girded himself with a towel, got down on his knees, humbled himself with his own vulnerability, and washed their feet.

When you have a brother or sister who is mired in sin, first and foremost, prepare your heart for humility through prayer. Ask Jesus to help you join Him in His humble approach. Ask Him to help you get down on your knees in humility before them. Ask Him how you might wash their feet with the water of His gentle words rather than drown them in it. Ask Him how you might gird yourself with the towel of mercy and tenderness. Your purpose isn't to humiliate them and beat them into submission. Your purpose is to restore them to a state of cleanliness before God. If you want to confront someone about their sin, you must not judge them. You must wash their feet.

Judging other people is about pride. It says I'm qualified to condemn and judge you because I'm better than you.

Now, one of the great ironies in the Christian community is how judgmental we can become of a brother or sister because of how judgmental they are. We judge them for being judgmental. Beware of this self-righteousness. Remember, even in the face of someone who is judgmental, humility and service is the key.

So, what's all of this got to do with mental health?

Love, joy, and peace, as always. Pride, in any manifestation, robs you of the fruit of the spirit (Galatians 5:22). If you allow yourself to get spun up about what somebody else is or isn't doing, then in your pride, you've allowed their behavior to rob you of the fruit of the spirit.

It also has to do with manifesting the Fruit of the Spirit in your life to others. God says the Fruit of the Spirit is love, joy, peace, patience, kindness, goodness, faithfulness, gentleness, self-control. To the extent that you yield your will to the will of the Holy Spirit, these character qualities will be manifested in your life.

The first three, love, joy, and peace, are about our own mental health. Love, as well as the remaining six, have to do with how we treat other people and the kinds of witnesses we are for Christ, also impacting our mental health. The more we can manifest this fruit, the happier other people will be around us, the more fellowship we will enjoy, the happier *we* will be in our own skin, and the better our witness will be to the believing and unbelieving world.

I heard one time that the word JOY is an acronym that stands for Jesus-Others-You. If you can put Jesus first in your life, then other people, and lastly yourself, then you've achieved the ultimate joy, and the ultimate mental health. It will drive out the pride, the selfishness, and the lusts that rob you of the fruit that brings you such supreme mental health.

Confronting your brothers and sisters about their sin is a responsibility we all share, but to do so in love, grace, encouragement, and humility is the way of Christ, and leaves you feeling uplifted and at peace.

7) Laugh Therapy

Laughing. Be aware that this is the one thing that can have the quickest effect on your mental health, and the one thing you're most likely to blow off and ignore as simplistic and irrelevant. Please don't do that. Take this one as seriously as you do the others. It has just as much basis in Scriptural truths, as well as medical science, and deserves just as much credibility. Please do this. It works.

Researchers at Loma Linda University in Southern California have found a physiological change in your body chemistry that happens when someone engages in a belly laugh,[28] one of those laughs that makes your body shake and makes others laugh along with you. It seems that it stimulates the production of beta-endorphins, the body's natural morphine. People will use illegal drugs and alcohol because they feel better for a season, but the damage those substances do to their bodies makes them worse off than they were before. But remarkably, they want that feeling so badly, to hide from the negative thoughts and feelings, the trade-off seems worth it. We're back to the monkey trap we talked about before.

But God gave us a way to experience that same high drug-free. There's no side-effect, no ill effects of any kind, and it's socially acceptable. Just laugh, and your body and mind both feel restored.

There is also evidence that it positively affects heart disease, as well as immunity from disease, and the effects can last as long as 24 hours after a good belly-laugh. Triple whammy. A God-sized remedy for mood disturbance, heart disease, and general disease of all kinds. That's our God. And to add to the benefit, it is fun and it doesn't hurt.

I'm very glad that science has finally caught up with God in this area. He said, "A merry heart makes a cheerful countenance" (Proverbs 15:13) and "a merry heart does good, like medicine" (Proverbs 17:22).

If you have a merry heart, then your body chemistry changes to affect your mental state, your heart, and your ability to fight off disease, all rolled up into one. What a deal.

Find time to laugh. Make time. Go to a funny movie, rent a stand-up comedian video, something. Get together with a friend who makes you roar. The more you laugh out loud, the better mental and physical health you'll experience. God said that a merry heart is good for countenance and general health. Medical science is finally coming around and is starting to agree with Him.

Laugh. Not the little snicker thing, but a rip-roaring belly laugh that makes the room move. You'll feel better inside and out. God said it, and you can count on it.

XV — IF ONLY I HAD MORE FAITH

The Truth And The Lies About Faith

Ok, I admit it, the truth is if we all had enough faith, we wouldn't need mental health therapy, we wouldn't need mental health books, and there would certainly be no need for this book.

And if pigs could fly...

See, the problem is, and the practical reality is, we *don't* have enough faith. That's just the way it is.

Did anyone beat David up for not having enough faith when he said, "My God, My God, why hast thou forsaken me?" (Psalm 22:1). Did anyone beat Moses up for lack of faith when he said, "But God, I am slow of speech. *I* can't go speak to Pharaoh!" (Exodus 4 10). (Actually, God did beat him up a little, but He still used him.) Where was Gideon's faith when he was hiding in the wine press threshing his crops? (Judges 6). God called him a "valiant warrior," but he sure wasn't displaying much valor that day. Did anyone accuse Peter of lack of faith for that gut-wrenching denial? (Matthew 26:69-75) In fact, Jesus prayed for him, encouraged him, and restored him. Many times Jesus said, "Oh, ye of little faith." Did He fire them as apostles? Of course not. He prayed for them, encouraged them, taught them, and their faith grew. Study Abraham, Hezekiah, and many others throughout Biblical history. Throughout their growth in faith, He used them all mightily.

Clearly, lack of faith was the problem in all of these cases. All of them and many, many more illustrate what happens when we have a lack of faith, and that increasing our faith should certainly be a priority in our lives. But they also show that, when we suffer in our faith, we're in good company, and God can still use us to accomplish His purpose.

Lack of faith is a common Christian disease. Clearly, we have to grow in our faith, and while we're doing that, we suffer from lack of faith. Just stands to reason. Truly, there is no end to our quest and our ability to grow in our faith. Also, as we go through some ups and downs in our lives, our faith will sometimes go through ups and downs as well. There are many examples in Scripture.

To have steadfast, consistent, and deep abiding faith is called Christian maturity. We can't be mature when we're newborns, we can't be mature if we've never had any appropriate upbringing, we can't be mature when we've followed bad examples, and so forth. And even the most mature Christians suffer crises of faith.[29] So, depending on where we are in our Christian walk, we will have more or less faith than someone else. That's just normal, so we can't beat ourselves up over it, and we can't beat others up, either.[30]

But having said all of that, please understand that there is no excuse for complacency in this area. In each of the above cases (Abraham, David, Moses, etc.), and in a whole lot more, God was merciful and faithful to help His children develop their faith.

So how exactly did He do that?

Well, remember that Abraham was told by God that he would be the father of a great nation when he was well into old age? He then waited another 25 years before Isaac was born - Abraham was 100 years old (Genesis 21:5). When Abraham was really put to the test and God asked him to sacrifice that very same son, Abraham was now well over 100 years old. He'd been following God for many, many decades with God showing him His hand and helping him develop his faith all along the way. I'd say he had a good reason for having a lot of faith.

And remember that Moses spent 40 years in Egypt learning their ways, and then He spent 40 years in the back-side of the desert learning how to raise a family and tend sheep after the Pharaoh threatened to kill him for killing an Egyptian soldier. Moses was 80 years old and had been through many years of training at the hand of God when God called him to get the Israelites out of Egypt. I'd say he's not a particularly fair example with whom to compare ourselves and our faith.

King David also went through a lot. He was assaulted by King Saul and had to run for his life (1 Samuel 19). He was hunted by King Saul, lived in caves, and had to use every internal resource he had to survive (1 Samuel 22 and others). By the time he took the throne, he had been through extreme hardships for over a decade, trusting and relying on God throughout the entire ordeal. God really worked with him to build his faith, and I think one could make the case that without this training time, David would not have trusted God the way he did, and he could not have been the great King he became.

There are many examples in the Bible of great men and women of faith (Hebrews 11), and there are certainly examples where God miraculously gave someone faith to accomplish a specific task at hand. For the most part though, the great Biblical heroes' faith was hard-won by years of trials and trusting in God. I think many Christians are too hard on themselves and others for their so-called "lack of faith." It takes training, and no one should expect an Olympic Champion in the first year of training. Relax, work hard, and give yourself a break.

Now having said that, there must be something we can do to help ourselves grow our faith without just waiting for God to dump trials on us.

You're absolutely right. There is. And as always, Jesus has the answer.

Let's examine a specific lesson. In Luke 17:4, Jesus had just told the disciples, "And if he sins against you seven times a day, and returns to you seven times, saying, 'I repent,' forgive him."

The disciples, in their horror of the weight of that, replied, "Increase our faith!" I can see their eyes as wide as saucers and their mouths dropped open with shock. It's almost a funny picture, actually.

Therapy with God

But Jesus, possibly even smiling at the scene Himself, said, "Yeah, you're right. You do have a faith problem (Luke 17:6 paraphrased). Let's see what might help. I'll tell you a story, and show you a real-life example. You see if they make sense to you."

The first story is about some 'unworthy slaves' doing what they're told to do (Luke 17:7-10). So what's that got to do with faith? God promises us the following sequence of steps:

1. As we are obedient to His word as a slave might be,
2. we will see Him at work in our lives,
3. we will experience great joy (John 15:10-11) as our lives improve,
4. we will start to trust Him more and more,
5. we will be motivated to increase our obedience out of our love and developing trust, and
6. the cycle will continue and pick up speed.

As we just step out and start doing what he's already told us to do, as a mere slave might, without questioning or hesitating, we will start to see the miraculous power our obedience has in our lives. From that newly developing perspective, we will learn to be more and more obedient over time from our hearts rather than just our obedience.

This is a message that, to start the process of increasing our faith, we must be at least as obedient as slaves. That obedience will result in our seeing God working in our lives, we will learn to trust Him, and our faith will grow.

But actually, there's more to this story. It also speaks to the slaves as being *unworthy*, and doing "*only* that which we ought to have done." Is that what we want? To be *unworthy slaves*? To *only* do what we've been commanded to do? In this parable, Jesus is also, in a gentle and subtle way, inviting us to be *more* than that. He wants friends and lovers, not slaves. How do you become more than a slave? Do more than *only* enough. Here's how: Seek opportunities to bless Him with something He didn't specifically ask you to do. Go out of your way for Him. Watch Him work through you and relish the fun of it. Just like two lovers trying to out-do each other with their gifts, go above and beyond.

Jesus is telling us that the minimum standard is total obedience as any slave would be expected to do. You get no thanks for that. But the ultimate is to go above and beyond that into blessings and gift-giving. Then sit back, and watch your love and your faith grow.

The second opportunity He has to help them learn about growing faith is in the incident with the lepers (Luke 17:11-19). Jesus told ten lepers to go and show themselves to the priests. Note that He hadn't healed them yet. Unhealed, they turned and left. There was obedience. It wasn't until they were on their way that they were healed. They were obedient to the command of Jesus and *then* they were healed.

But there's more. One of them returned to worship Him and thank Him. We might say, "But wait, Jesus told them to go to the priests, but this one disobeyed His command and returned. What's with that?"

That's the difference between a lover and a slave. The nine who were 'slaves' did exactly what they were told — obeyed the letter of the law. The tenth, who was in love with Jesus and was more in tune with what would bless Him, returned to honor Him. He wasn't even a Jew. Jesus' reaction to the man who returned was, "Where are the other nine? Go, your faith has made you well."

But wait, the other nine were healed, too, weren't they? Yes, they were. Their bodies were healed. But the one who returned, the one who knew Jesus well enough to know when to 'disobey' the command and return to Him to thank Him and worship Him, had the special blessing from Jesus. He got the 'extra credit' for the faith that not only healed his body, but saved his soul as well.

If you want to increase your faith, it's a four-step process.

1. Obey him absolutely and completely, regardless of the consequences, regardless of whether or not your agree, regardless of whether or not you understand.
2. Bless Him with extra acts of love and commitment.
3. Thank Him without ceasing for *all* things (good and bad).[31]
4. Worship Him for who He is.

Get those four words into your head:

- ➢ Obey, Bless, Thank, Worship;
- ➢ Obey, Bless, Thank, Worship;
- ➢ Obey, Bless, Thank, Worship…

Repeat them over and over. To the extent that you can do those four things and make them the focus of your relationship with Him, you'll see your faith, as well as your love for Him, grow in unimaginable ways.

XVI — VICTORY IN TRIALS

❦

Why Does God Allow Bad Things To Happen?

Why did God allow there to be evil in the world? We are God's creation, aren't we? Why couldn't He have just made us evil-free and then none of this horror would be happening? He's supposed to be all-powerful right? Either He's not as powerful as we're led to believe, He's not as perfect as we're led to believe, or He's just another abusive father who enjoys watching his children suffer. What's the purpose? What's the point?

I read a book once where the author was visiting a man he intended to interview.[32] On the outside of the man's office was a cartoon with two turtles having a conversation. The first turtle says to the second one, "If I got a chance to talk to God, I'd ask Him why He allows there to be so much evil in the world." The second turtle responded thoughtfully, "I'd be afraid He'd ask the same question of me." That one strikes a cord.

Now think about this next illustration. If you owned a dog and you came home from work each day and the dog met you when you came in the door and jumped up and down and licked you and loved on you, wouldn't you feel uplifted and loved? Filled with joy? If people were watching, wouldn't they see that you had a great relationship with your dog and that the dog really loved you? But what if you had the dog chained to the front door so he didn't have a choice but to be at the door when you got home. He was there alright, but what love would you receive from that? How would that glorify you? Where would your joy be, then? What would the people watching think?

God could indeed have made us sin-free. But to do so, he would have had to have made us choice-free. When Eve and then Adam chose to eat of the fruit, they were exercising the right of choice that God had given them. They were lured and lied to, true. But they had the choice to say no. Because they didn't, we have the sin nature that has been passed down. All of us — believers and non-believers alike — wrestle with the daily struggles of the 'Adam and Eve' within us. Only through the power of Jesus' Holy Spirit in us can we truly have victory over the nature that was handed down to us.

Our free will has left us with a world that is filled with sin, and with that sin comes evil and misery.

But you know all of that. That's what everyone says when we ask, "Why, God?"

Ok, given. There's evil in the world, but why doesn't God protect Christians at least? If He's an all-powerful loving Father and we're His children, then why do bad things happen to us?

Ok, good question. What if all Christians had God's total protection and nothing bad ever happened to us? What did Satan say to God? I touched on this in Chapter 7, "Thinking About What I Read."

> "Does Job fear God for nothing? Have You not made a hedge about him and his house and all that he has, on every side? You have blessed the work of his hands, and his possessions have increased in the land. But put forth Your hand now and touch all that he has; he will surely curse You to Your face" (Job 1:9-11).

So what if God made a hedge about us on every side and protected us from all evil? What Satan is telling us here is that people would say, "So what that you love God? Anybody would love God if He protected them and provided for them the way He does you. I'm not impressed. Your God doesn't offer me anything; I live in the real world." Or they would say, "You can't understand what I go through. You're no help to me. Your life is easy and cushy."

Or let's say nothing bad ever happens to you, and they become Christians because they see that God is taking such good care of you. They decide they like that deal and they want some of it, so they 'become Christians.' What would happen to their faith if their lives suddenly took a turn for the worse? Their expectation from watching your life is that God makes people happy and provides them with this wonderful life. They expect Him to do the same for them. Since God isn't making them happy, He's failed them, they stop trusting Him, and they reject Him. They saw God as the giant 'sugar-daddy' in the sky, and He stopped producing.

What if, on the other hand, those same people were watching us suffer? What if they saw that we deal with the same issues they deal with? The same pain, the same struggles, the same heartaches? And yet still, we have a peace about us and we love and trust God through it all. We lean on Him, receiving supernatural strength to deal with it all through Him.

Reflect on these passages:

> Acts 5:40b-42 — "...after calling the apostles in, they flogged them and ordered them not to speak in the name of Jesus, and then released them. So they went on their way from the presence of the Council, rejoicing that they had been considered worthy to suffer shame for His name. And every day, in the temple and from house to house, they kept right on teaching and preaching Jesus as the Christ."
>
> Matthew 5:11-12 — "Blessed are you when people insult you and persecute you, and falsely say all kinds of evil against you because of Me. Rejoice and be glad, for your reward in heaven is great."
>
> James 1:2-4 — "Consider it all joy, my brethren, when you encounter various trials, knowing that the testing of your faith produces endurance. And let endurance have its perfect result, so that you may be perfect and complete, lacking in nothing."
>
> 1 Peter 1:6-7 — "In this you greatly rejoice, even though now for a little while, if necessary, you have been distressed

by various trials, so that the proof of your faith, being more precious than gold which is perishable, even though tested by fire, may be found to result in praise and glory and honor at the revelation of Jesus Christ."

1 Peter 4:12-13 — "Beloved, do not be surprised at the fiery ordeal among you, which comes upon you for your testing, as though some strange thing were happening to you; but to the degree that you share the sufferings of Christ, keep on rejoicing, so that also at the revelation of His glory you may rejoice with exultation."

What do each of these passages have in common? They are all describing rejoicing, not in spite of the suffering, but *because* of it. And finally, Paul said:

"Therefore we do not lose heart, but though our outer man is decaying, yet our inner man is being renewed day by day. For momentary, light affliction is producing for us an eternal weight of glory far beyond all comparison, while we look not at the things which are seen, but at the things which are not seen; for the things which are seen are temporal, but the things which are not seen are eternal" (2 Corinthians 4:16-18).

But that was Paul, right?. What kind of suffering could *he* have gone through? Certainly, he was protected by God. In Paul's words, look at what he's referring to as "momentary light affliction" just a few short pages later...

"...in far more labors, in far more imprisonments, beaten times without number, often in danger of death. Five times I received from the Jews thirty-nine lashes. Three times I was beaten with rods, once I was stoned, three times I was shipwrecked, a night and a day I have spent in the deep. I have been on frequent journeys, in dangers from rivers, dangers from robbers, dangers from my countrymen, dangers from the Gentiles, dangers in the city, dangers in the wilderness, dangers on the sea, dangers among false brethren; I have been in labor and hardship, through many sleepless nights, in hunger and thirst, often without food, in cold and exposure" (2 Corinthians 11:23-27).

Paul ran the race well. People saw that his faith in God was persistent, consistent, and profound. And they learned to trust Paul's God, not in spite of his pain and misery, but Praise God, because of it. Paul had an eternal perspective (Colossians 3:1, Philippians 3:20-21, 2 Corinthians 5:20, and others). Paul's life had profound purpose, and part of that purpose was his suffering (Acts 9:15-16).

"But it's not like I'm suffering for Christ's sake?" you say. Oh, but you certainly are. Why? Because people are watching.

In your suffering, you need Him now more than ever. Show them — those who are watching — what a wonderful, comforting, faithful Lord you have.

Pastor Rick Warren[33] said, "Pain is not the problem. Pain without purpose is the problem."

> "Blessed be the God and Father of our Lord Jesus Christ, the Father of mercies and God of all comfort, who comforts us in all our affliction **so that we will be able to comfort those who are in any affliction** with the comfort with which we ourselves are comforted by God" (2 Corinthians 1:3-4).

Let me stop here again with a word of compassion: I know what you're going through may be tough, and possibly even devastating. Get help if you need it, and depending on the severity of your pain, consider medication to see you through the really tough times. God never promised us that He would keep us from all harm. He only promised us that He would be there with us through it (Hebrews 13:5), and that He would never give us more than we can handle (1 Corinthians 10:13). God has provided people and medical science to help us when we need it, so please make use of the rich resources He has provided.

But as Paul and many others wrote about and demonstrated with their lives, give purpose and meaning to your suffering and to your life. Use the comfort you get from God in your suffering as training so you might grow stronger now and comfort others later. Teach those who don't know the Lord to lean on Him in their suffering by leaning on Him in yours, and then showing them how it brings you peace in the storm. Show them that you love Him and trust Him and know that He'll see you through even this. Bring them to Him as your faithful, loving Father in times of trouble. Show them who He is. In Job, Satan showed you that your bad times can often be more productive for God's Kingdom than your good times. Rejoice that Jesus has considered you worthy of suffering in His name.

More Purpose Of Suffering

"So if that's true, what does it mean when the Bible says that God causes all things to work together for good (Romans 8:28), and God gives what is good to those who ask Him?" (Matthew 7:11).

Well, yes, those things are true. But His definition of *good* and yours might not necessarily be the same thing.

When your 5-year old son says he wants Pop Tarts for breakfast, it's not for his good if you give them to him. You know better than he does what he needs, and nutrition is important. But what if you were a neglectful parent and day after week after month you just gave him the Pop Tarts he asked for just to shut him up and get him out of your hair. Would that be loving? Would that be in his best interest? Of course not.

God loves us far too much to always give us what we ask for. We don't know best — He does. We want Pop Tarts, but He knows we need something better.

There was a mother who had to take her daughter to the doctor for a medical procedure. Because of the nature of the procedure, it wasn't advisable to anesthetize the child. Instead, the mother had to hold her down as the doctor performed this painful procedure. The child, too young to understand, looked at her mother as if to say, "I trusted you! How could you!" Brokenhearted and weeping, the mother continued to hold her precious baby down.

When God needs to allow bad things in our lives, He weeps and grieves for us (Judges 10:6-16). It was never his plan (Genesis 1-2).

Therapy with God

When Lazarus died and Mary and Martha wept for the loss of their brother, Jesus wept with them (John 11:35).

Weep with those who weep (Romans 12:15b). God asks us to respond to those who weep this way because *He* does. But like a good parent, God sometimes must allow things in our lives that we may not like, or calls us to experience certain things for a reason we may not understand.

However, the one thing we know for sure is that, "…God causes all things to work together for good to those who love God, to those who are called according to His purpose" (Romans 8:28). I heard a pastor say, "God don't waste your pain," So if there's purpose in your pain, what is that purpose?

We can't know for sure, however, there are some patterns. The following is a list of the reasons I've been able to discern through my research (and experience) as some purposes for our trials. Look over this list, and reflect on them as they might apply to you.

1. To discipline us for sin
2. To get our attention and draw us closer to Him
3. To help us learn compassion, grow, and strengthen, e.g., 'boot camp'
4. To redirect our lives
5. To give God glory

Consider them in order. It would be just too easy for us to assume that God is helping grow our character when in reality, we have sin in our lives that He is trying to purge. If you miss that, you'll be waiting an unnecessarily long time for that character development and the lesson to cease. Prayerfully eliminate them one at a time before proceeding to the next one for consideration.

Discipline

God will sometimes allow us to experience difficulties to send us the message that we have sin in our lives. Now this is not the everyday sin that we stumble upon as we live our lives. Examples of those might be that we occasionally jump on our children inappropriately, we show pridefulness when someone pays us a complement, we allow the angry word to come out of our mouths when someone cuts us off in traffic, etc. That's not to minimize or diminish those acts as sin, but once you're secure in your salvation, there are different degrees of sin and God's reaction to it.

The kind of sin that brings God's discipline into your life is the wanton, willful, disobedience that indicates a lack of fear of God and a lack of conscience toward disappointing Him. If you're a believer but you're an active gambler and you know it's hurting your family, then God may discipline you. If you have a foul mouth and refuse to give it up in spite of the Holy Spirit's promptings to you about it, then you may be subject to God's discipline.

If that's happening to you, rejoice, because it means God is paying attention to you. God rebukes those He loves (Hebrews 12:6; Revelation 3:19), and his rebuke of you is an indication of His love.

My daughter had friends in High School who, when she asked them what their parents would say about where they were going or how late they stayed out, would say, "My parents don't care enough about me to have a curfew."

What a tragedy. But God is a good and loving Father, and if you're being disobedient to Him, He cares enough about you to pay attention to how you're living your life, and discipline you if He deems it necessary.

If you find yourself in this place, then in addition to rejoicing for God's love, you also need to pray about deliverance. If you're in habitual, willful sin, then you need to stop. God has promised that no temptation will come upon you except as is common to man (1 Corinthians 10:13), that He will be faithful to both forgive us for our sins (Romans 8:1), and give us the strength to gain victory over them (Hebrews 2:18). Pray to Him for deliverance from your sin. Paul cried out, "Wretched man that I am! Who will set me free from the body of this death?" (Romans 7:24). The inference, of course, is that Paul is in bondage to his sin. If you're in habitual sin, 'bondage' is a great word.

So what's the practical application of that? Again, listen to Paul:

> So then, brethren, we are under obligation, not to the flesh, to live according to the flesh — for if you are living according to the flesh, you must die; but if by the Spirit you are putting to death the deeds of the body, you will live (Romans 8:12-13).

So if you're sinning, you must die? Not physically, of course. You must die to your fleshly desires and needs. You must die to your *self*. You must repent of your sins, which means to "agree with God that they're sin and turn your back on them."

King David struggled with sin and confessed it to God. How does he address it?

> When I kept silent about my sin, my body wasted away through my groaning all day long. For day and night Your hand was heavy upon me; My vitality was drained away as with the fever heat of summer. I acknowledged my sin to You, And my iniquity I did not hide; I said, "I will confess my transgressions to the Lord; and You forgave the guilt of my sin" (Psalm 32:3-5).

Pray to God. Confess your sins to Him. Tell Him you agree with Him and that you're turning your back on your sin. Mourn for your sinfulness (Matthew 5:4). And thank Him for the discipline and then for the forgiveness that is already yours through the death of His Son.

But that's not all.

The next step is *critical* to your full deliverance: *Tell someone of the same gender as you about your decision to give this sin to God.* If you keep it a secret, it'll just ambush you again. If it's been a habit, a life pattern, the temptation will be horrendous to return to it, and the enemy will do everything in His power to encourage you to do so. You *must* be accountable to another brother or sister. Confess it, and ask them to pray for you and with you, and to hold you accountable to them and to God for your decision to turn. I would suggest you establish a schedule for meeting with them to force you to touch base on a regular basis, weekly or more. In humble submission, ask for help from a brother or sister.

I emphasize that it must be a brother or sister of the same gender as you because, first of all, it won't work if it is your spouse. It needs to be someone who can be bold and honest with you about your behavior who doesn't have to live with you while you process the pain, and a spouse isn't the person to do that.

So if it's not your spouse, then, to become that vulnerable and intimate with a member of the opposite sex leaves you too vulnerable to the sexual pressures of the flesh. Don't trade one sin for another. Keep it clean, and always stick to a member of your own gender for this accountability.

Now, depending on the type of problem we're talking about, you might need professional help. If your problem is alcohol or drugs, sexual addiction, pornography, gambling, or any of a number of other addictions, please get help. These are very difficult problems to deal with when you *do* get help. If you don't get help, you put tremendous unnecessary obstacles in your way.

Ok, the final step to full deliverance of your sin is to ask forgiveness of and make restitution to anyone you might have hurt through your sin, providing that doing so doesn't do any additional harm.[34] Ask God for wisdom to discern who that might be (spouse, children, friends, coworkers, etc.), and then ask Him for the humility and the courage to take that step. It's easy to be pompous and arrogant and 'holier-than-thou.' Real humility requires a *great deal of courage.* You may need to pray for help in that area.

Finally, remember that even when the trial is because of sin, God can do a wondrous work through it in you. Some of the best witnesses for Him have a difficult past (Luke 7:36-50, 1 Timothy 1:12-16). Submit to Him humbly, and let Him do that work.

Get Our Attention

This one is very similar to Discipline, but the sin might not have a specific name. The primary sin here is 'distance from God,' which inevitably allows us to drift away from our focus of obedience and commitment to Him. In that sense, it is also sin and God is using our difficult times to help us turn it all around by drawing close to Him again. Many people move close and drift away in cycles as their lives get bad then good then bad then good, again. God wants us to get close and stay close, even when our lives are good (Deuteronomy 8:10-20).

Throughout the Bible, from the first "In the beginning" to the last "Amen," when God deals harshly with disobedient and adulterous peoples, His primary motive is to draw them back to Himself. Noah's flood, the plagues in Egypt, the wars in Canaan, even in Revelation, God's intention was one of mercy and love, meant to bring difficult and stiff-necked people to Himself. Those who refused would suffer consequences, possibly even death, but His intention was always the same: restoration.

As believers, He will do the same with us. If you find yourself suddenly in a terrible mess in your life and you're trying to figure out why God would allow that terrible situation, one of the options to consider is, 'Have I drifted away from Him? When's the last time I had my normal devotion time with Him? When's the last time I attended a church service? Do I chat with Him throughout the day? Am I being a good example for my family? Especially for my children?

If you can answer any of those questions in the negative, then God may be trying to get your attention with your current difficulty. If you know you're not particularly mired in any terrible sin and you're confident that this isn't discipline, then this is the next possibility to consider.

If this is true about you, if you've grown somewhat distant, then it's time to turn your life back over to Christ. Re-dedicate your life to Him. Pray the sinner's prayer again and go back to where you were when you were excited about Him.

In Revelation Chapter 2, Jesus tells the people of the church of Ephesus that He sees their works and that's good, but He takes exception to them because they've left (not lost — *left*) their first love (Revelation 2:4). He told them, first and foremost, to repent of the sin of having left Him, and then go back to doing whatever it was they were doing when they remember being in love with Him at first.

When you first dedicated your life to Christ and you were in that 'honeymoon' phase, what did you do then to express that love? Did you go to Bible studies or prayer meetings? Small group? Ministries of some sort? What was it that was *unique* to you that allowed you to express your love for Him?

Whatever that was, to recapture that 'love affair' with Jesus, go back to doing those things. That's the advice Jesus gave to the Church of Ephesus, and it's the advice He gives to us.

Jesus' letters to the seven churches present a picture to us of who we are as the church of Christ, as well as individuals. Read the letters to the churches as if they were to you directly. Make them personal and see what God is trying to tell you about your walk with Him. You just might have left your first love.

Help Us Grow And Strengthen

In ancient days, the farmers had a device they used for processing wheat. It was quite large and heavy. It was made of a series of logs, strapped together with twine, between each of which were large, sharp stones poking through the logs just far enough that the stones hit the ground when the device was put on the ground, but the logs did not. That device is called a "tribulum."

The purpose of the tribulum was to help the farmer purify the wheat to make it ready for grinding and bread-making. When the wheat harvest came in, they would spread it out on a circular concrete-like surface. The tribulum was then hitched to a horse or donkey and round-and-round-and-round the donkey would go, dragging this huge device over the top of the wheat. The purpose was to separate the wheat grains — the precious kernel of nutrition — from the chaff — the outer covering that was useless for food. Over and over and over the tribulum would go until the sharp stones would rub and scrape over the wheat, and the chaff would be completely separated. At that time, the farmer would go in and toss the mixture of wheat and chaff into the air. The heavier, more substantial nutritious wheat kernels would drop back to the cement, but the lighter, useless chaff would blow away in the breeze. The quality of the wheat that remained and was useful for food was dependent upon how heavy the tribulum was and how many times it made its rotation around the platform.

Wow. What a great picture. Of course the word Tribulum, which means "Threshing sledge," is far too close to the word *tribulation* to be coincidence. The purpose of the Tribulum was for the purification of the wheat.

So why does God allow tribulation in our lives? If it's not to rid us of sin in our lives, and it's not to get our attention because we've drifted from him, then it may be to purify us.

So how does tribulation purify us? God has a lot to say about that. Let's see what He says:

> James 1:2-4 — Consider it all joy, my brethren, when you encounter various trials, knowing that the testing of your faith **produces endurance**. And let endurance have its perfect result, so that you may be **perfect and complete, lacking in nothing**.
>
> 1 Peter 1:6 — In this you greatly rejoice, even though now for a little while, if necessary, you have been distressed by various trials, so that the **proof of your faith**, being more precious than gold which is perishable, even though tested by fire, may be found to result in **praise and glory and honor** at the revelation of Jesus Christ.
>
> 1 Peter 5:10 — After you have suffered for a little while, the God of all grace, who called you to His eternal glory in Christ, will Himself **perfect, confirm, strengthen, and establish you**.
>
> Luke 22:31-32 — Simon, Simon, behold, Satan has demanded permission to sift you like wheat; but I have prayed for you, that your faith may not fail; and you, when once you have turned again, **strengthen your brothers**.[35]

The other picture that beautifully illustrates this concept is in the refinement of silver. The silversmith takes the impure silver and puts it in a huge pot. He then proceeds to turn up the heat. As he turns up the heat, the silver melts and the impurities rise to the surface as "dross." The silversmith carefully removes the dross and throws it away. Then he cranks up the heat a little more, and more dross surfaces which he removes and discards. Then more heat, and more, and more until the silver is at the point of virtual collapse. The silversmith takes the last of the dross off of the top. How does the silversmith know when the silver is pure? How does our Heavenly Silversmith know when we're pure? That's easy:

When He can look into the super-heated, ready-to-collapse silver and see His reflection.

Pain without purpose is the problem. God loves us so much and wants only the best out of our lives that He is willing to put us through the grinder, under the threshing sledge, over the fire, to rid us of the chaff and dross in our lives, and yield the purity and beauty He wants for us that will glorify Him and ultimately bring us great, unspeakable joy.

If you're in the fire, know that God is there with you, know that there is purpose in it, and know that He is going to work all things to good if you just love Him and trust Him (Romans 8:28).

Redirection Of Our Lives

Before Paul's conversion, (Acts 9) Stephen was preaching to the council (Jewish leadership). They were so upset by his preaching, they stoned him to death. As he died, he proclaimed that he could see Jesus standing at the right hand of God. Jesus, normally seated at the right hand of God, *stood* to welcome Stephen into eternity.

So clearly, Stephen was not being disciplined for his sin — Jesus stood for him for goodness sake. God was not trying to get his attention to draw him close. He was about to be as close as he could possibly be. He was at the end of his life, so God wasn't trying to purify Stephen for any fruit he might later produce. So what was the deal?

Redirection (and certainly for God's glory - but we get to that next). Stephen's death wasn't about him. It was about the Gospel of Jesus Christ.

When Stephen was stoned to death, the Christians who were in Jerusalem were so terrified that they all fled to the country (Acts

8:1). They were convinced that if they stayed, they too would be captured and killed. Saul, later to be called Paul, proved them right. He became well-known for his zealous capture, torture, imprisonment, and murder of those who followed "The Way."

So what happened when they fled? The Gospel was spread throughout all of Asia. As they ran, they took the Gospel with them, redirected by God for His divine purpose.

When that same Saul was converted on the road to Damascus and became a fervent, if not ravenous, Christian, it was his intention to preach the Gospel to the Jews. He was a Jewish scholar, schooled in all of the Old Testament stories, and knew the Jews and their culture well. So Saul knew that God meant for him to witness to his Jewish brethren and help them see the light of Jesus.

But God had other plans. Whenever Saul, now Paul, would enter a new town, he would go racing over to the Synagogue to preach to the Jews. Many times, Paul had to run for his life, once even being lowered out of town over the protecting wall in a basket because, had they found him the following morning, they'd have surely killed him (Acts 9:24-25).

So what did Paul do? He eventually gave up on the Jews and started spreading the Gospel message to the Gentiles (Acts 13:45-47). As a result of Paul's rejection and threats by the Jews, he was forced to head for the country and preach to the Gentiles, fulfilling God's purpose for his life all along.

For more examples of this, refer to the stories of Joseph in the book of Genesis, and the books of Ruth and Esther. Notice how God allowed each of them to go through trials in their lives. Each of them suffered greatly, and each of them accomplished great things for God. Joseph and Esther saved the nation of Israel from complete annihilation, and Ruth became an ancestor to the Lord Jesus. God had redirected their lives through trials.

So clearly, God will use affliction and difficulties to get us where He wants us to go. So how's your job going? If you've eliminated the first three possibilities, is it possible that God is trying to move you somewhere else? How about your living situation in your community? Has it recently become an inexplicably difficult place to live? Maybe God has a divine appointment for you somewhere else.

The tricky part of this one is that you have to be painfully honest with yourself. If your life at work is difficult because you're rebelling against your boss or doing a poor job, then that's sin, and that's not about redirection of your life. If this is the third job you've had and they always turn out the same, then you need to look to yourself with an honest appraisal. If your living situation isn't working because of your own selfishness, then that's sin, and you have to work on that before you can think about redirection.

Now I will tell you that there are times when the temptation to sin is too strong to resist, and running from that situation may be an appropriate response. Joseph did that when Potiphar's wife was trying to seduce him (Genesis 39:12). He *ran*. I propose that he ran because he knew that the temptation was too big, the risks were too high, and running was his best alternative. Paul told Timothy to "run from youthful lusts" (2 Timothy 2:22).

If that's your story, then by all means run. But know that it's not about redirection. It's about your inability to resist the temptation to sin and that God has given you a way out (1 Corinthians 10:13). Redirection is so you can fulfill some higher purpose God has in mind for you somewhere else. They are two entirely different things.

Discernment is the key, and that's where prayer comes in. Before you assume God is trying to move you, you *must* reflect on your life to see if you're the problem. Communication with Jesus and open and honest evaluation of yourself are critical. Alcoholics Anonymous calls this self-evaluation a "searching and fearless moral inventory." It's quite cleansing. I recommend it for everyone. Conduct this inventory before you decide this trial is about redirection in your life.

So let's assume you've done that soul-searching evaluation and you really feel it's an issue of redirection. There's a very important step you need to take now. You need to get confirmation. The next chapter is on discerning God's will for your life, and it includes some specific steps as to how you must do that. They are critical steps, so don't just go on your 'gut feeling' and quit your job. You *must* get the Godly confirmation before you move. Be flexible, be ready to go, but get the confirmation first.

God wants you to be where He needs you to be to do the job He wants you to do. You need to remain open, honest with yourself, and flexible. If you received that confirmation that God wants you to move, could you? More than your ability, God wants your availability. Be ready to go when God says, "Go."

For God's Glory

I believe that this is the ultimate purpose for pain. To suffer for the glory of God is the highest of honors, and gives you the highest opportunity for your greatest triumph. I know this one is difficult to understand, and if you don't have the Holy Spirit living in your heart or have a supernatural love for God, then you couldn't possibly understand. If you're a brand new Christian, this one might be hard for you, but please bear with me.

So why is suffering for God's glory such a privilege? Because it's the only purpose for suffering that is uniquely *for* God. It's the ultimate, purest state of, *"it's not about me."*

So what exactly does the word *glory* mean? In addition to the majestic beauty and light that surrounds Him in all His glory, it refers to thought or opinion, reputation, praise, honor, splendor, light, perfection, rewards. When we bring God glory, we make Him *look good* to other people. The reason this is so important is because one of our primary purposes in life is to bring people to Him. Everything else we can do for God, worship and praise Him, fellowship in His name, pray to Him, sing for Him, everything else that's so important for us, we will be able to do in heaven. The only thing we cannot do is be His witnesses. Witnessing is only for bringing the unbelieving world into a relationship with Him. In heaven, that part of our work is over.

> The Bible is filled with stories where people suffered for the glory of God. In the book of Exodus, the Israelites were backed up to the Red Sea, no escape, and the Egyptians were bearing down on them with the intention of returning them to slavery. No hope, no weapons, no soldiers (Exodus Chapter 14). They complained to Moses bitterly.

God miraculously saved them, took them across the Red Sea safely, destroying the Egyptians in the process. Once on the other side, the Israelites sang and danced and praised God.

The parting of the Red Sea was a beautiful illustration to the Jews and to us of God's protection in our lives. God could have worked it out a different way, but He purposely directed them to have their backs up against the Red Sea with no hope so He could show His power and glory. Many of the nations in the surrounding areas heard that God parted the Red Sea for them. After it was all over, they were thrilled.

But how much better would it have been if, trapped with their backs to the Red Sea, they danced and sang praises to God for *what He was going to do* in this situation to glorify Himself? After all, God had a vested interest in seeing the Israelites saved. How surprised would the Egyptians have been had they come riding up on the Israelites with destruction in their hearts and seen them singing and praising in their trial. Might they have reacted differently? Might some of them have seen God a little differently?

In another example in the book of Acts (Acts 16:22-44), the Apostle Paul and Silas had been beaten with rods and thrown into prison. Rather than grumble and groan, they were "praying and singing hymns of praise" where all the prisoners could hear them. That night, there was an earthquake. The walls of the prison were broken down, the doors were opened, and the chains and shackles were released. When the guard, who was under the penalty of death if any prisoners escaped, saw it, he drew his sword to kill himself knowing his punishment would be worse. Paul yelled at him — from inside the prison with all the prisoners — and told him to stop, that they were all still there.

Still there? What's with *that*? Why didn't they *run!?*
Paul understood something about his imprisonment: It had purpose beyond that which he could see. When the doors were

opened and he *could* have escaped, he didn't because somehow he knew that God had something He wanted Paul to do with this. When the guard came and saw it, he *fell at Paul's feet* and asked how he could be saved. Paul said, "Believe in the Lord Jesus and you will be saved." As a result, the guard and his entire household were baptized and brought into the Kingdom of God.

Well, what about the rest of the prisoners, though? The Bible doesn't say anything about them, except that they were all still there. Why would that be? Why wouldn't *they* run? This was their big chance. Why do you think they stayed? What's your best guess? Scripture doesn't tell us why, but my best guess is that they were drawn to Paul and Silas and their strength and faith in God. They, too, understood that the salvation of their souls was of far more value to them than the salvation of their bodies. I believe they were simply drawn in.

So what did Paul do to draw them all in? How do we really glorify God in our trials? By trusting Him, loving Him, thanking Him, and praising Him *through* it, *before* it gets resolved. Reflect on the Enterprise, Alabama story with the boll weevil. As we go through our difficult times, we show the world the depth of our faith, we show them the faithfulness of our God, and we show them the reality of God in our lives.

Pain isn't the problem — pain without purpose is the problem. By praising God, Paul gave his pain purpose.

Job's life epitomizes this concept. When Job's entire life was stripped away — flocks, crops, herds, and even all ten of his children — he continued to love, honor, and glorify God. How did he do this? He remembered what all of the apostles knew. He remembered that in spite of his circumstances, his Redeemer lives (Job 19:25). Whatever else is going on in life, that's a truth and a hope we can all hold on to.

> Jesus' dear friend Lazarus lay dying. A messenger came to Him and asked Him to come quickly to save Him, saying "Lord, behold, he whom You love is sick." But when Jesus heard this, He said, "This sickness is not to end in death, but **for the glory of God**, so that the Son of God may be

glorified by it." Lazarus was sick, and actually did die to be resurrected again by Jesus, all for the glory of God and Himself. Scripture does not say God gave him the illness that killed him, but when He got sick and Jesus had the option of healing him, he chose not to — for the glory of God (John 11:3-4).

As He [Jesus] passed by, He saw a man blind from birth. And His disciples asked Him, "Rabbi, who sinned, this man or his parents, that he would be born blind?" Jesus answered, "It was neither that this man sinned, nor his parents; but it was so that the **works of God might be displayed in him"** (John 9:1-3).

If our faith isn't real or isn't strong enough, then we won't be able to honor Him and trust Him through our trials. We will question Him, become bitter or fearful, and possibly even reject Him. To glorify Him, we need to stick with Him and continue to trust and praise Him.

Learning how to praise Him *in* the trial is the goal, and one which will bring you immense relief and peace. That may seem impossible at this point in your walk with Him, but just remember that that is the goal. Learn to praise Him *in* the trial, not just after it's over and resolved. Praising Him in the trial glorifies Him, brings people to Him, and reminds you that He's still on the throne. If you can't do it from your heart, if you're faith just isn't there yet, do it out of pure obedience. Just do it and your heart will follow. You will find your own inner life being restored in the process.

If you can do that through your trials, then you are truly the best witness there is, and your rewards in heaven will be great. Martyrs will have the best experience in heaven because they have suffered to the ultimate for His glory. They understood the power, the abundance, and the honor of suffering for His name.

Give your pain purpose. Trust God, thank Him, praise Him in the midst of the storm, and draw them in.

Well, that's all well and good, but exactly how does one pull that off? Here I'd like to give you some practical guidance on exactly how to continue trusting and praising Him in the midst of your trial.

What He wants you to do is to turn it all over to Him. This is how you do that.

Turning It All Over To God

Ok, then. You're in the middle of a mess. Your kids are doing drugs, your spouse is spending all the money, your job is falling apart. "Ok, I can trust God," you say, "but do I just sit around waiting for the Red Sea to part? That seems so irresponsible."

It is. That's not what God wants you to do at all. When the world is falling apart around you, here's the list of what to do, in order, prayerfully relying on God throughout the process.

1. Do whatever you can.
2. Seek objective counsel.
3. Pray fervently, cry out to God.
4. *Then* turn it over to God (and keep praying).

Let's go through each of them in detail.

Do Whatever You Can

You probably know this story, but if you don't, you need to. There was as man who was standing on top of his roof because the river had flooded and the water was rising rapidly. A boat came by, and the captain said, "Hey mister! Get on board!" The man said, "No thank you, God will save me." The boat left, and the waters kept rising. The man was now up to his waist in water when a second boat came by and said, "Come on, man! Get in!" Again, the man said, "No thanks, God will save me." Finally, with water up to his neck, a helicopter flew overhead and yelled, "We'll send a basket down! Get in!" The man said, "No thanks. God will save me." Then the man drowned. When he got to heaven, shocked, he said to God, "I thought you were going to save me!" God said, "I sent you two boats and a helicopter. What *more* did you want!"

King Hezekiah was a man of vision. A practical man. He knew that Jerusalem would again, some day, be under siege. A 'siege' was where the enemy camped outside of the protective walls of a fortified city, preventing anyone from coming or going with the idea that eventually, the people inside, being prevented from bringing life-giving water into the city, would get desperate enough to come out, opening the door to opportunity for the enemy. To protect Jerusalem from this siege, King Hezekiah "stopped the upper outlet of the waters of Gihon and directed them to the west side of the city of David" (2 Chronicles 32:30). It was actually a conduit over 1,700 feet long, still in existence today. In so doing, the siege could last as long as the enemy wanted to stay, and the Israelites would never have to leave the protective walls of their city.

Now Hezekiah could have said, "My God will protect me!" But he knew something about God. He knew that God views our lives with Him to be a joint venture, a partnership. We need to participate. We need to trust and rely on God, but we need to do our part.

When Moses was backed up against the Red Sea with the entire nation of Israel, God said to him, "Why are you crying out to Me?" (Exodus 14:15). This was no time for prayer. You've already done that. This was time for *action*. Get to it, Moses.

God wants to team with us, not have us be Christian couch-potatoes and let Him do all the work. When Joshua crossed the Jordan River into Canaan, God was certainly capable of sweeping all of the inhabitants out of Joshua's way and giving the Israelites a comfortable place to settle, but He didn't. They had to fight — hard and a lot. As a matter of fact, it didn't even end with Joshua. It went on throughout the history of the Jews, through to this very day. God wanted to work *with* them, not *for* them. We're a team.

Don't exclude God as you go about trying to solve it yourself, but don't forget to do your part.

Think smart, work hard, pray hard, and do whatever you can.

Seek Objective Counsel

Once you've done whatever you can, or even while you're doing it, get some guidance.

Proverbs tells us, "For by wise guidance you will wage war, and in abundance of counselors there is victory" (Proverbs 24:6), and

"Where there is no guidance the people fall, but in abundance of counselors there is victory" (Proverbs 11:14).

No one is perfect or has all the ideas or answers. Nor can we truly view our situations objectively. Talk to someone you trust who will give you a wise, honest, and Bible-driven perspective. You're too close to the situation. You may be over-reacting. You may be enmeshed. You may have missed a clue. You might not be aware of resources that are available to help you.

King David was known as a 'man after God's own heart' and had many counselors (2 Samuel 17:15; 1 Kings 12:9). Moses was advised by his father-in-law as to how to judge the people of Israel (Exodus 18:19), and many prophets served as advisors to Kings as well (Jeremiah 38:15).

We are a nation of people who loves our independence. We have that 'rugged individualism' that has made America great, but it also leaves us feeling that to ask for advice or help is to admit weakness or even defeat. That's pride, and it is Satan's favorite weapon against us.

Talk to your pastor, talk to Godly family and friends, talk to your Christian therapist. See if there are any public resources you might bring to bear on the situation. Go on-line and do some research to see if there are other people who struggle with the same thing, see if there are any forums (websites where you can talk to other people on-line) pertaining to this topic. Satan wants you defeated, and he wants you thinking you can solve this by yourself. That's our nature, so it's an easy thing for him to sell us.

But God, as He shows us in His word, thinks otherwise. Those Proverbs, as well as the many examples He's given us through the Biblical heroes, show us the way. When you have to figure out how to wage this war, ask for help and guidance.

Pray Fervently

Paul says, "Pray without ceasing" (1 Thessalonians 5:17). Pray throughout every preceding step to ensure that you are in constant connection with God. One of the reasons David was a "man after God's own heart" was because he sought the Lord constantly. Except for that transgression with Bathsheba (2 Samuel Chapters 11 and 12), David never took a step without getting the Lord's guidance, and neither should we.

But there comes a point in the process where we need to *cry out* to Him. Kings David and Asa, and many others cried out to the Lord when things got bad. This does not imply that they weren't in constant communication with Him prior to that. They certainly were. But there came a point when they were surrounded by their enemies and all hope seemed pointless that they cried out to God.

As you read the stories about David and Solomon and Asa and the rest of the immensely powerful, God-driven people in Scripture, say to yourself, "What can I learn from how they operate? What do *they* do in their lives that I can put into practice in my own? How did their approach work out for them?" One of the things they did often was to seek the Lord constantly, and *cry out* when things got from bad to worse.

When you get to that place where you feel like there's absolutely nothing left for you to do, you've searched your own experiences, sought the counsel of others, prayed and reflected and read Scripture, and you can't think of anything else you can do, then that's the point at which you cry out to God as your Great Rescuer.

So how do we do that? Well, crying out to God is personal, and I would say no two people do it exactly the same. You and God have to figure out what crying out looks like for you. However, if you don't have a clue, then this might be a good place to start: Get on your knees and let your request be made know out loud. Tell God what's on your mind. Tell Him how bad it is. Ask Him how He wants you to handle this. Ask Him for help. Submit to Him with profound humility. Cry, shout out loud, whisper, scream. Some people stand and other's fall on their faces. I heart it said once that we'll all know Moses when we see him in Heaven because he'll be the one with the flat nose from falling on his face so much.

And if you haven't already done so, this may be a great time to fast. If you have never fasted, then please get some guidance from your pastor before you do. For some people, it can be dangerous, so be smart about it.

In the end, you have to determine what your version of crying out looks like, but when you feel that all human hope is lost, cry out to God.

And finally, turn it over to Him. Just leave it at the foot of the cross.

Turning It Over To God

Turning it over to God means laying it at the feet of Jesus at the Cross. Give it to Him. That wonderful prayer 'Footsteps' says it best. Where there are two sets of prints, you are walking side-by-side with Him. But where there is one, that's when Jesus has you in His arms or on His shoulders. When you get to the point where you can no longer walk, let Him carry you.

"Ok, so that's all well and good. I understand the concept, but *how* exactly do I do that?" you ask.

The practical reality is that very few of us have problems in our lives that we can literally hold in our hands, and neither do we have literal crosses that sit in the corner where we can place our box of problems. So what, exactly, do we mean when we say 'leave it at the cross?'

You've heard a lot of this already, so it'll sound familiar. First of all, trust that God is in the middle of it, He's watching, and He cares what happens. And where exactly does that trust come from?

1. **Talking to Jesus** through Scripture,
2. **Being obedient** no matter the cost, regardless of whether you agree or understand,
3. **Thanking Him frequently** as He works the little things in your life, and
4. **Fellowshipping** with other brothers and sisters who have Him working in theirs.

As you become more aware of Him being involved in the little things, you'll start to trust He'll be there in the big things. Here's an example of Jesus paying attention to little things.

When Jesus was turning the tables over in the Temple, whipping people, and throwing money onto the floor, he stopped in the middle of that tirade and *said* (didn't yell, mind you — he *said*) to those selling the doves "Take these things away..." Why did he stop that way and deal with the doves individually? (John 2:13-16).

Because, had He turned the tables of the doves over, He'd have hurt the doves.

They were in cages and couldn't fly, defend themselves, or even just get out of the way. They were totally vulnerable to whatever Jesus wanted to do to them, and he *asked* that they be removed. He cared for them enough to stop in the middle of what appeared to be an out-of-control rampage and deal with them individually and safely.

If He does that with a bunch of doves, you can be sure He will do that with you. If He is so aware of their presence and needs in *that* situation that he halts His thrashings to deal with them individually, He will deal with you individually, too (Matthew 10:31).

This is an example of personalizing Scripture. Learn to trust Him by seeing how He handles other situations and then generalizing them to yourself.

So the first step is to see Him in your situation, uniquely, individually, personally.

The next step, then, is to pray them onto the Cross. Pray this prayer:

"Lord, you know my needs better than I do. You are more familiar with this situation than I am. Father, you know I need your help and I feel like I've done everything I can in this situation. So I'm giving it to You. I'm leaving it at Your feet, at the foot of the Cross, so you can deal with it in any way You think best. You know what's going on in my heart, Lord, and that I'm in pain. Please, Father, help me in this situation, and help me learn to rest in Your protection, Your provision, and Your peace that surpasses understanding.

Help me learn to rest in Your arms for comfort, to trust You, and to leave the resolution up to You."

Pray that prayer twenty times a day if you need to. Pray fervently, from the depth of your soul. Let Him hear your heart, connect with Him, see Him with you taking action. Trust Him, and let it go.

Leaving It At The Foot Of The Cross

Ok, then. You've given it to God. Great. Excellent work.

And before you can turn around twice, you have it back again. If you're like me or most of the people I've ever counseled on this, putting it there is one thing, but *leaving* it there is something else altogether. You just can't seem to *leave* it at the foot of the Cross.

When you feel yourself taking it back, don't rebuke yourself. *Gently* say to the feeling, "No, I'm not going to deal with you. I've given you to the Lord, and I'm not taking you back. Father, please take this back from me again."

My biggest weapon against the thoughts and feelings coming back into my head is my memorized Scripture. Whenever I feel it creeping back in, I start reciting one of the longer passages I've memorized.[36] It takes so much concentration to recite the long passages that by the time I'm done, I can't remember what I was anxious about. It's gone, and I'm at peace. God promises us that His Word will not return to Him void (Isaiah 55:11) and that it will accomplish the purpose for which it was intended. If you turn to Him through your memorized Scripture, He will bring you peace. If you haven't memorized that much Scripture yet, then carry a pocket-sized Bible with you and steal off into a corner and open it up to Psalms. It won't take long for the feelings to pass as you read from David's heart.

If that doesn't seem to do it and you still take it back from God, then remember the steps you took to get to where you could leave it there the first time, and start over:

1. Do whatever you can again.
2. Seek objective counsel again.

3. Pray fervently again.
4. Turn it all over to God again.

If you find you're taking it back from God, then go back to step one. Is there something you didn't do the first time? Is there a possibility there's something you missed or did inadequately? Use your propensity to take it back to reflect on the situation again. It's very possible you missed something. Or maybe God is giving it back to you because He wants more from you.

So, reflect on it again, get some more guidance, hit your knees again, and once you've gone through all of that a second time, turn it over to God again.

And again, and again, and again if you need to. Each time you find yourself taking it back, go back to step one. Each time you take it back and start over, you will come to the conclusion faster and faster that there's nothing you can do. Before you know it, when you start to feel yourself taking it back, the process will go so rapidly that you'll hardly notice it happened at all.

Summary For Dealing With Trials

This was something of a long chapter, so I wanted to summarize before we move on to the next section. Here are the section headers for this chapter. Reflect on them for a bit, apply them to your life, and if there's anything here you just don't understand, then please go back and re-read it before you move on. They're just too important.

Why does God allow bad things to happen?

1. To discipline us for sin,
2. To get our attention and draw us closer to Him,
3. To help us grow and strengthen, e.g., 'boot camp,'
4. To redirect our lives, and
5. To give God glory.

Turning it all over to God

1. Do whatever you can.
2. Seek objective counsel.
3. Pray fervently, cry out to God.
4. *Then* turn it over to God and keep praying.
5. When you take it back from God, start over with step 1.

Then as a final thought in dealing with your trials, please remember two critically important things:

1. **Pain is not the problem: Pain without purpose is the problem, and**
2. **God will never waste your pain.**

XVII — WHAT IS GOD'S WILL FOR MY LIFE?

Discerning God's Will

Ok, we've gone over a lot of good, practical stuff for dealing with mental distress and trials in our lives. One of the therapies was to "Do," remember? The implication, of course, is to do what it is that God wants you to do with your life: To find and fulfill your divine purpose. So exactly how do we do that? How can I figure out what God wants me to be doing? How can I discern His will for my life?

Let's see.

Do What You Know

I heard a sermon on this topic one day, and the pastor said the most remarkable thing:

> "If you don't know what God wants you to do, do what you know God wants you to do until you know what God wants you to do."[37]

Brilliant. That comment changed my entire perspective of God's will for my life.

I've also heard it said that 95% of God's will for your life is in the Bible. Just do it.

We spend so much time thinking about how God is going to use us that we totally miss the point. The very question, "What is God's will for my life?" puts the focus back on me.

The very first step in fulfilling God's purpose, in doing God's will for your life, is to know Jesus, learn His commands, and be obedient.[38] If you're not doing what's already been written down in God's book, then why would He 'pile on' and give you something more complicated to do? He's already told us that (paraphrased), "he who is faithful in the little things can be trusted with the big things, but if you're not faithful with little things, I can't trust you with the big things" (Matthew 25:21).

Reading the Bible and learning how to be obedient to the Word is the first step toward hearing personally from God about His will. That's preschool through High School 'will.' College-level 'will,' that personal 'this is just for you' kind of communication from God, would make no sense to you unless you've learned the simpler obedience first. It's like giving a 4th grader a physics exam. First things first.

Joining Him In His Work

I agree with Mr. Henry Blackaby and Mr. Claude King who said in their book, *Experiencing God*, that the right question about God's will is, "What's going on around me, what is God doing, and where is He working now?" Then, the question becomes, "How can I join Him there?"[39] That takes the focus off of me and puts it squarely back where it belongs — on God.

When God called Moses to leave the wilderness and rescue the Israelites from the Egyptians, who was that about? Moses? Not in the slightest. It was about freeing the Children of God. It was about glorifying God in the process. Moses was a tool.

If we're not very careful, it can become about our glory rather than His. We want to have these wonderful, lofty ministries, public responsibilities, we want to be chosen by God for some special high calling, we want to dedicate our entire lives to setting the world on fire and saving it at the same time.

But what if God's will for your life is to be a church secretary and your job is to produce church bulletins and announcement letters in support of the head secretary? Would you be okay with that? No glory at all. Invisible. In the background. Nobody knows your name but the church staff and the people who come in to visit. But that's God's will for your life. Is that okay with you?

What if God's will for your life is to be a stay-at-home mother, home-schooling your kids. Would you be okay with that? Considered by modern society to be one of the most thankless jobs there is, we don't even acknowledge it as 'work.' "Does your wife work?" we ask. How insulting.

But what if that was what God wanted you to do? Nothing more glamorous than that. No glory at all. Other than your family and your small group, nobody knows who you are. Is that okay with you?

Think about it this way: See God's big picture for the church to be a huge tapestry. It's God's design; He's the artist. God is developing this wonderful tapestry, and it's going to be beautiful and perfect, God-perfect. Each of us is a single thread in God's tapestry, but when we're all in place doing our unique part, the tapestry is just unbelievable and screams the glory of God.

Of course, I want *my* thread to be the bright red or gold one that stretches all the way across the middle so that whenever God or anyone else sees it, they see my thread first. But what if in God's perfect plan for the tapestry, my thread is just a little gray one way down in the lower right corner. Maybe it isn't even all that long. Just an insignificant little gray thread.

But without it, God's perfect tapestry isn't perfect any longer. It may not be much of a loss, but any loss results in imperfection. Perfection isn't a range of conditions. There are no gray areas. Something is either perfect, or it isn't. For God's grand plan to be perfect, my thread, short and gray though it may be, *must* be there. The tapestry isn't about me, it's about God.

If you struggle with that concept, then you need to check yourself to see if your motive is to glorify God or yourself. If you're not sure, just spend some time in the Bible and some time in prayer with God. Ask Him to purify your heart.

Ok, so now that we have your perspective right, we need to get down to 'how.' One big question all believers, especially new believers, struggle with is how to hear the voice of God. Mr. Blackaby and Mr. King describe it as, "The Seven Realities of *Experiencing God*." Quoting *Experiencing God*, they are:

1. God is always at work around you.
2. God pursues a continuing love relationship with you that is real and personal.
3. God invites you to become involved with Him in His work.
4. God speaks by the Holy Spirit through the Bible, prayer, circumstances, and the church to reveal Himself, His purposes, and His ways.
5. God's invitation for you to work with Him always leads you to a crisis of belief that requires faith and action.
6. You must make major adjustments in your life to join God in what He is doing.
7. You come to know God by experience as you obey Him and He accomplishes His work through you.[40]

Each of these Realities is described in more detail in *Experiencing God*, and they've done a much better job doing so than I could even attempt.

However, I would like to take this space to address Realities #4 and 7, specifically, hearing the very voice of God, and obedience.

Mr. Blackaby and Mr. King say that God speaks through the Holy Spirit, and that the mechanisms the Holy Spirit uses to speak to us are:

1. the Bible,
2. prayer,
3. circumstances, and
4. church.

The bottom line about this list of ways God speaks to us is this (again, quoting *Experiencing God*): "No one of these methods of

God's speaking is, by itself, a clear indicator of God's directions. But when God says the same thing through each of these ways, you can have confidence to proceed."

Let me amplify that point. Don't run off and make a major change in your life if you read a verse or have a dream that you feel 'tells' you that you need to leave your family to fend for themselves and run off to Africa to feed the poor. Don't smirk — that's actually happened. If you get life-changing direction for *any* of the items on that list, you *must* confirm that direction with the others before you can proceed. If you get confirmation from all four, then you can confidently make your move.

Now, that's not to say that you can ignore the promptings of the Holy Spirit as you read Scripture. You don't need to check with your pastor and pray fervently about forgiving someone of an offense. If you feel prompted in an area of obedience and the Scripture is clear that it applies to you in this situation, then just go do it. If you have *any* doubts about its applicability or it's going to cause an upheaval in your life or someone else's life, then by all means, check with your pastor and the other sources first.

Now, having drawn that distinction, we'll take each of the items individually.

Hearing From God In The Bible

As you read through Scripture, remember my mantra:
slow down, meditate, pray, apply.
When you do that, you give God a chance to speak to you directly. You think about how this verse or section applies to your life. You check yourself to see if you're being obedient. You chat with Jesus about it.

Remember that the Bible is not only a revelation of how God wants us to live, but much more importantly than that, it's a revelation of the person and character of Jesus Christ, Himself. More than anything else you do with Scripture, you want to get to *know Jesus Christ*. As you reflect and meditate, think about how this verse or section helps you know Him better — how He thinks, how He reacts, who He is.

As you get more and more familiar with Him, you'll grow closer and closer to Him. The closer to Him you are, the more likely it is that you're going to hear from Him personally.

God is relying on your relationship with Him *through Scripture* to communicate with you. If you're skipping that step, none of the other means of communication are going to be very available to you.

Critical point: God will *never* give you personal direction that in any way violates His Bible. To do otherwise implies there is something imperfect in the Bible, or that He left something out that He is revealing to you alone. That would never happen. Whenever you think you've heard from God, you *must* filter it through Scripture before you act.

Second critical point: When you read something in Scripture and you believe God has spoken to you through it with direction for you to act, and especially so if it is a big change of some sort, make sure that you have checked other sources to ensure that you have interpreted the Scripture and God's direction correctly. Make sure it complies with the Scriptural definition of what is 'righteous.' God would never ask you to do something that fails that test. Check commentaries, check with your pastor, check with Godly friends. Don't run off half-baked thinking you've been told by God to do something through Scripture, only to find out later that you totally misunderstood what it meant.

So as you read Scripture, and especially as you slow down, meditate, pray, and apply, you will start to notice something interesting. You will find that you'll be reflecting on a passage that never really had much meaning to you the other 10 times you've read it, over and above the obvious Biblical meaning. But then this time, on the 11th time, something amazing happens. Suddenly, like a light has come on, you see how it *directly* applies to you, and how you can use it in a particular situation in your life.

That's the Holy Spirit speaking to you, into your spirit, directly into your heart. When that happens, you are hearing the very voice of God: Be *very* excited!

If you've never had that happen, be patient. As you implement the techniques you've learned in this book, you will. God wants to speak to you, but he needs you to slow down and listen for Him.

But remember that your responsibility doesn't stop there. When God speaks to you directly, it usually means there's something He needs you to do, which often means there's something you need to change in yourself. Once the excitement of hearing from God dies down a little, you might hear yourself saying, "Oh, no. You want me to do *that*?"

You need to be obedient at this point. He's not likely to keep talking to you and giving you more instructions if you can't obey the one thing He's already given you to. It's *critical* for you to be obedient to what He has told you to do before He's going to give you more.

If you've heard from Him in the past and you're wondering why you haven't heard from Him in a while, you have to ask yourself, "Have I been obedient to the last thing He told me to do?" If not, then that may be why.

If, however, you *were* obedient and haven't heard from Him for a while, then the guidance I've heard is, "Then just keep doing the last thing He told you to do, continue to read and get to know Him better and better, and be patient." We go through seasons where we are just 'in the wilderness,' as was Moses for 40 years, where God is preparing us for His next instruction. David was 13 years in the caves while God was preparing him for the monarchy.

To hear from God through Scripture, slow down, meditate, pray, and apply.

Hearing From God Through Prayer

Prayer is the most intimate time you will have with God. That's why, in addition to my formal prayer time, I like to 'pray without ceasing.' If you've never attended a Bible Study or read a book on prayer, I'd highly recommend you do so. Different denominations have different perspectives on prayer as well, so trust the church where God has planted you and seek their guidance.

In the mean time, I'll give you a few thoughts that might help you now.

First, as is the case with Bible reading, just slow down.

I heard a woman one time talking about this concept, and she said that she was very frustrated that she never felt like she was hearing from God. She would pray and pray and pray and pray and pray, and then end up saying, "God? How come you never talk to me?" And just as clear as day, she heard Him say, "Well, if you'd ever shut up, I could get a word in!" (Those were her words — I don't know if God actually used the phrase 'shut up'). She realized she never hesitated or paused in her prayer time to just *listen*.

Slow down and listen as you enter into the presence of God through prayer. You'll hear from Him a lot more often.

The next thing you need to be aware of is this: Prayer isn't about getting God to bend to your will — it's about getting your will to bend to God. I've said it before, but it bears repeating: More than any other single thing, prayer is about reporting for duty.

As you pray, remember that God isn't a vending machine: You can't put in your quarters worth of prayer and get your candy out of the shoot. God has a plan for you. He has a perfect and beautiful plan tailor made for your life (Ephesians 2:10). Your prayers, therefore, should reflect that you're 'armed and ready for battle' with whatever new step He wants you to take. As Jesus prayed right before He went to the cross, "not what I will, but what You will" (Mark 14:36).

Another thing to remember about prayer is that occasionally, God will actually grant a prayer that is outside of His will (Numbers 11:4, 10, 19-20; Numbers 20:20-22). Be careful what you pray for so as not to kindle the Lord's anger toward you. Read the referenced passages carefully so you understand what these people did: Don't repeat their mistakes.

However, that's not to say you can't ask. Definitely ask. When a teenager comes to their parent to ask if they can do something, the parent feels blessed because the very question acknowledges the child's submission to and respect of the parent's authority in their life. God loves for us to come to Him with our requests. He delights in granting what He can when it doesn't interfere with His plans.

The point of the Old Testament passages is that these people were complaining, demanding, and had selfish, ulterior motives that showed a lack of respect for God and a lack of trust in His divine plan. Jesus, on the other hand, in the prayer just quoted above, had actually made a request of the Father. He said, "Abba! Father! All things are possible for You; remove this cup from Me;" It was after He had appealed to His Father that He demonstrated His utter obedience to God by adding, "but not what I will, but what You will."

The safest way you can be confident that your request is in His will and that you're hearing from Him is to be absolutely neutral on how you want it to work out. If you are praying for a husband or wife, be absolutely neutral as to who this person might be or when they might show up. If you are praying about a new job, tell God that you just want His will to prevail in this circumstance. If you beg and plead, He just might grant it to you, but it might not be what you really want.

If you struggle with that objectivity, then make *that* the subject of your prayer. "You know my heart, God. I *really* want this new job. But more than that, I want to be obedient to your voice, trust your plan, and follow your lead. Please change my heart Lord so I can be objective and either go to the new job or stay where I am and be totally open to hearing your guidance in my life in this area. Help me be objective so I can hear from you clearly, and stay within your will."

Remember that your life is about Him and not you. It's about His will and not yours. It's about lifting Him up and not yourself. Keep your prayers and your motives focused on His will and His purpose, and you will hear from Him.

The second big pointer I have about prayer is to make it real. Be real. God doesn't want your flowery prose, He wants your heart. Talk to Him like He knows who you are. Talk to Him like you know who He is. Draw near with confidence to the throne of grace (Hebrews 4:16) and let your requests be made known to God (Philippians 4:6).

I attended a Bible study on prayer once, and the illustration they gave was very illuminating. It told a story of a CEO of a major corporation. He was one of those high-level executives that have several layers of secretaries before you can get to him, but on his desk, was this special phone that only his children had the phone number for. Everyone knew that if that phone rang, all activity in the room stopped as the CEO answered the phone so his kids could talk to 'Daddy.' There was nothing in his life more important to him than being available for his precious children.

God, our heavenly 'Daddy,' has that phone, and we have the phone number. The question in the Bible study was, "If that's true, then why don't we pick up the phone more often and call him?" One of the wise and unashamed women in the study said, "I never hang up." What a great picture. She is on that special phone with her Daddy all day long.

That's the kind of relationship He wants with us. Not irreverent, but real. He's your Daddy. Call Him. He'll stop what He's doing and chat.

Hearing From God Through Circumstances

The third major way God can speak to us is through our circumstances. This is very akin to the 'Redirection' we discussed in an early chapter about trials, but it doesn't necessarily have to involve suffering. It could simply be a change of some sort in some aspect of our lives.

There are many examples throughout Scripture where people heard from God through circumstances. Paul said that he had been forbidden by the Holy Spirit from preaching the Gospel in Asia, forcing Him to go to the Phrygian and Galatian regions (Acts 16:6). Paul didn't share with us exactly how the Holy Spirit forbade him, but clearly, his circumstance prevented him from going to Asia, and as a result, he preached the Gospel in Phrygia and Galatia, following the will of God.

When Moses was leading the Israelites out of Egypt, "the Lord went before them by day in a pillar of a cloud, to lead them the way; and by night in a pillar of fire, to give them light; to go by day and night" (Exodus 13:21). Although Scripture doesn't give us the exact mechanism, keep in mind that they were in the wilderness. In the wilderness, it's hot during the day and cold at night. God's cloud would have made a wonderful refreshing shadow in the heat of the day, and His fire would have provided them with warmth and light during the night. As the cloud moved and they became hotter in the heat, they would naturally have moved to remain under the shade. The reverse would have been true at night. Thus, if nothing else, their own desire to remain comfortable would have propelled them to stay with the cloud and fire, and as a result, they would be directly in the will of God.

The circumstances could be as simple as your becoming more aware of a need of some sort. If you suddenly find yourself in the middle of a traffic jam and you look over and see broken down homes with children in bare feet and you feel your heart break, that may be God speaking to you through that circumstance that He needs you to get involved in serving the poor.

Another example might be that your spouse is transferred to a new job. As a result, you have to move to a different community and to a different church. When you get there, you find that they are in need of someone who has exactly the skills and Spiritual Gift you have to lead a desperately needed ministry. Sure, you could complain about the inconvenience of having to move and leave your church family and the community you know: but if God's hand is in it, then you can rest assured that there is something there that He needs you to be involved in, and if you're open to it, it will glorify Him and bless you.

Sometimes God will use our circumstances to position us where He needs us to be so we can get involved in His on-going work. Remember, it's never about us — it's about Him and *His work*.

Hearing From God Through The Church

If you're not plugged into a church body, please understand that, among many other reasons for attending church, you are blocking one of the greatest opportunities God has for speaking to you directly. I strongly recommend that you make that a very top priority in your

Christian walk, as well as in your attempt to improve your state of mental health.

Churches are made up of many different components that God will use to speak to you. First and foremost, consider the pastor and his weekly message. I cannot tell you how many times I have come out of a church service and said, "Wow. He must be following me around. That sermon was *directly* for me!" I haven't spoken to a Christian yet who hasn't had the same experience as well. Go to church and listen for the voice of God through your pastor.

The second way God will speak to you in your church is through Community Groups or Small Groups. These groups are typically 8-15 church members who get together on a regular basis to do Bible Study, fellowship, ministries, or whatever. The benefit of these groups is to allow people in the church to get to know one another and become aware of each other's needs. Your awareness might be an invitation from God for you to offer them support or encouragement. The group may also be involved in ministries that have been brought to their attention through prayer. If you're not involved in a Small Group, you are missing out on another prime way that God will seek to speak to you.

Another mechanism God will use to speak to you is through the programs and ministries that the church has made available and supports. Be alert to what's going on in your church. Mr. Blackaby and Mr. King say, "When God reveals to you where He is working, that becomes His invitation to join Him. When God reveals His work to you, that is His timing for you to begin to respond to Him."[41] When you become aware of a need and feel drawn to that need, that may be God speaking to you through that circumstance.

The final critical component of being involved in a church is the accountability. People in the church will tend to keep you humble. If you try to make it about you, they will typically let you know that it isn't. That keeps you safe and protected from your own flesh.

Remember that doing God's will is not about you. If you're not very careful or have no accountability, that's an easy trap to fall into. Remember that Satan wants to ruin your witness and he can do so through your church involvement as easily as he can anywhere else. Many people who thought they were following God's will into a ministry have fallen victim to the temptations of Satan to make it about themselves. This is always an extremely risky place to be. Ask Jim Bakker.[42]

Hearing From God Through Obedience

When you have a choice between two options and one of those options is in the will of God and the other isn't, then the decision you make will determine the extent to which you are able to hear from God.

First of all, when Adam and Eve sinned, what's the first thing they did? They hid. When we have something to hide from God, we hide. We hide our faces, we hide ourselves, and we try to hide our hearts. We block Him by not thinking about Him, not reading His Word, and not praying to Him. He becomes more and more distant.

Until you purpose in your heart to start obeying His commands, regardless of whether or not you understand or agree with them, and regardless of the consequences to you, you will be very unlikely to hear from God concerning His will for your life. You may be subject to His discipline, but you're not very likely to be getting many marching orders.

If, on the other hand, you *do* choose to be obedient to Him, then you are not going to be hiding from him, and you are going to learn to trust that His direction is in your best interest. You may not always like it, it might not always feel good at the time, but you will *always* know it's the right thing to do.

If you find yourself hiding from God, then come out of the trees into the light of His Son. Repent of your disobedience, recommit yourself to obeying Him, and listen for His still small voice in your heart. As the prodigal son's father raced across the open field to wrap his loving arms around his returning wayward son (Luke 15:11-32), so God will wrap His loving arms around you to welcome you back into the fold. Why did the father see his son "a long way off?" Because he never stopped looking, waiting, and hoping. Jesus gave us that story so we would know the heart of God when His children repent and return.

Your obedience glorifies God. Much of God's commands fly in the face of the wisdom of the world. Without your faith in His reality and sovereignty, you would never be able to pull it off. Your obedience is your testimony to the others who are watching that He is very real to you.

So how does obedience relate to mental health? In the context of this section, obedience equals peace, contentment, and inner joy. It means a cleaner, purer relationship with God, and opens the channels of communication. When you have an open, honest, clear channel of communication with God, His voice will keep you ever-aware of His presence; it will bring you peace and joy, and He will give you purpose in your pain and purpose in your life. Your obedience will grow your faith, and your faith and your ever-deepening relationship and communication with Him will bring you that contentment, peace, and joy.

XVIII — EXAMPLES FOR REFLECTION

❦

Ok, now the rubber *really* hits the road. We're going to work, painstakingly, through some specific Biblical examples to show you exactly how you can think about Scripture as you read to do two critical things:

1) fall in love with Jesus, and
2) apply it to your life

This chapter is to show you what I mean when I say, "how to think about Scripture." I'm going to walk you through my thought process as I read. The following chapters show you specific examples of ways to look at specific problems or issues, but this chapter is to show you how to use your daily reading, regardless of where you are in the Bible, to allow God to speak to your heart.

According to a class I attended at church on how to study the Bible, to really get the most out of it, it's a three-step process. In my experience, to know these steps and use them will help you understand what you're reading better, and apply it to your life more effectively. There are many good books on how to read the Bible, so if you're so inclined, please avail yourself of what's out there. In the mean time, the steps are:

1) observation,

2) interpretation, and
3) application.

Observation means to review a section to see if there are any clues as to what the author's focus was. Think about the following questions as you read:

1. Who's writing the book?
2. Who is he writing it to?
3. What's happened or is happening to him?
4. Can you infer something from the author's own experiences and what he's writing here?
5. Is a word repeated several times throughout the section?
6. Are there terms like "But" or "Therefore" that indicate that something is compared or contrasted, or something is linked in a particular way?
7. Are there general themes running through a section of Scripture?

One of my favorite phrases in the Bible is, "But God." Be on the lookout for those because it means that there is a very exciting transition that it taking place. Something awful had been the situation, "But God" comes in and everything changes. Stop and meditate on them when you see those.

Make sure you determine the context of each section you are studying. Read several verses before that section, and several verses after. If you're not already doing it, get into the habit of studying verse-by-verse through a chapter. Start at the beginning of a book and work your way all the way through. And when you start at the beginning of a new chapter, always go back and read several verses leading into the chapter. It's amazing how often one thought has led into the next, but we miss it because we just start the next day with the beginning of a new chapter.

Once you've made some important observations about it and feel like you have the structure and flow of the section down, then try to figure out what the author wanted you to know from this section. Interpretation isn't up to you: It's up to the author of the book. Your job is to figure out what *he* meant — not what you'd *like* it to mean or what you think it *might* mean. Much of this can be discerned by comparing it to other sections of Scripture that deal with the same thing. Scripture validates Scripture. Check with how the same author treats the same subject in different chapters or books, and determine how different authors address the issue.

Once I feel I've spent enough time and gotten as much as I'm going to from a section of Scripture, the next thing I typically do is check myself against the scholars. I'll check a few commentaries to see if I'm on-track or off-track, or if I've missed anything. The commentaries I use are fairly common, but I know there are lots of options so you don't have to stick with mine. The key is to check with several so you don't get only one person's perspective.

Specifically, the commentaries I use are:

1) The Bible Knowledge Commentary from Dallas Theological Seminary,
2) Matthew Henry's Commentary,
3) Jon Courson's Application Commentaries (Old and New Testament),
4) Spiros Zodhiates Word Studies (Old and New Testaments), and
5) Jamison-Faucett-Brown Commentary.

You may have your own resources that you use, and that's fine. I'm not even sure these are necessarily the best ones, and I think some of the scholars may even cringe at my choices. They're simply the ones that are available at the Christian Book Store where I shop, so they're the ones I use. Just spread the wealth around and check several sources before you settle into an interpretation.

Now, exactly how much time you spend in the Bible before you go to commentaries is open for debate amongst the pastors I've listened to. I've heard some pastors say you *never* go to the commentaries until you have allowed the Holy Spirit to do His work in you and through you through Scripture, and I've heard other pastors say, especially if you're a young Christian, that the risk of misinterpretation is high enough that if you are focused and meditating on a section of Scripture, go to the commentaries early in your work and let them guide your interpretation. Then you can meditate further and work with the Holy Spirit to allow Him to drive the application to your life.

You and the Holy Spirit can decide how you should handle that process.

So, let's get started. If you don't already have your Bible open, now's the time. I'm not going to quote the sections I'm discussing, so you'll need to read them in your own Bible first.

Read John 1:1-14

Start by reading the Gospel of John Chapter 1, verses 1-14. Read the entire section first, and then come back here to see how to apply the "slow down, meditate, pray, apply" process. If you haven't already done so, go read that now.

Great. Now, let's see how it works:

John 1:1 — "In the beginning"

Let your mind wander back in time. Way back. Genesis starts with that same phrase. "In the beginning, God created the heavens and the earth." Here, we see, "In the beginning was the Word."

As you read the passage, you discover that "The Word" John is referring to is none other than Jesus Christ, Himself. So *this* "In the beginning" is actually referring to the time *prior* to the Genesis "In the beginning." Genesis is referring to the beginning of *time*. Here, we're looking at the status *before* time existed. It actually means "prior to the beginning…" because God is eternal.

"In the beginning was the Word, and the Word was with God…" The Greek word "In" here implies that, in the beginning, this situation already existed. Jesus was already with God eternally. There was no time when God existed and Jesus did not. All the way back as far as "In the beginning" could possibly refer to, which is infinity, eternity, Jesus was there.

"…and the Word *was* God." John jumps right to the deity of Christ. That's the whole purpose of John's Gospel — to teach us that Jesus is God in the flesh. He tells us that right up front.

Just think about that for a minute. Close your eyes and let that concept roll around in your head. Jesus, who walked on the earth, touched people physically and spiritually, ate with them, drank with them, walked with them, performed miracles in front of them. *That* Jesus was God. Actually, that's wrong. I should have said that Jesus *is* God. He arose. He's alive. Right now, eternally. He's still in His glorified body, and He's still God.

Slow down, meditate, pray, and apply. Let the magnitude and the majesty of that sink into your soul.

Verse 3 says *all things* came into being through Him. He is the Creator God. The earth, the stars, the grains of sand, insects, bacteria, everything. *All* things. Even the wicked for the day of evil (Proverbs 16:4). Ponder that, and try to feel the enormity of our God. Don't ever forget His enormity. The goal is to make Him personal, but don't ever diminish Him in size.

Reflect and meditate on Jesus' enormity. Talk to Him about it.

Verse 4 — "In Him was Life..." Science is spending millions or billions of dollars trying to search out the origin of life. All they need to do is read this verse. In *Him* was life. He was the beginning of life. Reflect that later on He said, "I am the Way, the Truth, and the Life." All life began in Him and with Him. He was the seed that started all life. We *all* sprang forth from Him. He was Adam's Father. In the beginning...

And yet, here He was, walking among us — asking <u>us</u> to believe in <u>Him</u>. He is very life itself, and yet He humbled himself to come down and *ask* us to believe in Him! The enormity of it all...

Verse 5 — "The Light shines in the darkness..." What happens when light shines in darkness? What happens to the darkness? What *is* darkness but the absence of light? So if there is darkness, then that means we are devoid of light. But when the light comes in, the darkness is destroyed.

Is there darkness in your life? Maybe some light but pockets of darkness? Light doesn't discriminate on what it illuminates. If it's there, light will shine on it. Light flies out of the light source and strikes whatever is in its path — unless, of course, there is an obstacle in the way.

Are there obstacles blocking the light in your life? Verse 9 says that Jesus lights *every* man in the world. So why are there people in the dark, people who don't believe in Him? What's blocking the light? To escape the light that's coming your way, you have to either duck behind something or move something in between you and the light source.

Is there something blocking the light from reaching you? Jesus is the light. Come out into the open and let Him shine His light on your face.

Meditate on Jesus' light for a minute. Feel the warmth. Drink it in. Feel His love on your face.

Verses 10 and 11 — He came unto His own, but His people rejected Him. They blocked the light. They moved out of the way and hid behind an obstacle. Why would they do that? Why would they not want the warmth and the light? What would that obstacle have been? What might it be for you?

Stop for a minute. Ask Jesus why someone would block His light? Ask Him to help you remove any obstacles you have that are blocking His light from reaching you to the full.

Verse 12 — But those who *did* receive Him became God's children. What does it mean to be someone's child? How would your life have changed if you didn't have your parents? If you didn't have *any* parents? Maybe you didn't, and the question brings up some difficult feelings. God has invited you to become *His* child. As children, you have a closer relationship than an acquaintance, or even a friend. You have access that other people don't have. You have an expectation of closer attention. You have the expectation of provision. You also have the expectation of loving discipline. Good, loving parents train their children, and sometimes that training brings discipline. If you're not being disciplined by your parents, then you won't feel very loved. What would God's discipline feel like to you? Do you think you'd recognize it as discipline? Or would it just feel mean and ugly? Could you tell the difference?

Compare your own parents to God as your heavenly Father. Think about what you would expect the differences to be. Embrace God as your *real* Father and let Him love you in His perfect way.

Reflect and meditate on what it would feel like to be God's child. Respectfully call Him "Daddy," as Jesus did (Mark 14:36).[43] What would that mean to you? What *does* it mean to you?

Finish the rest of this section in a similar manner, reflecting on each verse and what it means to you personally. Remember to talk to Jesus about it throughout.

Read Matthew 11:2-9

This is about John the Baptist struggling with who Jesus is. Read the whole section first.

Now let's reflect a bit:

Verse 3, John says, "Are you the expected one, or shall we look for someone else?"

Huh? What does *that* mean? John "leapt for joy" inside his mother's womb when Mary, with Jesus still in her own womb, came to visit John's mother, Elizabeth. As an adult, John announced Jesus with, "Behold, the Lamb of God" twice as Jesus approached him at the river. He claimed to have seen the dove ascending and lighting on Jesus. He certainly heard God's voice say, "This is my Beloved Son in Whom I am well-pleased."

He knew that Jesus was the Son of God better than anyone. So why would he ask a question like that??

Reflect on this. Ask Jesus about it. John had been in prison for a while, and he certainly had to understand that his life was in danger. He'd been hearing many, many stories about Jesus' miracles, and he and Jesus were second cousins. John had *baptized* Him, after all. If Jesus was going to perform a miracle on anyone, certainly John could expect that he would be included. And yet there he sat in a dank, dark, dungy prison.

Stop and think about what that must have been like for John. What must he have been thinking? If that were you, what would *you* have been thinking? Put yourself in John's shoes.

Now go back and re-read Jesus' response. How would you have taken his response? How does Jesus' response apply to you?

When you are in the 'prison' of life, do you wonder where Jesus is? Do you think He's abandoned you? What were John's expectations of Jesus? What are yours?

"Blessed is he who does not take offense at me." Do you take offense at Him if He doesn't do what you expect? Does your faith hold up? It seems John — the great John the Baptist — has a crisis of faith.

What's John's real question here? I think rather than, "Are you the One?", John is pleading, "Aren't you going to save me?"

By His reply, Jesus said, "No, John, I'm not. And you won't understand why until you are safely in the arms of God. Then you'll understand, and I will see you when I get there[44]."

Do we understand when God says, "no" to us? Do we have a crisis of faith?

Yes. Sometimes, yes.

Then we're in good company.

But blessed are we if we are not offended by Him.

Read Matthew 12:46-50

When I first read that, I was very puzzled. I thought Jesus' answer was, well, *rude*! I thought, 'Now I *know* Jesus isn't trying to set an example for us to disrespect our parents. It's just too important to Him. It's one of the *Ten Commandments* for goodness sake! What's going on here? "Lord, what's going *on* here?"

Think for a minute. Meditate for a bit about why Jesus might have reacted that way. If you said, well, Jesus is demonstrating that we're supposed to be more loyal to those who are obedient to Christ than to our family just because they're family, okay, I agree with that. But does that justify being rude? I mean, we're talking *The Virgin Mary*. And He didn't even send word out that he'd be there in a bit. He just blew them off. I was very puzzled.

I just left it there the first time I read it, and several times after that, and tried not to dwell on it. But it always sort of stuck in my throat.

So reflect on that for a minute to see what you might be able to come up with on your own.

Now turn to Mark 3. Remember what I said about comparing different Gospel's versions of the same story? This same story is in Mark 3 as well. Read Mark 3:31-35 now. It's the same story, right? Now read verse 21 above it.

Jesus knew very well what they were thinking, and He was going to have no part in it. They thought He was "out of His mind!" If He'd gone out to them, they'd have hauled Him away to who knows where. They didn't want to talk — they wanted to take custody of Him. It never occurred to me that these were His brothers with His mother. Mary couldn't have, but the brothers could have come inside to speak to Him. They didn't need Him to come out at all! When I first read it, I didn't trust Jesus enough, or I didn't trust my own understanding of what I was reading. I was young in the faith, and confused. I didn't make that mistake again.

This passage got me over a very big hump when I discovered it. I realized, just because I don't understand a passage doesn't make it wrong, it doesn't make it invalid, it doesn't make it inapplicable to me or my situation — it just means I don't understand it yet.

Very humbling, indeed, but a critical step in my growth.

Let's do one more.

John 1:29, 36

We'll go back to John Chapter 1 again. Read verses 29 and 36.

If your Bible has margin notes with cross-references, you should have a cross-reference to Isaiah 53:7. Any time you have margin notes with cross-references to the Old Testament, try to take the time to check it out. Go there now and read that verse, and read it in context. As a matter of fact, read the entire Chapter 53 in Isaiah.

What was John the Baptist thinking when he called Jesus, "The Lamb of God?" What does Isaiah say about lambs? Could that relate to Jesus? What does that tell you about his crucifixion? Isaiah was written 700 years *prior* to the birth of Jesus. Why is Isaiah speaking in past tense, sounding almost like he *knew* this man?

What are your thoughts now about Jesus being the "Lamb of God?" What did John know about Jesus in those early days? What could he see was going to happen to Him?

Let's go deeper. Notice the word "pleased" in verse 10. I looked it up in my Greek dictionary, and it's not a poor interpretation of the Hebrew. It literally means, "to be pleased, to delight in." Think about how that could be. Then go on-line and look up "Roman scourging" and "Roman crucifixion" in a search engine to get a sense of what Jesus went through. Brace yourself: It's not easy.

Then reflect again on that word, 'pleased.'

Exactly who was it who died on that cross? Jesus, yes. But Jesus was God incarnate. God felt every stroke and piercing. God suffered with His Son. Have you ever watched someone you love suffer? If your child needed a kidney to live, would you be pleased to give it to him? Of course you would, because you would know that the end result would be your child's survival. And so God was pleased to crush His Son because of what the end result would be: Eternal fellowship with you.

Reflect on the enormity of all of that, and fall in love with Jesus.

XIX — TOPICAL EXAMPLES: OLD TESTAMENT

Before I get into the topical examples, *please* don't skip the earlier chapters of this book. Without the foundational changes in the way you regard Scripture and Jesus, this is just another 'program' that will die on the vine. Plus, I've included many of the passages I use in therapy in the pertinent texts, so to skip the foundational chapters will be to miss some of the really good stuff.

The essence of this book is to teach you how to *personalize* Scripture and draw close to Christ through it. In this chapter, I take specific sections of Scripture and show you how you can take what might seem like distant stories about other people and make them about you, for you, and to you.

You are the hero of the Bible. You are the villain. You are the damsel waiting to be rescued, and you are the champion who will rescue her. You are the confused disciple, the prodigal son. You are Peter sinking into the sea and James and John wanting to rain fire down on the Samaritans. You are the good Samaritan and the injured Jew needing help. You are the Pharisee who passes him by.

You are Lazarus, risen from the dead.

You are all of these people. We all are. Learn to see yourself in these stories that way. When you do, the Bible will become the most exciting book you have ever or will ever read, and it will truly transform your life.

Let's walk through some specific examples to show you how. Needless to say, this is far from a complete list. All I'm trying to do here, as with the rest of this book, is to whet your appetite for more. Allow the Holy Spirit to show you those that apply directly to you, and let Him be your tutor.

I'm not going to include footnotes any longer for quotes I give. I'd like you to start finding them on your own if you'd like to see them. If you don't know how to do that, refer to the Appendix called, "How to Read Your Bible," and look specifically at the section called, "The Concordance."

Ok, Lazarus, let's go.

Misinterpreting Or Adding To Scripture

Read Genesis 3:1-7

Precept: Understanding what God meant by a certain passage of Scripture is *critical* to knowing how to respond to it. When we either add to or detract from what God meant, we wind up going off in all sorts of dangerous directions.

Illustration 1: Look at Adam and Eve. God told Adam that they could eat of any tree in the garden except the one in the middle, the tree of the knowledge of good and evil, or they would die. Easy enough.

Adam heard the command, but we have no evidence of whether Eve heard it from God, or from Adam. Since we know she hadn't been created when God first told Adam and it isn't likely He felt it necessary to repeat Himself for Eve's sake, it's a pretty fair bet she heard it from Adam.

Then comes the serpent. First, he questions what God *actually* said. Since Eve heard it from Adam and Adam got it from God, then Eve didn't have the confidence to stand her ground. Either she didn't trust Adam to have explained it well enough, or she didn't trust God to really mean what He said, or she didn't trust herself to have heard it right. In any event, she entered into a dialogue with the enemy.

The first thing the enemy does is to try to confuse. "Indeed, has God said, 'You shall not eat from any tree of the garden'?"

She knew that wasn't right, so she tried to correct him. "From the fruit of the trees of the garden we may eat; but from the fruit of the tree which is in the middle of the garden, God has said, 'You shall not eat from it or touch it, or you will die.'"

'Or touch it?' When did God say *that*? Go back and see where God and Adam had that conversation. Do you see that part? "Or touch it?" It's not there. She added that herself. So what happened next?

"…she took from its fruit…"

She touched it, and she didn't die. "Hmm," she might have thought. Ok then, since she didn't die when she touched it …

"…and ate;"

In her mind, she didn't die when she touched it as God said she would (or so she thought), so God must have lied about eating it, too. Since she didn't truly understand the command, she couldn't know how to be obedient to it. Satan set the trap and she fell in.

Why Adam didn't stop her, we can't know for sure. We can surmise, but the only thing we know for sure is that Eve didn't understand what God had said, so she blew it. Then she ate and didn't die, and Adam went along with her. The Apostle Paul said she was "deceived," which is clearly true. But she set herself up by not knowing what God had really said.

When she added the "or touch it" part, legalism was born. When you take God's commands and subtract from them, then you are just being disobedient. But when you take God's law and add your own twists and nuances to it, you are setting yourself and others up to be deceived just like Eve was. The Pharisees did that, and Jesus rebuked them for it.

Lesson: See yourself as Eve in the story. Then Adam. Personalize it by saying "When do I do that? Do I twist Scripture? Do I really know what God wants of me? Do I add to what I've read? Do I let other people influence my thinking about what I know to be true? Do I try to impose my understanding on others?"

We need to read Scripture with the idea that we are searching for God's truth. We need to really understand what *He* meant by what He said, and we need to be careful not to let man add to it or subtract from it and influence what we do. You have a responsibility to God to be obedient, and that responsibility doesn't diminish just because you don't know what His commands are. As the officer will tell you, "Ignorance of the law is no excuse." It's easy to see why subtracting from the law would make us vulnerable, but this story shows us that it's just as dangerous to add to it. Truth is truth. More or less than that is a lie.

Know for sure what God has said, don't listen to people who question it, and don't add or subtract from it. Protect yourself from the traps of Satan by knowing for yourself.

God Feels Distant

Genesis 3:8-10
Precept: Sin, current or unconfessed old sin, will keep you from experiencing the full presence of God.

Illustration 1: If you feel like you have more distance from God than you'd like, one of the things you might check is whether or not there is sin in your life. Before Adam and Eve sinned, Adam would walk with God, side by side. But when Adam sinned, he hid from God.

> "They heard the sound of the Lord God walking in the garden in the cool of the day, and the man and his wife hid themselves from the presence of the Lord God among the trees of the garden."

Lesson: So here you are again. See yourself as Adam, 'the man and his wife.' When you sin, do you feel ashamed and hide from God? If we have something we know we need to confess to God but we don't want to, we hide from Him. So how much fellowship and connection can you have with someone from whom you are hiding?

The book of James says, "Draw near to God and He will draw near to you." The implication is that you have control over how close you are to God. You draw first. If you have sin in your life and you're ashamed to face Him, then it's going to feel to you like He's left you. It's not Him — it's you.

Get right before God. Turn your face to Him and confess to Him and to whomever else you might have offended or hurt through your sin. Repent and make restitution. Get back into the Word so you can know what He wants you to know and you can hear from Him again.

Illustration 2: Another section of Scripture that serves to illustrate this same concept is in Revelation.

Read Revelation 2:1-5

"I know your deeds and your toil and your perseverance..."

Jesus is acknowledging their good works, but it's not enough. If you're hung up on ministries and activities but your relationship with Jesus is suffering, then Jesus says your endless good works aren't good enough.

"...But this I have against you, that you have left your first love."

Note that He doesn't say you've *lost* your first love. You've *left* Him. You did it yourself. But grace upon grace, our Lord doesn't admonish us, He doesn't torture us with silence, and He doesn't rub our noses in it. He just jumps right in to the solution.

"Therefore, remember from where you have fallen..."

What were you were doing when you were first saved and on fire for your new faith?

"... and repent ..."

Agree with God that what you're doing now is wrong and talk with Him about how you can turn it around. Confess to Him what you did that got you where you are now.

"...and do the deeds you did at first;"

If you're feeling distant from God, He wants you to know how you can restore your relationship with Him. It's right here in the text. Think about how your young Christianity manifested itself in your life, and if you see it as relevant, do that again. Did those things draw you closer to Jesus? Did they light the fire in your belly for God? Go back, do the deeds you did at first, and reconnect with the Lord of your life.

Lesson: God doesn't want your shame. He wants your confession, your repentance, your love, and your fellowship. Turn back, and walk with Him in the cool of the day.

Blaming Others For Your Mistakes

Genesis 3:8-13

Precept: When we blame others for our mistakes, we step outside of the full restoration and blessings of God.

Illustration: Adam and Eve ate the fruit and got busted. When God questioned Adam, what did he say?

"The woman…"

He blames his wife first. He seems to have forgotten that *he* was the one to whom God gave the command. He never mentioned that. Way to love your wife, Adam.

"…whom *You* gave to be with me…"

Then he blames God. Not only is Adam not repentant, he's blame-shifting. Not only is he hiding from God, he's hiding from the truth.

"…she gave me from the tree…"

Back to the wife again. He wants to make sure he spreads the blame everywhere available except on himself.

"…and I ate."

Finally, Adam squeaks out a bit of a confession because he knows he doesn't have a choice at this point. This is not the dialogue of a repentant heart.

But what about Eve?

"The serpent deceived me..."

At least she's a little closer than Adam was as to who was to blame, but she's still deflecting.

"...and I ate."

She didn't blame God, and she didn't blame Adam, but there's still not much repentance in her words. She's making excuses and deflecting, but she's not blame-shifting.

So where do you fit into that scenario? Do you make excuses or deflect? Do you blame-shift? What would have been a better dialogue? Let's try it again and see if we can help Adam:

God: "Have you eaten from the tree of which I commanded you not to eat?"

Adam, falling on His face before God: "Oh, Lord God, please forgive me. I am weak and I did disobey your word. I knew exactly what it was You wanted me to do, and I didn't do it. I am so deeply sorry for hurting You and for disobeying Your word. I am deeply ashamed for not preventing my wife from doing the same. This is entirely my fault, Lord. Please forgive me."

Hmm. I often wonder what decision God would have made had Adam approached it that way instead of the defensiveness and blame-shifting. I guess they'd have had to be evicted anyway because they were now in a decaying state (they will surely die), and God couldn't allow them access to the Tree of Life. But I believe it would have been different somehow.

What did your parents tell you when you were growing up? "If you'll just confess to me what you did, even if it was wrong, the punishment won't be nearly as severe as it will be if you lie or hide it from us? Just tell us the truth!" Remember that lecture?

Lesson: In response to this reading, ask yourself, "When I sin, do I defend and blame-shift?" Or do you confess it up to God openly and honestly? No one is responsible for your sin but you. Not another single person on the face of the planet. "She disrespects me and makes me rage," "He ignores me and makes me react that way." Nope, sorry. "That woman" or "That man" isn't to blame for your sin, and God won't hold them accountable for it. No question he'll hold them accountable for their own sin in this situation, but He will *not* hold them accountable for yours. That belongs to you.

So confess your sin to God with courage, repent, and see how He responds.

Is It God's Wrath Or Is It His Love?

Precept: Sometimes when we're going through tough times, we think we're being punished. But do we know the difference between God's wrathful hand and His loving touch? Sometimes we don't.

Read Genesis 3:22-24

Illustration: When Adam and Even ate of the fruit of the tree of the knowledge of good and evil, they condemned themselves to a body that would decay, grow old, wrinkle, and fall apart. Anyone who's over 40 knows what that means. That was the consequence of the fruit they ate.

> Then the Lord God said, "Behold, the man has become like one of Us, knowing good and evil; …"

Definitely not God's long-term plan for us.

> "…and now, he might stretch out his hand, and take also from the tree of life, and eat…"

Even though they had eaten from the wrong tree, the other trees were still there. There was nothing stopping them from eating again.

> "…and live forever…"

This was supposed to be an 'either-or' decision for Adam. To eat from both of them would be a total disaster. Their bodies were going to decay, and they were going to live in a world that knew evil and shame. To live forever in this state would be worse than the worst possible hell.

"…therefore the Lord God sent him out from the Garden of Eden…"

"Therefore…" I think that sometimes we miss that connecting word. It says, "Therefore." So remember when I said earlier, if you see the word "therefore," check to see what it's there for? So what is it connecting here? That beautiful word is telling us that if Adam, in his fallen state, eats now of the Tree of Life, he'll live that way for all of eternity, and God can't allow that. You could slightly amend that statement to say,

"Therefore, since He loves Adam and Eve and can't allow the possibility that they might spend an eternity in those decaying bodies and that evil world, the Lord sent him out from the Garden of Eden…"

Out of God's *love*, not His wrath, God sent Adam and Eve out of the garden. The first thing God did was to cover their nakedness, their shame, with the first blood sacrifice. He then stationed angels outside the entryway to prevent them from having access to the Tree of Life. He knew He had a plan to restore them to full fellowship with Him through Jesus Christ, but it couldn't happen now, and it couldn't happen this way.

Lesson: You know it had to be devastating for God to evict Adam and Eve from His beautiful garden. He had walked with Adam in the cool of the day. They were friends, companions. And then God had no choice. Adam had to go. To have done otherwise would have created a situation infinitely worse for Adam and Eve. God knew that, and in His love, as torturous as it must have been for Him, He did the only thing He could do: He sent them out.

When you feel like you're in the middle of God's wrath, is it possible that He's actually showing you His love? You know Adam and Eve didn't understand what had happened. From their perspective, they were being punished. We have the advantage of being privy to the conversation that the three persons of the Trinity had with one another, but Adam and Eve didn't. We heard God's heart. They didn't. All they knew was their pain.

When you feel yourself being confused about your situation and feel like it is God's wrath, return to this section and reflect on what Adam and Eve must have thought, too.

I've Done So Many Awful Things That I'm Not Worthy To Be Saved

Precept: Man's heart is evil. Period. And God knows it, loves us anyway, and solved that problem for us.

Read Genesis 6:5-6 and Genesis 8:21

Illustration: When God decided to flood the entire earth, He did so because He'd regretted making mankind.

> "Then the Lord saw that the wickedness of man was great on the earth, and that every intent of the thoughts of his heart was only evil continually. The Lord was sorry that He had made man on the earth, and he was grieved in His heart." (Genesis 6:5-6).

So that was it. Total annihilation. Wow. That's pretty harsh. He really takes this sin and evil thing very seriously.

So then you might say, "But what about me? Frankly, I'm not sure the flood solved very much. The world looks pretty evil, and as for me? I know I'm a terrible sinner, and as a matter of fact, with the things I've done, I can't imagine for a minute He'd forgive me and accept me into the Kingdom of God. I'm just so unworthy and evil. Look what He did to *them*."

Well, the good news is that God agrees with you. You're a sinner, and you're not worthy. Listen to God's comment *after* the flood, and his justification for never flooding the planet again to destroy it.

"...and the Lord said to Himself, 'I will never again curse the ground on account of man...'"

Ok, that's good so far. But look at his reason.

"...for the intent of man's heart is evil from his youth..."

Huh? That was His reason for destroying it in the first place. What's *that* supposed to mean?

Lesson: What that means is this: God knows us, gang. He totally understands we are evil from our youth, and He can destroy the planet a hundred times, and that's never going to change. Our salvation isn't because we've finally been punished enough and figured out how to be good: It's because God loves us anyway. So what's the difference between the situation before the flood and after?

"Then Noah built an altar to the Lord, and took of every clean animal and of every clean bird and offered burnt offerings on the altar. The Lord smelled the soothing aroma; ..."

Noah offered a burnt offering and God smelled the soothing aroma. The significance of the "burnt offering" is that the entire animal being sacrificed is burned up on the altar. In all of the sacrifices the Israelites were required to make to God, only the burnt offering required that total burning up of the flesh. In every other case, someone got to eat some of the animal that was being sacrificed. The burnt offering, though, was completely consumed by the fire.

God wants us to die to our flesh, burn it up completely on the altar of our love for His Son. He wants to smell the sweet smelling aroma of our life wholly given over to Him: total abandonment, total repentance, and total surrender.

You're right. You're a sinner. You're not worthy. God agrees with you. It's a good thing it isn't about that.

Gossiping About Other's Sin

Precept: Gossip is sin, and it destroys. People's lives are cursed when they do it, and people around them are cursed as well.

Read Genesis 9:20-27

Illustration: Do you find yourself talking about other people's sin? I know you know that you're not supposed to do that, but do you know how strongly God feels about it? Here's Noah again, after the flood.

Noah got drunk. Here's the upstanding, righteous man Noah, the only man on the entire face of the planet who was worthy to be saved. His family was saved because of their relationship to Him. There's nothing there that speaks of their righteousness — just Noah's. And now he's drunk and naked.

Do you know of any good, supposedly upstanding, righteous Christian people who have gotten caught in a terrible sin? How did you react to them? What did you do? What did you say to others about them? Reflect on that for a minute.

Now look at what Ham, Noah's son, did.

"Ham, the father of Canaan, saw the nakedness of his father, and told his two brothers outside."

Now, we don't know if he went, "Wow — guess what guys!" or if it was a reverential concern and asking for help. The text doesn't say. It just says that he told them.

So what did they do? They went in backward so as not to disrespect him by looking at him. They held a blanket between their shoulders to prevent anyone else from seeing him, and covered his nakedness with blanket.

When he awoke, somehow he knew what Ham had done. He knew Ham had looked at him, and he knew Ham had told, so he cursed Ham, right? Wrong. He cursed Canaan, Ham's son. Ham's son was cursed because of what Ham had done. You want to hurt someone? Hurt their children. Just ask God.

When we gossip, we need to know that it not only affects the one about whom we are gossiping, but it affects those to whom we are gossiping, and it affects our children, as well. Whether we like it or not, our children are cursed — maybe not directly by God — but cursed nonetheless. If we believe gossiping is appropriate and acceptable, our children will learn from us, and live what they learn. We do it, then they do it, and everyone gets burned.

So what did Ham do wrong? Rather than do whatever he could to cover his father's sin, he looked, and he talked. Even if he couldn't cover it alone in this case, the brothers proved that the *most* he would have had to do is tell one of them. But he told them both. That speaks to his heart. He wanted to be *in the know*. He wanted to be the guy with the scoop. He wanted to make himself look bigger by making Dad look foolish to the brothers. This was either a big joke, or a big opportunity to be 'one with the boys' as he *knew* something they might want to know.

It was gossip, pure and simple. There was nothing positive about it, and nothing loving. The Apostle Peter says that, "Love covers a multitude of sins" (1 Peter 4:8). This was pure gossip, and his son got cursed.

Lesson: Do you find yourself talking about other people's sin? About other people's troubles? About other people's *anything*? Understand that if you're talking, then that's your clue that you need to be doing. If you can't *do* anything, then talking about it won't help, either. It's just gossip.

So how does this apply to mental health? It's about maturity, purpose, contentment. If you're worried about what's going on in other people's lives, but can't do anything to help them, then that speaks of a heart that needs to be distracted from its own life. If you're a gossip, then what you *really* need to do is look inside and see what hurts and why you need to be distracted from it.

Contentment says, "I wish everyone else well, too." Gossip says, "My life is terrible, so I need to focus on everyone else's terrible life to feel like my life isn't that different from theirs, and so it isn't really that bad."

If you're a gossip, let that be a red flag to you that there is something amiss in your own emotional life, and deal with it. You'll be much, much happier, more contented, and less of a gossip if you do.

Check yourself whenever you enter into a conversation. Ask God to bless your conversation and protect you from gossip. If you ask Jesus to join you in every conversation you have, you'll gossip a whole lot less. As I've said so many times, pray Him into the room with you. He is your best protection from gossip.

One Foot In The Church And One Foot In The World

Precept: God wants all of us, wholly dedicated in our hearts, to Him

Read Genesis 19:23-26

Illustration: When the Angel of the Lord told Lot and his family to leave Sodom (symbolic of the sinful world and our sinful pasts), he said, "Don't look back." In spite of the warning that the entire place was going to be destroyed, the angel had to literally drag Lot and the family out for their own safety. Lot's wife, who notably had no name, was so reluctant to go, so afraid she'd miss something, she couldn't stand it any more and in spite of the angel's command, she looked back.

You know the story. She turned into a pillar of salt. Gone. Wow. Pretty harsh.

So why did she turn into a pillar of salt??

Remember the section on 'exaggeration and emphasis?' I made the case that God is using the history of the Jews to make some very big points to us to get our attention in a very big way. This is one of those examples.

In verse 17, the Angel of the Lord said the following:

"Escape for your life! Do not look behind you, and do not stay anywhere in the valley; escape to the mountains, or you will be swept away."

That was an unambiguous warning to make your decision, make it in *not* be ambivalent. *Do not look back!* Her actions betrayed her heart. She *was* ambivalent, she *did* miss her old life, and she looked back.

Lesson: When we leave the world of sin, when we are liberated from that bondage, *don't look back*. God knows that we will have a certain tendency to *long* for the wrongful fun of the past, the bad company we may have kept, or the opportunities we used to have for making destructive choices. He wants us to know, in a *very big way*, that we can't have it both ways.

No question, Jesus wants us to come to Him 'just as we are.' We do not have to 'clean up our act' to give our lives to Him. He knows we're coming pre-packaged with our sin, our faults, our history, and our habits. He's not asking that we give everything up before we join Him in the Kingdom. He will help us work on those things in His timing, and He will be there to help us as we struggle and grow.

But what we do need to understand is this: Although we are going to be bringing a lot of junk with us into the Kingdom, we are not to look back with that *longing* that says, "I'm not sure I'm making the right decision. I sure wish I still had *that* in my life." If that's where you are, then you need to rethink your position. God doesn't want luke-warm love. He wants your whole heart, no regrets. If He doesn't have that, then you won't be obedient to Him. If you're not obedient, there's no way you can be content and at peace. You will have life-long insecurity, pain, and conflict. His insistence that you give it all to Him is His way of loving you.

I've had people tell me that they don't want to be Christians because then they'd have to give up the things they like to do. I tell them, "I can do anything I want! I'm totally free to act in any way I want, treat people any way I want, get away with anything I want. I've never experienced such liberation and freedom." The catch of course, is that having now left the old world and been re-born into a new life with the Holy Spirit living in my heart, I want very different things. And I really, really *want* those new things now. It's not fake, and it's not just obedience or self-discipline. It's truly the desire of my miraculously transformed heart.

This story shows you visually, with emphasis and exaggeration to make the point, that He wants your undivided attention. What kind of a point would it have made if her husband had said to her, "Now you know, wife, the Angel of the Lord said not to look back.

You probably shouldn't do that." Would that have gotten your attention? Would that have made the point?

A pillar of salt. I don't know about you, but that makes the point to me loud and clear. If I hear myself saying, "Wow, I remember when I used to…," I immediately decide if that 'used to' glorifies God or not. If it doesn't, I don't look back.

Idol Worship

Precept: "You shall have no other gods before Me. You shall not make for yourself an idol, or any likeness of what is in heaven above or on the earth beneath or in the water under the earth. You shall not worship them or serve them; for I, the Lord your God, am a jealous God… " (Exodus 20:4-5a)

Read Genesis 22:1-19

Illustration: Abraham and Sarah had Isaac when Abraham was 100 years old. They had longed for a son their entire lives, and God had never blessed them with one. Then, miraculously, He opened Sarah's womb, and when she was 90 years old, she bore Abraham a son.

Then some years later, God says, "Now I want him back."

What??! Did I hear you right, Lord?? But You said… You promised! Remember, "Father of a great nation??" How can I be a father of a great nation with no children, Lord!? I don't understand…

But of course, Abraham didn't say any of those things. He didn't need an explanation, and he didn't have to understand. He arose *early* the next morning and headed out to be obedient to God.

What was God up to? Why did He put Abraham through this test, only to stop him from killing the boy in the last moment?

Well, there are many valid answers to that question. The one we're going to focus on here, though, is the one that has to do with your mental health.

What we're talking about here is idol worship. Abraham had waited his entire adult life — possibly 80 years — for a son. God had told him 25 years before Isaac was born that He was going to give him one, but then he had to wait. Finally, finally, a son.

Now, given the circumstances, do you think Abraham might have been protective? Possessive, maybe? What about even deeper than that. Is it possible that Abraham *worshipped* Isaac?

God wasn't testing Abraham to see what he would do. It seemed like that, but that's not what it was. God knew exactly what Abraham would do. God sees the beginning and the end simultaneously. He knew he would be obedient. It wasn't about that.

Again, what it is really about is somewhat complicated having to do with current events as well as prophesy, but for this book, it's about idol-worship.

God wants to be God. Period. No ifs, ands, or buts. I believe Abraham did indeed worship his son, and because of that, God needed to do some work in him.

So, imagine walking up to the mountain with the knife in your hand and the wood tied to your son's back. What would have to be going on in your heart for you to be able to put one foot in front of the other. Sure, Abraham trusted God, and he knew he was going to be the father of a great nation, and he knew he was going to be obedient to God's commandment. He knew those things because he'd walked with God for many decades. He believed God, and he had learned through tough times to trust God.

But what about Abraham's love for the boy? Did that change, step by step? One step, then the next, brought him closer and closer to putting a dagger in his son's chest and a torch to the wood.

Was there a point at which Abraham 'let go' of him internally? Was there a point at which Abraham said, "I have to disconnect somewhat emotionally or I'll never be able to go through with it." Was there a point at which he said, on some level, "Ok, God. You're God and Isaac is not."

I submit to you that Abraham made this cataclysmic transition at the point at which he raised the knife. At that point, Abraham put God utterly and completely back in charge. There was no more worshipping the boy. Abraham had to choose, and he chose God. God was Abraham's God, and Isaac was *God's* son.

Lesson: Do you have an Isaac in your life? Do you have something that competes with God for your attention? Your affection? Your loyalty?

How about your spouse? How about your children? Your job, power, money? What about your ministries? Or maybe a couple of less obvious ones. What about your depression? What about your bitterness and unforgiveness? Have they become gods and idols in your life?

Look at it this way: What do you spend your thought-life on? What do you spend your time and energy on? What do you spend your money on? What priorities do you have in your life? If God isn't your god, then who or what is?

God is a jealous God. That doesn't mean the same thing to Him that it means to you, though. It means that He is jealous *for* you — on your behalf. He knows that the very best thing for you is to put Him first in your life. Not your spouse, not your children, not your career. When He's God, you're happier, your family is happier, you're available to serve him, you're a better person, you're a better witness, and everyone wins.

Get rid of your "Isaacs." Give them all to God. If he wants you to have them back, he'll give them back to you. But you'll always know Who they *really* belong to. The fact is, they belong to Him whether you 'give' them to Him or not. You may as well acknowledge it and receive the peace it brings.

God is God, and that's the only way He will have it. He loves you that much.

Impulsive, Life-Altering Decisions

Precept: Make your life about God, not yourself and your wants.

Read Genesis 25:27-34

Illustration: Esau and Jacob were twin sons of Isaac and Rebekah. Esau was the older of the two, and as such, had a right to the firstborn's birthright, or double portion of the inheritance, as well as the father's blessing. That was a huge deal in those days. It often meant the difference between success and failure in life, between freedom and bondage.

Esau asks Jacob for a bowl of stew, claiming to be starving. Jacob says, "Sell me your birthright."

Esau says, "I'm going to starve to death anyway, so I may as well sell it. I swear."

So here we are in this story: Esau was hungry, so he sold his birthright to his younger brother for a bowl of stew. Jacob did indeed get the inheritance and the blessing.

When Esau realized what had happened, he wept bitterly, begging for a blessing from his father. This was not to be. There is only one blessing, and it was now Jacob's. This was an enormous mistake for Esau, one for which he paid dearly his entire life, and one for which Jacob suffered greatly for many years as well. The two brothers split up, Esau hated Jacob, Jacob ran for his life, and the family was split wide open.

So what was the big deal about the stew anyway? Was it worth it? Esau said he was starving, but was he? He had just been out in the field, and you can go for at least 30-40 days without food before you starve to death.

So what was really going on, then? Esau wanted what he wanted and he wanted it right now. He was spoiled. In that moment, he didn't care what it cost him. Instant gratification without the slightest concern for what the future consequences would be. Very poor judgment, snap decision, life-changing event — one from which there was no way back. No changing his mind, no do-overs.

What happened? In one moment, one poor decision, the need for instant gratification, he lost everything that was rightfully his. He lost his future.

Lesson: Some of our decisions are like that. Sometimes, we would like to take them back, but we just can't. No changing our minds. No do-overs.

Esau over-reacted to his desire for stew because he was hungry and saw it as "starving."

"I *love* him so much, I just *have to have him! I'll do anything to keep him.*" Then the baby's on the way, and college is out of the question.

"I am really mad at my parents right now, and I don't want to think about it. Let's get high." And on marijuana laced with PCP, you jump out of the moving car.

"Come on, let's race! What're you, chicken?" And the headlights that you thought were in the other lane, weren't.

Esau didn't stop and think. We often don't stop and think. Sometimes, those impulsive decisions have life-long, irreversible consequences. They did for Esau and his entire family: Will they for you?

My Faith Isn't Happening Fast Enough

Precept: Faith is grown over time. Work with Jesus, but give yourself grace.
Read Exodus 23:27-30
Illustration: This is where God is telling the Israelites how He is going to help them when they cross the Jordon River into Canaan, the land flowing with milk and honey in which they are going to set up their new nation.

At the time of the crossing, Canaan was filled with all sorts of other peoples. The Midianites, Canaanites, Amelekites, and tons of other "ites." But God promised the land to Israel.

So in verses 27 and 28, He's telling them how He is going to evict the nations before them. But then in verses 29 and 30, He says,

"I will not drive them out before you in a single year..."

And then tells them that the reason is because they couldn't handle it. They need to grow into the new land slowly.

"I will drive them out before you little by little, until you become fruitful and take possession of the land."

"Little by little." Let that phrase roll around in your head for just a minute.

God is telling them that this 'take-over' deal is a partnership. They have to become fruitful and *take possession* of the land, and as they do that work, He will drive out the enemy before them. They're a team, and God is going to drive the enemy out, but only little by little, to the extent that the Israelites become fruitful and 'take possession.'

Lesson: Be patient with yourself as you do this work. The biggest obstacle to mental health recovery is impatience. Work with God, be fruitful, go to war with the enemy, and know that as you do your part, God will continue to drive out the enemy before you, and you will get your Promised Land.

Ok, that's all great theology, but how does that work out in my life in a practical way?

For instance, let's say you have a mental health disorder. You're depressed and you're considering taking medication. But you hear yourself or others say, "Just trust Jesus and you'll feel better and you won't need medication." Or, "Why do I need to lean on therapists and drugs when I should be leaning on Jesus?"

Leaning on Jesus is certainly the goal. That's my passion, and that's what this book is all about. We also have to understand that the level of faith and trust that it would take for a person to never get depressed or need medication is the complete conquest of the Christian Promised Land. God is faithful, and He will continue to work on your faith as long as you continue to partner with Him, but He isn't likely to give it all to you in one big chuck.

He's going to do it little by little, as you work with Him, as you partner with Him, as you do your part. Be patient with yourself as you go to war with the enemy and take the Promised Land by storm. But also understand that there are rivers to cross and battles to be fought and until you've won a few more battles, you just might need a little help.

If you're depressed, be comforted. You're in good company: David was depressed; Elijah was depressed; Paul was depressed; Martin Luther was depressed; Charles H. Spurgeon was depressed; Abraham Lincoln was depressed; and many, many others as well. Jesus even said His soul was grieved to the point of death.

Give yourself a break. God could have annihilated the Israelites' enemies with a single swipe of His hand, but He chose not to. He wanted them to earn it by learning how to trust Him, lean on Him, and partner with Him. These are skills that would become invaluable in the centuries to come as they continued to fight battles and grow as a nation.

As He works with you in your current battles as you struggle to take the Promised Land, God will deliver your enemies to you, but He just might decide to do it "little by little." Be patient with Him, trust Him, and be patient with yourself.

Remember, the Apostle Paul said, "We comfort others as we are comforted by God." The implication is that there are times when we need to be comforted. If this is one of your times, then just know that there will come a time when you'll be on the other end of that comfort and you'll be comforting others. These are the times that you will lean on and learn from during those times.

Your pain, legitimate in the eyes of God, has purpose. Partner with God, get the help you need, and be patient as you work.

How Come *They*'re Blessed?! Haven't I Been A Good Christian?

Precept: God is sovereign and has the big picture that we don't have. He gives us what we need to fit into that big picture, but it isn't always what we want.

Read Psalm 73 in its entirety.

Illustration: We often get confused when we see unbelievers who are seemingly blessed by God with their lifestyles and His provision of them. The Bible tells us that the rain falls on the wicked as well as the good, which means that God doesn't discriminate when He brings the life-giving rain. Everyone benefits. But nonetheless, we are troubled when we struggle and they're endowed with wealth and comforts and good health and the like.

We get envious, and sometimes a little resentful.

Lesson: First of all, know you're in good company. Look at Asaph struggling with the same issue.

But then look how he resolves it in His mind. He says, " Until I came into the sanctuary of God; Then I perceived their end" (v 17). He recognizes that they will come to "their end," and that even with all of their possessions, they don't have what he has: God. We have to remember the same thing: We have Jesus. Whatever they have in terms of temporal worldly possessions pales in comparison to the wonder and glory of our greatest possession, our Lord.

The truth is that we need to pray for them. When people of the world fall, they fall hard. They don't have the hope we have. They don't have the assurance of their final destination that we have, so they have no choice but to make as much out of this world as they can. It's all they've got. Rather than be envious of them, my heart breaks for them.

When you see someone who doesn't know the Lord, but they have a wonderful home, a great job, a wonderful family, fabulous opportunities for fun and excitement, just remember their real plight is underneath. It's in their hearts.

Regardless of how much 'stuff' or privileges they have, they will never have what you have unless they give their hearts to the Lord. They will always have that 'empty place' that only He can fill. They will always know something is 'missing,' but won't have a clue what. Their eternal destination is separation from God. For many of them, the very reason they are so motivated to pursue success like that is because of that deeply penetrating empty hole in their soul. When life takes a dive, they will take a dive with it. They have no other choice.

Asaph knew that in spite of how it appears on the surface, we have something they can't comprehend.

When you see an unbeliever who appears more fortunate than you, weep for them, and pray for them.

Praising God In The Middle Of The Trial

Precept: Understand that God knows what you're going through, and He's still in control.

Read Jonah 1:17 - 2:1-10

Jonah had been asked to go to Nineveh to tell them that their destruction was at hand. Nineveh was an extremely evil and violent place, and Jonah had no intention of seeing them saved from God's wrath. He ran and was subsequently thrown into the sea.

"And the Lord appointed a great fish to swallow Jonah, and Jonah was in the stomach of the fish three days and three nights."

We read that and think, "how *horrible* to be in the belly of a great fish!" But Jonah was a dead man. He'd been thrown overboard in the middle of a raging sea, way too far from shore to swim back. But God had other plans for him. We think "swallowed," Jonah thought "rescued."

Jonah *could* have thought his situation had just gone from bad to worse. Drowning is one thing, but being fish-food is something else altogether. So what did Jonah pray?

"But You have brought up my life from the pit, O Lord my God."

Jonah was still in the belly of the fish! What did he mean, 'brought my life up from the pit'?

If I were in the belly of a fish, great or otherwise, I'm not sure that would have been my first thought. From my vantage point, Jonah was still *in* the pit!

But Jonah realized that God was God. Jonah knew that he had repented in his heart. He chose to trust God at this point, so he praised Him. From the belly of the great fish, Jonah praised God for what He had *already done*! Extraordinary.

What I see in this story is a man fully surrendered and submitted to God, whatever happens. The story doesn't give any indication that Jonah knew he would be spit onto dry land. He may or may not have, but it doesn't matter. No matter how this situation might seem on the outside, Jonah had surrendered to God, totally and absolutely, and it was all good.

"I have been expelled from Your sight. Nevertheless I will look again toward Your holy temple."

Jonah's heart was once again turned toward God. He had fully repented of his sin of rebellion, and could now again look toward and draw close to God. Jonah loved God and was willing to do whatever God wanted at this point. And He praised Him.

When you're in the middle of the belly of the great fish, where's your heart? Do you say, "fish food" or do you say, "rescued." Do you see God's bigger picture for your life, or are you mired in the here-and-now struggle?

Lesson: God has a plan for your life. The Scriptures say that over and over. You're a part of a much bigger plan that you could never see or understand. God's ways are higher than our ways. God wanted Nineveh saved and He chose Jonah to bring them that message. Jonah couldn't see the big picture, but through his trial, he came to trust God.

Trust God. I know sometimes that's hard when you feel like you're drowning or going from bad to worse, but God knows what He's doing, and He loves you a lot more than you love yourself. He knows what's going on in your life, and He's working it all out for good — for you, but more importantly, for Him. Jonah's life wasn't about him, and your life isn't about you. Your life has purpose in God's great plan, and it just may include some time in the deep, or even in the belly of a great fish. Rest in that, and praise God.

XX — TOPICAL EXAMPLES: NEW TESTAMENT

In this section, I present, in a very similar fashion as in the last chapter, how to learn specific lessons and concepts from the New Testament writings. Some of the concepts are the same as I presented in the Old Testament section because I wanted to give you a taste of the consistency of themes between the two Testaments of Scripture. This is an example of how the Bible is one book, not two, and not 66. As you see the same themes running throughout both Testaments, you will start to personalize the miraculous nature of Scripture more and more. These are just a very small sampling of the hundreds of examples where this is the case. My hope with this is to whet your appetite for more.

You may also recognize some repetition from some of the teaching chapters earlier in the book. Again, I believe repetition helps drive home a point, and I also wanted to let these three Examples chapters stand on their own to some extent. I am trying to make this book easy to read, easy to reference, and a good learning tool. Some occasional repetition facilitates that goal.

So here we go.

I Feel So Guilty About What I've Done In The Past

Precept: Guilt feeds into the devil's plan for your life. God wants to set you free from this guilt.

Read Philippians 3:7-14.

Illustration: Paul is describing his life as a Jew in the passage immediately preceding the one referenced. In it, he is telling the Philippians what a great Jew he was and about all of his accomplishments. Then he says, 'but it's all a total waste, and I have given up everything for Christ.'

He goes on to say that the way he has been able to do that, is to focus on the future, not on the past. "One thing I do," Paul says, "forgetting what lies behind, I press on..." Paul sees the 'upward call in Christ Jesus' in his sights, and he isn't going to allow himself to be distracted by anything.

Lesson: I press on. Get that phrase locked into your brain. "I press on."

You may have heard the phrase, "Go for the brass ring." It is referring to javelin training where the horseman has a very long spear, and racing down a track, he tries to spear a small brass ring hanging on a rope at the end of the track. If he succeeds in getting his javelin through the brass ring, he wins the big prize.

Now, imagine this horseman racing down the track, and see him repeatedly turning his head to look back to where he just came from, twisting his body to strain to see behind. What do you think the probability is that he will hit the brass ring? If you said, "Zip," I'd agree with you. He keeps taking his eyes off of the ring, and therefore the prize. He has no hope.

Now of course, Paul's writings are talking about his accomplishments, and for you who have accomplished much, these verses are for you, too. But this section is about guilt, and it works just as well for that. Guilt is Satan's weapon against you. As long as he can keep you looking back and wracked with guilt, he knows you'll never hit the brass ring of your upward call in Christ Jesus. He has won. The more you "press on," the more you will be in God's game plan, and fulfilling your purpose on earth. That's the last thing Satan wants, so he will use whatever means at his disposal to ruin your life - including your guilt.

Paul imprisoned, tortured, and killed Christians just because they were Christians for his own personal political gain. He had a lot to feel guilty for. But it didn't matter. He had a job to do and the devil wasn't going to stop him.

God has a plan for your life. Paul is calling it, "the upward call in Christ Jesus." Your guilt is one of your worst enemies in fulfilling that plan. Satan will always tell you, "Yeah, but look what you did? What if they find out about your past? You know you're the only person that ever did that, don't you? You know *these* people wouldn't do something like that. They're *righteous*!" The last thing Satan wants is for you to focus on your 'brass ring,' so he will distract you with whatever tools he has.

I heard someone once say, "When Satan reminds you of your past, just remind him of his future."

God wants to set you free. Romans 8:1 says, "...there is now no condemnation for those who are in Christ Jesus." Keep your eye on the brass ring of your calling, and don't give the devil dominion over your thoughts.

Let your past be in the past, and just press on.

I've Been Such A Sinner, God Could Never Forgive And Save Me!

Precept: God is forgiving and loving and desires a relationship with you. There's nothing you've done or could do that's so big that He can't love you and use you.

Read Matthew 1:1-16.

Illustration 1: If the above fear reflects your heart, then you're in very good company.

Matthew Chapter 1 is a very boring genealogy: the infamous list of "begats" that we hear so much about in the Bible and hate to read.

But there's something different about this one. There are actually four women in that list. That's absolutely *unheard* of in Jewish genealogies. Genealogies are to show the *male* line of descent. Women didn't count enough to be listed, so they never were.

But here we are in the first chapter of the first book of the New Testament, the genealogy of Jesus Christ, and we find four women.

Extraordinary. That was the first clue to the people of Israel that something big was changing in the way women were to be regarded.

But wait — there's more. Guess what kind of women these were? You guessed it — sinners.

The four women are Tamar, Rahab, Ruth, and Bathsheba.

Tamar was the daughter-in-law of Judah, the father of one of the twelve tribes of Israel. But look at verse 3 again. It says that Perez and Zerah were born to Judah and Tamar. How can that be if she is his daughter-in-law?

When Tamar's two prior husbands (Judah's two eldest sons) died, one after the other, Judah promised his third son to Tamar when he came of age to be her husband.[45] Many years later, long after he'd come of age and Judah had gone back on his promise to her, Tamar decided she couldn't wait any longer. She dressed up as a prostitute and seduced Judah into having relations with her. Perez and Zerah were born of that union, and Perez, the child of a make-believe prostitute and a deceiver, became an ancestor of Jesus.

Rahab was a prostitute who lived in Jericho. When Joshua and the Israelites went across the Jordon River to spy out Canaan, Jericho was their first stop. Rahab had heard what Israel's God had done for Israel and so believed in the one true God. Because of that, she hid the spies of Joshua when her town's people came to find them, and she lied about their whereabouts. In spite of her lie and extremely sinful past, God blessed her and her family by saving them in the annihilation of Jericho, and including her in the genealogy of our Lord.

Ruth was the daughter-in-law of Naomi. Ruth was a Moabitess, a member of the people called the Moabites. They worshipped false idols and were enemies of the state of Israel. The enemies of Israel were her people. She left them to be loyal to Naomi, a Jew, after all of the men in their family died, and God blessed her by taking care of her physical needs and made her an ancestor of Jesus.

Bathsheba was an adulteress and had an affair with King David. It is true that King David had one of his men bring her to him, but God doesn't say, "Thou shall not commit adultery unless it is with the King at his command." Adultery is adultery. We are to be obedient to God first and foremost, and then to the authorities in our lives after that. There's nothing in Scripture to indicate she objected or resisted, but whether she did or not, she conceived a child through David.

Then, to cover up the affair, David had her husband murdered. David and Bathsheba lost the first child, but they were later married and were blessed with Solomon, the son of an adulteress and a murderer, who is in the genealogy of Jesus in Matthew.

Lesson: That's an amazing list of women. If you see yourself as a 'sinner' and that leaves you feeling unworthy of the love of Christ, then please understand that God honored each of these women, not because they were righteous in their own right, but because they overcame extreme obstacles and came to love and honor God as their God. And to make sure we didn't miss it, He included them in the first chapter of the first book in His New Covenant that would change the world forever.

Be uplifted, and let God love you, fellow sinner.

Illustration 2:
Read 1 Timothy 1:12-16, Acts 26:9-18
Both of these sections are the Apostle Paul talking about his life before he became a Christian on the Road to Damascus.

> "...formerly a blasphemer and a persecutor and a violent aggressor."
> "...I had to do many things hostile to the name of Jesus of Nazareth."
> "...not only did I lock up many of the saints in prisons... but also when they were being put to death I cast my vote against them."
> "...force them to blaspheme..."

Lesson: Wow. That's some pretty bad stuff. Did you ever murder someone for being a Christian? Have you ever forced someone to blaspheme, condemning their soul to hell?

Paul describes himself in Timothy as the "foremost of all" sinners. He wrote that under the inspiration of the Holy Spirit, which means it's the way he really, honestly saw himself. The Holy Spirit inspired those words, and the Holy Spirit is incapable of lying.

God brought him into His kingdom specifically *because* he had done all of those things. Why would He do that? Because God wants you to know that there is no sin on the face of the planet so severe as to be beyond His ability to forgive. As the worse sinner of all, Paul is an example of the kind of love and grace that God has. What God wants you to hear is, "If I'll save Paul, I'll save you."

I'm A Christian, But I Keep On Sinning! Surely God Will Condemn Me *Now*!

Precept: We are all sinners, and we all sin. God will keep on forgiving us and working with us to help us, however weak we are in our sinful flesh, as long as we are submitted and surrendered to Him.

Read Matthew 5:6, Romans 7:14 through 8:2

Illustration 1: We often *hear* Matthew 5:6 as "blessed are those **who are righteous,** for God will love them."

Is that the way you receive that? Is that what you've been taught? Is that the practical application of that verse in your heart? But that's not what it says at all. It says:

"blessed are those who **hunger and thirst...**"

The emphasis is on the hungering and thirsting. That's what blesses Jesus, and if that's your heart, if you hunger and thirst for things of God, if you hunger and thirst to be righteous in God's eyes, then you are blessed. Why?

"...because they shall be satisfied."

Satisfied. That sounds good. You want that. But just how will you be satisfied just because you 'hunger and thirst?' What does a deer do when it's thirsting? It finds a source of water. What does a bear do when it hungers? It seeks out a river filled with salmon.

If you're hungering and thirsting, then you'll just naturally go where the food and water are. Jesus said, "I am the bread of life," and "He who drinks the water I provide will never thirst."

Jesus doesn't require righteousness, although that is certainly the journey we're on. He knows we're a work in progress, but if we're not hungering and thirsting, then the seeking has stopped and we'll perish. If we *are*, however, then we will be satisfied through Him and His Word, and we will be blessed.

What about the Romans verses? When the Apostle Paul wrote those words, he had been a Christ follower for over 20 years. Look at how he describes himself. He is being very clear that he is still a sinner. This is not him recounting history. These are current events. What he wants to do he does not do, and what he doesn't want to do he can't stop himself from doing. "Oh wretched man that I am!" he exclaims. Does that describe the way you see yourself?

Then, in 8:1, he says, "Ah, all of that is true, but guess what? Through the blood of Jesus, there is no more condemnation." If you see yourself as a sinner and you hate it, then Romans 8:1 is your verse. As a matter of fact, read all of Romans Chapter 8. It's a miracle of grace.

Lesson: Yes, mourn for your sin and work toward righteousness, but be refreshed through the salvation Jesus brings with the blood of the cross. He paid the price for your sins — past, present, and future — and what He really wants from you is not your works or your inadequate righteousness: He wants your hungering and thirsting for Him. Get into the Word, bless God, and be blessed by Him.

I've Rejected God. He'll Never Take Me Back.

Precept: You've sinned, terribly. You've rejected Him and taken the opportunities He's given you and squandered them. But when you want to come back to Him and have a truly repentant heart, He will *run* to meet you and throw a party.

Read Luke 15:11-24

Illustration: Remember that the stories Jesus tells have spiritual meaning in addition to the practical application here on earth. This story is about God and how He feels about his 'sons,' no matter how they behave.

Many people see this as a story of an unsaved man coming to a place of salvation, and it certainly works for that. But I submit it works just as well for a 'backslidden' Christian. Consider this:

Nowhere in Scripture are unbelievers referred to as 'sons.' Also, nowhere in Scripture does it imply that unbelievers receive or have a right to an inheritance of any kind. No question it applies to the initial moment of repentance and salvation, but I believe it also applies to the rest of us who walk away from God for a season.

Note a couple of things here. At the end of his rebellion, the son had gotten to the absolute bottom of the pit for a Jew: feeding pigs. Unimaginable. Sometimes we need to be there to really see ourselves clearly. Once he was there, though, and could see what a state he was in, did he say, "I know. Dad's a good man. He'll take me back. I'll just apologize and I'm in. He'll forgive me."

He didn't say that or anything like that. He said, "Father, I have sinned against Heaven and against you. I'm not worthy to be called your son, and you can treat me any way you want. I have no excuses, no blame-shifting, no explanation of any kind. I am totally under your authority and I will accept whatever punishment you feel is appropriate, including becoming one of your slaves" (paraphrased).

I love the father's response to this: none. He didn't give him one. He didn't even give the comment the dignity of a reply. He simply ignored the plea, embraced him, kissed him repeatedly, restored him to full son-ship, and threw a party.

Note one other thing as well: Before the son made it home, when he was still "a long way off," his father saw him. Now remember that his son had been gone a long time, and the father would have had to have gotten on with his life. He had another son to deal with; he had a farm to tend to. Life goes on even when things happen we don't like.

So why was he able to see him from a long way off? Because he never stopped looking. He never stopped waiting. He never stopped hoping his son would return. That's God's heart.

Lesson: God wants you to be His own, whether you've never given your life to him at all, or you've strayed far from the path. Just repent, way down deep inside where your love and fear of God have died, and let God resurrect you to a fully restored relationship with Him. Come back, and the angels in heaven will rejoice and throw a party in your name.

I Suffer From Anxiety

Precept: Worry and anxiety are pain in advance. They're not God's best for us.
Read Matthew 6:25-34, Philippians 4:4-8
Lesson: This is another example of why really, truly *believing* that the Bible is the inerrant, perfect, personally authored Word of God is so terribly critical. Without that deeply-held conviction, the above passages make no sense.

There is *peace* in those words, if you believe that God is God and they come from Him.

Do you worry? Do you feel the anxiety of the day? You're not alone. The world is filled with people scurrying around filled with dread and anxiety and worry.

But does that make it a good thing? Does it make it Godly? Of course not. It breaks His heart.

But to allow the words of this section of Scripture to change your heart, you need to totally believe that God wrote them, not some old gray-haired guy who might have written Jesus' and Paul's words down wrong, or inserted their own thoughts into the mix.

Knowing that the Bible is the actual, inspired Word of God can only come through many hours of reading it. There's no other way. You have to read and read and read and read and read. Remember to visit with Jesus there and pray Him into the room. *Read every day*, even if it's just for a little bit. Even if it's just a single verse. Talk with Him. The more you do that, the more it's going to sink deeper and deeper into your heart that it's His voice speaking directly to your heart.

Remember that the miracle of Scripture is that it's a Spirit-to-spirit communication. It isn't about head-knowledge. It isn't about your *thoughts* about it. It's between your spirit and His. Be patient with yourself and little by little, you'll get it. Little by little the light will come on. You can't force it, and you can't believe what you don't believe. You will never truly and deeply believe that God wrote the Bible because this book told you, your pastor told you, or anybody else in your life told you. But if you work the program, if you read every day, you'll know.

Eliminating anxiety isn't a quick fix, and just reading these passages sounds like more of an admonition than it does a real, practical help. But the point is to drive it into your heart through meditation, repetition, memorization, and application. Drive it in like a carpenter slamming a nail into a board. Stroke by stroke by stroke, the nail goes deeper and deeper into the board. Each time you recite these verses, you're driving them a little deeper into you heart.

The writer of Psalms said, "Your word I have treasured in my heart, That I may not sin against You" (Psalms 119:11). He knew what we need to know. Treasure God's word in your heart, and watch your heart learn to trust God and relax.

Now remember, though, if your anxiety is toxic and life-altering, please seek professional, medical, or therapeutic help. Not all anxiety is environmental. Sometimes it's physiological or could even be the result of some other medications you might be taking. There's no shame in getting help, and possibly even taking anxiety medication if that is what is called for. It doesn't mean you don't love God.

But whether you seek professional help or not, read these sections of Scripture every day, and as often throughout the day as you can. Write them down on an index card and carry them with you. Read them whenever you feel the anxiety creeping up. Memorize some or all of them if you can. Drink the beautiful words of God in. Swim in them. Make them yours.

Stay in the Word and let His healing message sink into your heart. Then the words of Jesus will heal you. Little by little, maybe, but please be patient with Him. Don't give up, and they'll heal you.

I Feel Distant From God

I actually covered this in Chapter 19, "Topical Examples: Old Testament," but I'm putting it here as well to include this wonderful

New Testament illustration. You can refer back to the Old Testament one as a refresher if you'd like.

Precept: God wants to be close to us, but He won't force himself into your heart.

Feeling distant from God is, of course, a serious mental health issue. If you feel distant from God, then you feel alone, unprotected, unloved, lost.

But if you're a Christian, then the likelihood is that there was a time when you were close to Him. So what happened? This story illustrates what can happen.

Read Matthew 8:28 - 9:1, James 4:8a

Illustration: Jesus came to the country of the Gadarenes and healed two terrifying and violent demon-possessed men. The people of the town came out, and were so frightened — not of the demon-possessed men — but of the power that Jesus showed in healing them. They didn't understand and were frightened. So what did they do? They evicted Him. They asked Him to leave.

And what did He do? He left. Jesus is a gentleman. He will stay where He's welcome and wanted, but He'll leave if He's not.

Lesson: If you're feeling distant from God, is there a possibility that you subtly asked Him to leave? Of course you would never consciously do that, but is there a possibility that you are in sin and would rather He didn't watch? Is there a possibility that you've become distracted by the world and you don't have time for Him? Is it possible that His presence makes you uncomfortable for some reason?

Jesus knows your heart. If on some level, you'd rather He not be too close right now, He'll honor that desire and not force His way in.

If you're feeling distant, the best way to get back into that warm, peace-filled relationship with Him is to get back into His Word daily, pray without ceasing, re-engage in church, worship with abandon, join a small group. And ask Him if there's anything in your life that you need to evict, and be willing to evict it if He says 'yes.' Draw close to Him again and He will draw close to you.

My Marriage Is Terrible.

Boy, I resisted putting this in here, but I guess I have to. First of all, I'm not a marriage counselor so I have no confidence in my ability to tell you how to fix your marriage. If your marriage is in trouble, you and your spouse should seek professional help from a certified Christian marriage counselor who will bring Christ into the center. Be aware that it must be a Christian. The secular world's perspective on marriage is totally wrong, and doesn't honor God as being at the center of the marriage.

Now, having stated my disclaimer, I guess I do have a few words to offer.

Here are the passages I take people to for marriage issues:

- Ephesians 5:18-33
- 1 Peter 2:17 - 3:15
- Colossians 3:18-21

Let me caution you here. First of all, this is *impossible* without the indwelling of and submission to the Holy Spirit. If you try to pull this off in your own strength, you will fail, your marriage will get worse, and your resentments will grow out of control. If Jesus and the Holy Spirit are not the center of your world and the source of your motivation, then you must pray for that to happen first, and make that a priority in your life.

Second, most people read those passages and miss the big points. Husbands say, "SEE!? You're supposed to be *subject to me!*" and wives say, "Yeah, but you're supposed to love me the way Christ loved the Church, and He *died* for the church! I don't see you dying for me, so I don't have to be subject to you!"

Ok, my friends, let's look at the rest of those passages and see why both of these perspectives are totally wrong.

First of all, it says, "be subject to one another," men. Conveniently, a lot of men seem to skip over that part. It also says that husbands are to live with their wives with understanding, to show her honor, regard her as a fellow heir <u>so your prayers are not hindered</u>! That's pretty heavy duty, gentlemen.

Then it says, *all* are to be harmonious, sympathetic, brotherly, kindhearted, and humble in spirit; not returning evil for evil or insult for insult. You are to keep your tongue from evil and your lips from speaking deceit, turn away from evil, do good, seek peace and pursue it.

Remember that your goal, as husband of the family, is to emulate Jesus. Jesus was a servant-leader, not a tyrant.

The Colossians passage says, "Husbands, love your wives and do not be embittered against them." In my practice, I've seen Christian husbands who are demagogues, ordering their wives around, controlling what they do, being demanding and demeaning, yelling often, all under the banner of "you need to be subject to me," and they wonder why their wives are depressed and angry.

Husbands, be honest with yourself now. Do these verses describe you? Pray to God that your eyes be opened to what He sees in you.

Now wives, although the above verses are your husband's responsibility as much as they are yours, God *did* say we are to be subject to him. It doesn't say, "if he's a good man, respects you back, is kindhearted and humble in spirit." It doesn't give you any "ifs" at all. It just says be subject, respect him, be gentle and quiet in your spirit. He is responsible to God for how the marriage and the family operate, but you are responsible to God for doing your part.

As I said early in this book, this is the key: *No husband can be the leader of his family without his wife's permission.* To make it work, you must be a team. To be a team, there *must* be a team leader. God has chosen your husband for that role, but you must cooperate with God by being subject to your husband's authority, and giving him your permission and your blessing, even your encouragement, to lead.

Allowing your husband to be the team leader means that you will honor and support any final decisions that are made regarding the family. He cannot ask you to sin, and if he does, you *must* refuse. Refer to the story of Ananias and Saphira in Acts for Scriptural backing for that. It doesn't mean you don't have a voice, and it doesn't mean you have to be a namby-pamby, house-mouse doormat. Speak your mind clearly and respectfully, as a Vice-President would to his President, not as a slave would to a master.

Therapy with God

Husbands, regard your wife as your Vice-President rather than your slave, and she will respond in ways you cannot possibly imagine. Ask her advice. Respect her opinion. Give her some control. Give her freedom within the bounds of the marriage covenant. Trust her and trust that God will guide her. Don't treat her like one of your children. She isn't — she's your gift from God. You must treat her that way. Peter says to treat her as if she was a "weaker vessel." That means to treat her like a precious, easily broken vase in your hands. Lead, yes, but treat her with gentle kindness, not oppression.

Remember though wife, your husband is responsible for the family, and must have the final say. He <u>must</u> confer with you to be obedient to God's heart, but in the end, if you don't agree, the final decision is his, and you must honor and respect that decision, and do what you can to ensure the decision's success, even if you don't agree. That is what God is asking of us.

Now, let me say here that when I first read that section, I said, "What!!??" I'm a woman of the 80's mind you. I was all liberated and educated and earned my own money and could use an electric saw and all, and the *last* thing I needed was some man telling me what to do. And to make it even worse, *I'm older than him!* I really wrestled with it. It was my biggest stumbling block as a new Christian. However, God is my God, and He said that's what I must do, so after a bit more deep-breathing and wrestling with God, that's what I did. Ugh.

It took some time for it to become natural. At first, it was out of pure obedience to God, and I have to tell you, it felt humiliating. After a while, though, I could really feel my husband starting to respond to my gentler and quieter heart. Over time, our previously-difficult marriage became one of great communication, cooperation, peace, and love. My respectful submission to his God-given authority with a "gentle and quiet spirit" has opened the path for him to be the "servant leader" God wants him to be. I'm much more at peace, and I have come to deeply appreciate the great wisdom of the hierarchy God has set up. It was a huge struggle for me initially, and I still have a way to go, but in the end, God was right again.

But what if your husband is just an oppressor or a demagogue? What do you do then?

Note: Please be assured that this passage is not referring to the emotionally abusive, controlling, oppressive, isolating husband or wife. If that describes your situation, spend some time on-line educating yourself as to what emotional abuse is and see if it applies to you. If you believe it does, see your pastor. Get help from a good Christian Counselor who understands emotional abuse. Many church leaders, and even many Christian Counselors don't, so be discerning and hunt around. Let them read what you are reading and educate them. Get help, because that environment does not honor God, and it will kill your spirit and your marriage. Jesus asked you to be His witness. You need your spirit and your marriage intact to do that. Get help.

But I do want to spend some time discussing the tamer version of the demagogue for a minute. I'm going to discuss this issue using the husband as the example of the oppressive spouse because that's typically the case. Let me assure you, though, that women can be oppressors just as easily. Women, if you are the tyrant, please know that it is not okay, it is not God's will, and you will be held accountable before Him. Whoever the oppressive spouse is, please understand you have work to do, and you need help to do that work. Get help.

Ok, then, we are talking about the spouse who doesn't mean to be mean or a tyrant, but he is. He doesn't have a clue how to love his wife, and he has taken this "be subject to me" thing just a little too far. Let me reiterate: You, oppressed one, *must* have a solid relationship with Christ to survive this. Work diligently on that as your first line of defense. Men, read *Wild at Heart* by John Eldridge, and women read *Captivating* by John and Staci Eldridge, for practical guidance on making that work for you. And then swap them and read each other's.

So the point, and the solution to this problem, is to bring Jesus directly into the center of your marriage in a big, big way. To help you see this visually, imagine a large triangle on the white-board in your mind. See "Jesus" written at the top corner of the triangle, put the husband's name on the lower left, and the wife's name on the lower right. As you, husband, "look" at your wife, and you, wife, "look" at your husband from your perspective corners, you are as far from each other as you can be. As you see each other through your own eyes, as you focus on each other's characteristics, you will see the negative more and more, and you will feel a separation. But now visualize each of you looking up the triangle toward Jesus. As you each move up that triangle toward Jesus, drawing closer and closer to Him, look at what happens to the distance between you on the triangle. As you each draw closer to Christ, and become more and more obedient to him, you also, almost without realizing it, draw closer to each other as well. As you move closer to Jesus, you will start to see each other through His eyes rather than your own. Before you know it, the two have become one with Jesus at the center.

They key is, each of you must stay focused on Jesus and your obedience to Him, not on each other, and not on yourself.

Now, let me caution you. Don't let this become just another way of beating up your spouse. "I'm reading the Bible every day and going to church, but *he* isn't!" "I'm trying to be the servant leader Christ asks me to be, but *she* isn't following me!" Remember that those comments are still you each looking toward each other and not toward Christ. The key is to focus. Focus on the work He is doing in *you and you alone*. Give the Holy Spirit a chance to work in your spouse as they see the changes happening in you.

The referenced passage in 1 Peter says that if your husband is being disobedient to the word, your chaste and respectful behavior will win him "without a word." That works both ways, men.

> Romans 12:20 says, "If your enemy is hungry, feed him, and if he is thirsty, give him a drink; for in so doing you will heap burning coals on his head."

That means that if you are doing the right thing and your spouse isn't, your Godly behavior will give the Holy Spirit the opportunity to speak to his spirit and convict him of his sin against God and against you.

Lean on Christ and He will give you the strength to carry out this seemingly impossible task. Let Him fill you up so you'll have strength and love to overflow onto others, including your 'hard to love' spouse. The first 17 chapters of this book showed you how you can do that.

Husband, help your wife with this. Again, Christ was a *servant* leader. He washed his disciples' feet and loved them by spending time with them, instructing them, listening to them, and dying for them. When was the last time you washed your wife's feet, figuratively or literally? When was the last time you died to something you wanted to do to spend time with her and serve her, and just show her that you love her and she's worth it? You say you don't love your wife? Go back and re-read the section on agape love. To lead your wife the way God intends, husband, you must love her with action, you must serve her, and you must die.

Both of you must remember that your life and your marriage aren't about you. It isn't about your comfort, and it isn't about your happiness. It's about God. Period.

Please understand that your marriage has a higher calling and a higher meaning than just two people living together and making babies. It has a higher calling than you being blessed by God with the 'perfect' spouse to be your companion in your adult life. Your marriage is actually a reflection, a mirror-image if you will, a 'first fruits experience' of the marriage of Christ and His bride — the church.

When God said that wives should be subject to their husbands, He wasn't just establishing a hierarchy that works on earth. He was demonstrating, in a physical, earth-bound example, the relationship that we as the church are to have with Christ, our Bridegroom. When God said, "Husbands love your wives the way Christ loved the church," He was giving us an opportunity to show the world the character and the love of Christ in a physical, practical way.

Our marriages are living, breathing examples of that beautiful relationship we have with Christ. You've heard people say, "It's not a religion — it's a relationship." Our marriage relationship says, "See? This is what that means."

You, husband or wife, have a very important responsibility to show the world that our relationship with Christ is indeed that — a relationship. It's decidedly *not* a religion, just as a marriage is so much more than just two people living together under a set of rules.

Without the relationship, it's just rules. He brings home the paycheck and she tends the children. Or she brings home the paycheck and he tends the children. Whatever. Just rules.

As is the case with marriage, Christianity is so deeply and profoundly more than that. Your marriage is the best example you have that that is true. View it as the 'first fruits' of the glory of the marriage of the church to Christ: the first little glimpse of the full glory of our relationship with Him.

So how does that play out in a practical way? Each of you has to learn how to die to your *self*. Agape love is that love of choice, remember? My agape love for you is a choice I've made to make it about you, not me. I'm not focused on you meeting *my* needs, I'm meeting yours. If each of you operates that way, then there will be no more fighting and no more self-defense. Peace, harmony, contentment.

"So what if one of us isn't operating that way?" you ask. Well, remember, if it is bad enough, get help. But regardless, lean on Jesus. He's the lover of your soul. He's the one who will lift you up when you feel beat down. He's the one who esteems you enough to die on the cross for you. He is the One who fills your love tank so you have plenty left over to fill others'.

Regardless of how wonderful your spouse is, they will never be able to fill all of your needs. In spite of what Tom Cruise's character Jerry Maguire says, your spouse will never complete you. Only Jesus Christ can do that. We let Hollywood convince us that if we don't have that 'complete me' love with our spouses, the marriage is second-rate, and possibly doomed. That's a lie straight from the pit of hell. Don't believe it. A poor marriage is Christ's greatest opportunity to show the world that He truly is a God of resurrection. Lash yourself to Him and let Him do His work.

"Ok, so exactly how do I do that? What does 'leaning on Him' really look like?" If you've read the rest of this book, you know the answer already. But for a memory jog, here it is again…

> Read Scripture daily, memorize and meditate on what you read, pray Him into the room, chat with Him without ceasing,

re-engage with the church, fellowship with other believers, find your purpose, serve.

Enter into that loving relationship with Jesus and you won't feel the loss of a poor marriage relationship so deeply. Know that regardless of how your spouse treats you, you always have Christ as your Bridegroom, your brother, your counselor, your friend. Spend time with Him daily, and He will fill that void. That's a promise.

If one of you takes the initiative and makes those changes, the other spouse can't *help* but to change in response. It's like the mobile over the child's bed. If one animal is pulled down, the entire structure swings and sways. It can't stop itself. Families are like that. The difference with families, though, is that as the movement slows down and eventually stops, it's in a whole new, and hopefully healthier, place. You start the process by changing, and your spouse will respond. It may never be perfect, but they just can't help but change in response. I've seen it over and over.

Lower your expectations of your spouse and get your fulfillment from Jesus Christ. Get into the Word and learn how God wants *you* to be in your marriage. Take a class on being a Godly wife or a Godly husband. Do your part, and God will be faithful to comfort you and bring you peace — and hopefully that peace and comfort will come in the form of your spouse coming around. If not, you still win with your obedience to and closer relationship with the Lord.

Remember that you are going to be held accountable for how you respond to and contribute to your marriage, not the success or failure of the marriage itself. You are accountable for your part, your spouse is responsible for theirs. God is watching, and so is everyone else.

The other promise from God is that He will use your difficult marriage in productive ways. God won't waste your pain. Refer back to Chapter 16, "Victory in Trials." God understands the pain you are experiencing. He knows what you're going through. Trust Him, cry out to Him, believe that He loves you. If your spouse is mired in sin, understand that they are accountable to God before they're accountable to you. Whether they are a believer or not, God is working in them. If there's something you can do, then do it. But once you've done what you can, turn it over to God and leave their dysfunction at the foot of the cross. Engage with Christ and see the work God will do in you through that trial.

Develop a very close relationship with Christ by including Him in everything you do. If you get into the pattern of chatting with Him, visiting with Him, reading your Bible with Him, and the rest of it, then His presence in your life will give you ever-increasing peace. I know there are times when you want Jesus to have skin on, and if that's an option for you, then please do that. Get out and engage. Get with family, friends, groups of like-minded people. If, for whatever reason, that's not an option for you, then just know He's there with you and for you, and He's ready to give you comfort through your two-way communication with Him through prayer and His Word.

Final note: Again, if you're in danger, physically or mentally, absolutely get help. Don't stick around and keep yourself or your children in harms way. Talk to your pastor, get legal protection, do what you need to do. Press charges for assault if you need to. Take care of yourself and your kids. If your spouse tends toward intimidation and violence, but they've never actually struck you, don't let that lead you into complacency. I've heard of women where that was the case, and the first time he struck her, he beat her to the point of near death. If your husband throws things, punches walls, shakes or pushes you, or screams violently, talk to your pastor, get out if you can, and get help, even if he's never actually hit you. A lot may be at stake.

Now that's not necessarily to say you should file for divorce. Leaving to get safe and let things settle down, and filing for divorce are two entirely different things. Please consult with your pastor about that as well before you make any rash or final decisions. Pray about it. Consult with Godly friends. God is a God of resurrection — even in your marriage and in the heart of your spouse. I've seen amazing miracles when Jesus was brought into the center of the marriage.

In the end, loving God *through* your marriage is the greatest blessing there is. Develop the strength and faith to be obedient by just *being* obedient and seeing what miracles God can do.

Where Is Jesus In My Situation?

Precept: Jesus is always aware of your situation, but might be waiting for you to cry out to Him for help.

Ever wonder where Jesus is in your situation? Do you ever feel alone — like He's just left you there to deal with it by yourself?

Read Mark 6:45-52

Illustration: Jesus had just miraculously fed 5,000 men (plus women and children) from just a few loaves of bread and a couple of fish. You would have thought His disciples would have understood the power of Christ by now and reached to Him for help, but they just strained at the oars. The phrase 'evening' means some time between sunset and midnight. The phrase 'fourth watch of the night' means somewhere between 3-6 am. So that means they had been fighting a raging storm for somewhere between 6-9 hours! So Jesus, seeing them straining at the oars, walked on water to them.

But wait — check out verse 48 again — the last phrase: "And He intended to do what?!"

Why would He *do* that! Couldn't He see that they needed help?

So what happened next? They cried out. They weren't even really crying out to ask the Son of God to help them. They were just crying out.

The text says that "immediately" He comforted them with His words, got into the boat, and the storm died down. While they were willing to "strain at the oars" in their own power, He was willing to let them. When they cried out, He was there.

Lesson: So how long do you wait before you cry out to Him? How long do you 'strain at the oars' alone?

We are trained in American culture to be 'fiercely independent,' and unfortunately, we are.

But Jesus is a gentleman. If you don't cry out to Him, He'll allow you to deal with it on your own and in your own way as long as you want. He won't force himself into your situation.

Learn from the incident of the loaves. Reflect on times in the past when He fed you from what seemed to be nothing. Cry out to Him, invite Him into your current situation, get into His Word, and lean on Him. He will calm your storm, one way or the other.

My Christian Walk Isn't What I'd Like It To Be

Precept: The world can be a huge distraction, keeping us from our walk with God.

Read Luke 8:4-15

Illustration: Do you sometimes look at yourself and wonder what happened? You used to be so 'on fire' for the Lord, and you've become lukewarm. Ministries have lost their appeal, you haven't been to a Bible study in months or longer, and your Christian friends don't even seem all that appealing any longer. Does that describe you?

Here again I want to refer to "The Parable of the Sower." In it, Jesus is describing several different kinds of soil and the effect of that soil on the seed that is thrown onto it. Graciously, He also explains to us exactly what each of them means in our own lives, so we don't need to guess.

I've heard this parable described different ways, but the most common is that the first three soils represent different kinds of unbelievers, and only the fourth kind is the true believer.

However, I find it to be a much more useful parable if you consider it in accordance with some other sermons I've heard on it. I prefer to think of it where only the first soil is the true unbeliever, and the others represent different types of walks with Christ.

They all have wonderful messages we can apply to our lives, but the one I'd like to focus on here is the third soil: the seed that fell among the thorns. In this case, the thorns choked out the seed and they produced no fruit to maturity.

Does that describe you? Are you not producing mature fruit right now? Have your ministries fallen by the wayside? Are you not discipling anyone, including yourself? Jesus wants you to know that there are thorns in your life, and they are choking the fruit right out of you. But what exactly are those 'thorns'?

"...worries and riches and pleasures of this life..."

Read that list again. Worries, and *riches*, and *pleasures*! Two out of the three elements on this list are *good things* in our modern culture! Riches and pleasures? What could be wrong with *that?* Jesus says plenty. If you're not very careful, they could be the very things that are choking the spiritual life right out of you, choking out your fruit, keeping you from serving Him, and keeping you from growing close to Him.

So what might they look like? Clearly worries will choke us. We have lots of worries in our lives, and to the extent we focus on them to try to resolve some problem in our life, we won't be able to focus on the Kingdom of God. We all know how that works.

But what about the riches and pleasures? How do they interfere with our fruit?

Let's just look at a couple of examples. Let's assume you have a big boat. One of those really expensive ones. You've earned the money, you tithe just like you're supposed to, so you didn't see anything wrong with having it. After all, the family loves it and it gives you a chance to spend time together. That's good, right?

Absolutely. But what if the message you give yourself is, "We have to spend time on the boat every weekend, otherwise we can't justify the money we spend every month. Why have it if we're not going to use it?"

What, then, if somebody from your church calls you and says they need you for a new ministry they're trying to start. You now have to choose. You've spent all this money on that boat, so you really need to use it, but here's this ministry opportunity. Conflict, confusion, there's a fork in the road and you must choose which direction you will take.

Or you have wealth — lots of it. You actually give more than a standard tithe to the church, so you feel good about that. But the wealth requires some management. You have to pay attention to your investments, you have to spend a lot of hours at work managing the projects you run. You're providing for your family, right? But when do you spend time in your Bible? When do you go to a good Bible study? Do you have any accountability partners? Are you involved and engaged with your Christian brothers and sisters? Do you sit with your family and study and pray with them?

You work very hard, but what Godly fruit do you have to show for all your efforts? God says that it's all going to burn up in the last days if it isn't about eternity. Is your life about eternity, or the temporal 'riches and pleasures?' These are very big questions you need to ask yourself.

Check yourself. Are you allowing the thorns to choke the Word of God out of you? Are your priorities straight? What do you spend time on? What do you think about?

Worries and riches and pleasures. Jesus wants you to know that they can kill your fruit.

Example Wrap-up

There are literally hundreds and hundreds of these kinds of personal application stories in Scripture. As you read, *become* each of the individuals in each of the stories and see if the Holy Spirit speaks to you through the characters and the situations.

The Bible is personal, it's powerful, it's transforming. Make it uniquely yours as God intended it to be. When you do, Jesus Christ will become the love and Lord of your life, your Greatest Counselor, your Comforter, and your Friend, and the Bible will indeed become for you the greatest mental health book on the face of the planet.

Intermission Verse to Ponder: "When you have eaten and are satisfied, you shall bless the LORD your God for the good land which He has given you. Beware that you do not forget the LORD your God by not keeping His commandments and His ordinances and His statutes which I am commanding you today; otherwise, when you have eaten and are satisfied, and have built good houses and lived in them, and when your herds and your flocks multiply, and your silver and gold multiply, and all that you have multiplies, then your heart will become proud and you will forget the LORD your God ..." (Deuteronomy 8:10-14).

SECTION 5

******

SUMMARY

XXI — SUMMARY

The Cheat-Sheet

My prayer is that you've learned something to help you fall in love with Jesus, and to help you apply Scripture to your life in a practical, transforming way. If not, that's okay. Just go back to the beginning of the book and start over! (Just kidding... Um, actually, no I'm not.)

So now that we've gotten through it all, I want to acknowledge that that's a lot of material to remember. I have a hard enough time remembering it all, and I wrote the thing. So what I want to do here is to summarize the essential elements of this book to refresh your memory, and to give you somewhere to turn when you're just trying to remember what on earth I said. This is your 'cheat-sheet,' so to speak.

The goal of this book was to help you fall in love with Jesus and to help you apply His precepts to your life. The Bible is, in fact, the ultimate mental health book, and to the extent you can apply it to your heart that way, you will see miraculous things happen. Trust Jesus, get on His shoulders, and take the most exhilarating ride of your lifetime.

Here, I will summarize the salient points of this book to allow you to reflect and refresh your memory.

> 1. **Be assured of your salvation** — Without the indwelling of the Holy Spirit and a solid relationship with God, none

of this will make sense to you, and it will be impossible to make it work.

2. **Find out what your Spiritual Gift is, and put it to use** — God says to "go and do" to get yourself out of your mental distress. Don't sit around waiting for mental health to come knocking on your door: Go out and *get* it.

3. **Spend time in your Bible daily** — Remember that it's a *love letter* from God. Read carefully and lovingly, meditate on it, pray about it, memorize it, and apply it to your life. *Become* the people in the stories and see them as videos in your head. Don't become legalistic, but 'hunger and thirst' to be obedient and kill off the sin in your life. Learn how to search for buried treasure in your Bible as you might for hidden silver or gold or precious jewels.

4. **Spend time with the Lord "without ceasing"** — In addition to your more formal prayer time, chat with him throughout the day as you live your life. Include Him in everything. Consult with Him routinely. Invite Him into the room.

5. **Remember the Old Testament** — The Old Testament isn't just a wonderful history of the Jewish people. It is, among many other things, a precious revelation from God to help us see visually what He is trying to teach us in the New Testament. Regard it as a critical first section of a single volume, not a separate, optional, history of the Jews that has limited applicability to your Christian walk. Find its jewels and treasures, and let it transform your life.

6. **Seek God-esteem, not self-esteem** — Remember that your life is the product of God's plans for you. Your history, your parents, your childhood are all a part of how God is preparing you to serve Him in His Kingdom — on earth and in heaven. When you feel yourself thinking negative thoughts about yourself, remember that you are a child of the living God, the Creator of the Universe. He *chose* you to be in His family. His promises apply to *you*. You are an inheritor alongside His Son. You are a prince or princess, the child of the King of Kings. You are His friend, His partner

for all of eternity. Don't ever forget that, and boot your self-esteem problem to the curb.

7. **Re-evaluate your perspective** — See this world and things of the world as temporal, fleeting, like sand through your fingers. See things of God as eternal. Remember that God's blessings are internal, not external. Keep the two straight. Ask yourself, "Is this of God or of the world?" and make your life focused on things of God. See the world through His eyes.

8. *Use* **your trials to help you grow** — Regard the difficulties and trials in your life as boot-camp and battles in the great spiritual battles Paul talks about. Grow through them, understand that God is not punishing you, and He's not the enemy. Let the enemy be the enemy in your life. Partner with God *through* your trials to defeat your enemy, in whatever form he comes, and make Satan powerless on earth. We are to storm the gates of hell, and you need training to win. Your trials are that training.

9. **Remember that your life isn't about you: It's about God** — Put your focus on honoring God, enriching His reputation to others around you, and glorify Him in all you do. Worship Him in your song, your praise, your prayers, your relationships, your work, your study of His Word. Keep Him at the center of *all* things.

10. **Remember that God wants you to succeed** — God has a purpose for your life. When you succeed at accomplishing your purpose, you serve His grand purpose for the body of Christ. If you are focused on *His* will rather than your own, He will give you the gifts, talents, history, support, and power to succeed. Work with Him, cooperate with Him, focus on Him, and be obedient to Him, and you are guaranteed to be a fantastic success. To do so, you will manifest His peace and thrill and wonder and glory in your heart and in your life.

11. **Remember the love and grace of God** — God is a God of love, grace, forgiveness. God is a God of resurrection, power, victory. God is a God of second chances. God is a

God of mercy. *Receive and share* that love and enter into His Promised Land of a grand and glorious relationship with Him.

12. Fall in love with Jesus — See Him as a *person* you can fall in love with, in addition to your God whom you love. Remember the differences between agape and phileo love and apply them to your relationship with Jesus. Let His love wash over you, refresh you, open your eyes and cleanse your heart, and let your relationship with Him bring you the love, joy, and peace you seek.

God bless you for getting to this point. You are a true champion and will achieve your goals of a new and exhilarating relationship with Christ. Your perseverance has brought you here, and your perseverance will take you to Him, as well. Congratulations. I am so proud of you I could burst.

Let me wrap up with this one final thought-gift: Recall the discussion of the word "treasure" where we defined blessings from God as "that deep, inner contentment, peace, complete satisfaction, and fullness in God." When you ask Jesus into your life and then experience His presence with you, side by side throughout your day, you experience that blessing. The more you think about Him, pray to Him, worship Him, give to Him, and love and obey Him, the more His presence will permeate through you, and the more you will receive His sublime blessing over your life. How much blessing you receive is completely up to you.

Think of your heart as a treasure chest with only so much room. The more you treasure Jesus and allow Him to fill your life, the less room you will have for focusing on things of the world. The more He increases to fill your heart, the more His love and light will fill you, and the less you will hunger for the comforts and hurt for the sorrows and trappings that bind you. The more He is part of your thought life, the less you will have the unrighteous and hurtful thoughts and desires, and the more you will feel blessed in His fullness. The more you walk with Jesus in your life, moment by moment and hour by hour, the more peace and joy on earth you will experience, and the more His light will shine in you and from you. As others see that light, they will be drawn to you, and will want what you have. God's blessings will flow from you and expand and grow through them. You will be building friendships in this life, and you will be "laying up treasure in Heaven."[50]

Let Him be your Therapist, your Wonderful Counselor, your ever-present Comforter, and your cherished Friend. Let Him guide you, fill you with His love, and set you free.

* * * * *

Please leave me an e-mail at sue@TherapyWithGod.com. I would love to hear how you've been able to apply this book to your life, and how your relationship with Christ has grown.

Note To Professionals And Counselors

My prayer is that you have been blessed by this book and that your practice will be enhanced by it, as well. In our profession, our first and foremost goal with our clients is termination. I have found in my practice that the more my clients allow me to use Scripture during sessions and the closer they draw to Jesus, the faster they get back on their feet and are able to terminate therapy. I pray that you find that to be the case, too.

As much as we'd love to work ourselves out of a job, we know that will never be the case. There will always be hurting people who need a hand up and some encouragement. I pray this book can be used as a resource to help you in that journey with your clients.

God bless all of you. May the peace of Our Lord Jesus Christ reign supreme in all your hearts, and may you be His witnesses throughout all the earth.

SECTION 6

****

APPENDICES

APPENDIX A — THE GOSPEL OF JESUS CHRIST

Heaven Is A Gift From God

Since a solid relationship with Jesus Christ is the best mental health therapy there is, I wanted to make sure that what that means is clear.

Consider these words from the Bible.

> Eph 2:8-9 "For by grace you have been saved through faith; and that not of yourselves, it is **the gift of God**; not as a result of works, so that no one may boast."
>
> Titus 3:4-7 "But when the kindness of God our Savior and His love for mankind appeared, He saved us, **not on the basis of deeds which we have done** in righteousness, but according to His mercy..."
>
> Romans 10:9 "...if you confess with your mouth Jesus as Lord, and believe in your heart that God raised Him from the dead, you will be saved."

It breaks my heart to hear people say, "I'm a good person," or "I hope I'm good enough to get into heaven."

If you hope your good deeds and your good life will ensure you will receive a place in heaven, then you need to know that God requires perfection (Psalms 5:4-6, and many, many others throughout Scripture). He requires absolute, total, life-long perfection. That means you can never have told a single lie, white or otherwise; never stolen even the slightest thing; never had a single evil thought or selfish motive; never coveted anything you didn't need. Nothing, ever. The Bible says that over and over. God can't be in the presence of sin, and He cannot look upon sin, and He's a perfect, righteous judge. If you have ever done any of those things or many more, then from God's perspective, you're wearing your sin as if it were a sweater you cannot ever take off. Because He can't look at sin and you're wearing that 'sweater,' He can't allow you in heaven. You may feel that's harsh or not fair, but it's just the way it is. Scripture is extremely clear on that, and God gets to make the rules.

The real reason that even the smallest sin condemns us is because, in reality, even the smallest sin is an outward expression of an inward problem. The problem is that from God's perspective, the sin means that we've rejected His authority in our life. If we make a decision to separate ourselves from God's authority, which then results in sin, then we have decided to live life outside the will and presence of God, and God is simply honoring that decision.

Throughout the Old Testament, the Jews sacrificed animals to pay the penalty for their sins. The animals were required to be "without defect."[46] Absolutely, totally and completely perfect. The Jews couldn't pay for their own sins because they weren't without defect. Even their own deaths wouldn't have been enough to save them from hell because to sacrifice something that is imperfect is unacceptable to God. The centuries of sacrifices commanded in the Old Testament were to get the Jews' hearts prepared for the concept of a substitutionary sacrifice. A substitutionary sacrifice is where something else can be substituted and sacrificed to pay for my sins, but that 'something' must be perfect.

The rules about sacrifices are God's way of telling us, through the Old Testament pictures, what He requires. You can't pay your own penalty for your sin because you're not perfect. You're not a "lamb without defect." I've never met anyone who described himself as perfect, and I know I'm sure not. We can't be. Nobody is. If it were up to our own efforts and goodness, we'd all be without hope.

But God knew that and gave us a way out. He gave us Jesus. Not Christianity — Jesus. Jesus died completely sin-free, perfect, as an acceptable sacrifice unto God to pay the price for our sins.

God sent His Son to die on the cross for us. Jesus was that perfect sacrifice, the "Lamb without defect" that was required for an acceptable offering to God. When He died, He said, "It is finished." What was finished? The total atonement for the sins of every man, woman, and child on the face of the planet who repent of their sins and give their lives to Him.

Remember that Christianity is not a religion. A religion is a set of rules, a way of living your life, a way of thinking. There are many, many religions of the world, but true Christianity isn't one of them. Christianity is a relationship — a wonderful, glorious relationship with the living Jesus, the Creator of the Universe, which transforms a life full of senseless pain, misery, and efforts to be a 'good person' to one of profound purpose and hope (Philippians 3:8; Ephesians 3:14-19).

Once we understand His sacrifice, and once we've received His salvation, then our efforts to 'do good' are borne out of our love affair with Him. They become our opportunity to show Him we love Him back. Rather than our attempt to earn His love or earn our way into heaven, they become our precious gift back to Him.

Many people will say they believe in Jesus, and they truly do, but let's think about that for a minute. Is that enough? Don't forget that Satan believes in Jesus. James 2:19 says, "...the demons also believe, and shudder." Satan *knows* that Jesus is the Son of God, the resurrected Messiah. He's met Him face-to-face in the physical and spiritual world. There must be a difference between our belief and his.

One of the differences is faith. Satan's belief doesn't require faith. He's actually seen Him, so he knows the truth. Faith is not a factor.

The other difference is submission and trust. When the Bible talks about believing in Jesus, the Greek word literally means "to totally trust as if dependent upon; to turn your ship in that direction." In the same context, you might 'believe in' a loving parent, a great coach, a best friend whom you know will 'be there' for you. It doesn't mean you believe that they exist — of course they exist. It means you put your eggs in that basket. You become vulnerable to them. They have the potential to hurt you, but you know they won't. You know they'll be there if you need them. You *Believe* (capital B) in them.

I heard a story once that illustrates that point. A man had ridden a bicycle balanced on a rope over the Grand Canyon many times and people had watched him do it. They loved the spectacle of it. He was standing on the side, ready to go again, and people were all excited. He looked at the crowd and said, "Do you believe I can do this?" They all cried, "Yes! Go!" and clapped. He said, "Are you sure?" as if to taunt them and spin them up. Again they cried "Yes, do it!" and applauded again. And then he said, "So who will get on my shoulders?"

Your belief means you will get on his shoulders and trust Him.

It also means that you choose to agree with Him. If He says it's sin, then it's sin, and your desire is not to do it. You mourn for your sin, you repent of it, and you ask Him for forgiveness for having done it. That means that you "turn the other direction," or make a conscious decision not to do it any more. That's not to imply that you won't slip up, but it means that it is your *intention* not to slip up again, and you ask the Holy Spirit to help you make that happen in your life.

Will you get on Jesus' shoulders and let Him carry you through life? Will you trust Him and agree with Him? That's the Gospel of Jesus Christ. If you will get on His shoulders, agree with Him, and *Believe* in Him, then you will spend life on earth as well as all of eternity in the company of the Creator of the universe. That's the Good News of Jesus Christ. That's as good as it gets, and it's a fabulous ride.

If you're ready to do this, look to Him and pray this prayer from your heart, and know that you mean it from the depths of your soul. Speak it directly to Him. He's listening, He's waiting, and He will *run* to embrace you.

> "Dear Jesus, I know I've sinned against you, and I'm sorry. Please forgive me for being disobedient and rebellious, for doing things my way and thinking I could earn my way into heaven. I thankfully receive Your sacrifice on the cross for me as the complete and absolute atonement for my sinful past. Please come in to my life and take it over. I give it to you. I trust you, and I want to be yours. Please save me."

If you prayed that prayer and truly meant it, then welcome to the Kingdom of God, Christian. You've just made a decision that will secure your place in eternity and will transform your life on earth (John 10:10). Please tell a fellow Christian of your decision, and get into a loving, Bible-believing and Jesus-loving church. Refer to Appendix B, "I'm a new Christian — Now what?"

If you can't pray that prayer quite yet but would like to believe, then pray the 'skeptics' prayer:

> "Ok, Jesus, I'm not sure I believe in You at all, and it almost feels silly to be praying. But if you're there, please let me know. I'm open to the possibility, but I'm just not ready to jump in. If you're there, let me know, and give me the faith to believe in You."

If you prayed that prayer, then I know that God will be faithful and will let you know He's there. When that happens, then come back here and pray the first prayer and join the Kingdom of God. I rejoice in your openness and what God is going to do through your life!

But My Sins Are Too Many

I've had people say to me that their sins are too many or too severe, and that God would *never* be able to forgive *their* sins.

Jesus addressed that issue specifically in two separate occasions. In the first one, a woman had come into him while he was eating lunch with a Pharisee,[47] Simon. The woman, a 'sinner,' which is a euphemism for prostitute, came in and poured expensive perfume on his feet, washed them with her tears, kissed them and wiped them with her hair. The Pharisee was horrified that a Rabbi would allow this sinful woman to touch him.

Jesus addressed the Pharisee by telling him a story of three men. A money-lender had lent 50 denarii[48] to one man and 500 denarii to another. When neither of them could repay him, he forgave both debts — wiping them completely off the books. Now which of the two men would love and appreciate him and his generosity more, Jesus asked? Of course the Pharisee knew the answer — the one who owed him more and was forgiven more.

> He then looked at the woman washing His feet and said, "He who has been forgiven much, loves much; but he who has been forgiven little, loves little."

Your sins, many and severe as they may be, are the *very* thing that will glorify God when you turn to Him. As you have been forgiven much, you will love much, and glorify God much.

If you've been a terrible, horrific sinner, then He wants you to know that you're the best witness He has. Come to Him and tell your story.

A second example Jesus gave was of two men praying: a Pharisee and a Tax Collector. The Pharisee was saying (paraphrased), "God, I sure am glad I'm not a sinner like this Tax Collector! I fast twice a week and give to the poor" (Luke 18:10-14). The Tax Collector, on the other hand, was on his knees saying, "Oh God, I am such a sinner, I don't deserve your grace and mercy!" Jesus said, "I tell you, this man went to his house justified rather than the other; for everyone who exalts himself will be humbled, but he who humbles himself will be exalted."

The Pharisee didn't see his sin and so couldn't repent of it. The Tax Collector did both, and Jesus honored him for it.

You are a blessed one of a few who has actually been given the privilege by God of seeing your sin. Now just repent of it, turn your life over to Christ, and feel His forgiveness wash over you.

Now to really seal it, let me tell you about Saul. Saul was a Pharisee. Pharisees wore the big fancy robes, walked around like they were better than everyone else, and were the teachers of Scripture to the 'lowly' Jewish people.

After Jesus was crucified, rose, and ascended into heaven, the Christian movement took off. One of the prominent Christians, Stephen, was stoned to death for telling the Pharisees about Jesus. Saul was in "hearty agreement" (Acts 8:1) with putting him to death, and as a matter of fact, he noticed that the senior Pharisees were impressed. He saw this as a way to advance politically. Saul became ravenous for the persecution, arrest, prosecution, imprisonment, and death of all Christians — men, women, and children, alike.

But then, on the way to Damascus to arrest some more, he met Jesus face-to-face in a flash of light. "Saul, Saul, why are you persecuting Me?" was Jesus' question. At that moment, Saul, the ambitious, murderous, violent Pharisee became Paul the Christian, Paul the Apostle.

Saul, now called Paul, described himself as "a blasphemer, a persecutor, and a violent aggressor" (1 Timothy 1:13), as well as "foolish, disobedient, deceived, enslaved to various lusts and pleasures, spending our life in malice and envy, hateful, hating one another" (Titus 3:3).

Paul reflects on his life past, and says that it's *because* he was so bad that God saved him. He puts it this way:

> "Yet for this reason I found mercy, so that in me as the foremost [sinner], Jesus Christ might demonstrate His perfect patience **as an example** for those who would believe in Him for eternal life" (1 Timothy 1:16).

At this point in Paul's life, he saw himself, under the inspiration of the Holy Spirit (which means it *cannot* be false humility or it would be a lie), as the worst sinner of every person on the face of the planet (1 Timothy 1:15). And it was *because* of this, because he was the best example of a horrific sinner that Jesus Christ saved him.

Jesus saved Paul so that from that point forward, *no one* could say, "My sins are too big for God."

Not even you.

APPENDIX B — I'M A NEW CHRISTIAN — NOW WHAT?

So you've prayed the Sinner's Prayer and given your life to Christ. Congratulations and welcome into the church of Christ and the Kingdom of God! I rejoice with all of the angels in heaven that you have joined us.

But now what? What should you do next? I'll attempt to give you some guidance here so it doesn't seem so out of reach. It's really not all that hard, but so many people are left hanging there, feeling like they might do it 'wrong.' If you've given your heart to Christ, then you're secure, so there isn't any 'right' or 'wrong' way to do it.

However, there are some approaches you can take that will leave you in the spiritual wilderness a lot longer than you need to be. We want to move you quickly into God's Promised Land of a fulfilling and wonderful relationship with Christ, so here are some ideas.

Get A Bible

Let me be very clear at this point.

The most important job you have to do is to fall madly in love with Jesus, and be totally and absolutely filled with joy for knowing Him!

The reason your joy is so critical is because it motivates you to know Him more and spend more time with Him, and because people are watching. When other people see you moping around miserable and depressed and wracked with guilt, they see nothing in your God that they don't already have in the world. For you to draw them in — your fulfillment of the Great Commission — you must present to them a God who brings them something they *don't* already have — that deeply-rooted joy and peace, in spite of their circumstances, that only He can bring.

So exactly *how* do you do that? By reading the Bible and finding Jesus in there. Read your Bible with the intention of finding out who He is and of entering into a fully-satisfying relationship with Him. That's the goal of your reading the Bible. Not to educate yourself about doctrine, find out about the Jews, or any of a dozen reasons people will read Scripture. Your job is to fall madly in love with Jesus, learn to have that Godly fear of Him, and feel the joy and peace He gives in the inner-most core of your being.

As the first step to this glorious goal, you need to get a Bible. If you already have a church, then you might want to find out what they use and use that, but if it takes you several months to find *your* church, then don't wait. Go ahead, refer to Appendix C, "How to Select the Right Bible," and get started. Appendix D, "How to Use the Bible," will help you learn where to get started with the Bible and how to proceed.

Get Into A Church

Beyond getting a Bible, the single most impacting thing you can do is to get into a Bible-believing, Bible-teaching, Jesus-loving church. I've said it several times throughout this book, and I want to underscore it here: *Please find a home church.*

So exactly how do you find the right church? Just like you do anything else — you shop around. If you take a year to find just the right church where you feel at home and it becomes your family, then it takes a year.

Now, having said that, let me caution you about being a 'church gypsy.' Searching for your home church is one thing, making a conscious decision never to have a home church is something different altogether. You *must* have a home church. There is just way too much support they provide, training you can get, and friends and family you can make to miss out on that. If you 'church hop,' then that says you have no intention of getting serious and getting involved, and that will leave you in the Christian wilderness, wandering around aimlessly, your entire Christian life. You don't want that, and God doesn't want that for you.

Now, not every church is built for every person. Certainly, every person should be welcome in every church, but not every church is going to be a good fit for you spiritually. If you go into a church and it doesn't feel warm and welcoming for you, then please just say, "This church isn't a good fit for me," and start again next week somewhere else. If you get in there and they never bring up Jesus or read from the Bible, then it definitely isn't the right church. If they're not Biblically-grounded and Jesus-focused, then move on.

When my husband and I were in church-hunting mode, we often went to two sermons a Sunday and occasionally on Saturday night as well. For several months, we went to a different church every week or twice a week. Some were bad experiences for us, and some were luke-warm, and a few were wonderful. That's probably pretty normal, so don't give up. Keep up the search until you find your home. If you find one that has possibilities, go for several Sundays in a row to get a sense of it. If you have a friend who recommends a particular church, then by all means check it out. Remember, though, that it has to be a good fit for *you*, and that might not be the same church as your friend's.

Get Involved

When you are a brand new Christian, the tendency is often to either get neck-deep in ministries and Bible studies, or not to get involved at all. Resist both of those temptations. Once you've found a church home, talk to the pastor or one of the elders about how you might get involved in something you can handle. At this early stage in your Christian walk, it's far more important that you get involved in some good Bible studies so you can grow in your relationship with Christ and learn how to read the Bible than it is serving in a ministry. Get involved in the studies first, and then branch into ministries later. Trust and rely on your pastor's guidance on this.

Small Groups

Once you have your home church, get involved with people at the church. Most churches these days have what they call "small groups" or "community groups" or something like that. These are groups of up to 15 or so church members who get together on a weekly or bi-monthly basis to fellowship and study the Word together. They pray together and lift each other up, and they help each other when the needs arise. It is truly the best way to turn your church into your family. You just need a closer connection than sitting in the pew on a weekly basis can provide.

So, to list them out:

- ➢ Get a Bible.
- ➢ Get into a Bible believing, Bible-teaching, Jesus-loving church.
- ➢ Get into a Bible Study.
- ➢ Get into a Small/Community Group.

And fall in love with the Lord.

APPENDIX C — HOW TO SELECT THE RIGHT BIBLE

My first recommendation in selecting the right Bible is to get into a good Bible-believing and Bible-teaching church and find out what the pastor uses. That's the Bible you should probably start with if you have a church.

However, if you don't have a home church yet, or you'd like to find something that's a more personal choice and better fit for you and you're content to just deal with the differences from your church, then I've added the rest of this section for you.

As of this writing, bible.crosswalk.com has 27 different versions of the Bible listed on their 'using' pulldown menu. That's pretty daunting when you're standing in the book store trying to figure out which one to buy for yourself, so I'll try to help you narrow down the possibilities.

I'm only going to hit on a few of them here, largely because these are the ones I'm familiar with, and can speak more knowledgably about. I'm no expert on versions of the Bible, though, and if I've misrepresented any of them here, I offer my sincere apology. I urge each of you to go on-line and do your own research to fill in any holes I've left.

Basics Of Bible Versions

So here's my best attempt at explaining them from my humble perspective.

The reason there are so many versions of the Bible is because different people have different needs, different ways of studying, and different desires and goals.

The first thing you need to be aware of is that there are 'translations,' and there are 'interpretations.'

This explanation is a little simplified, but it will do for our purposes here. A **translation** is where the translators have taken the original languages, Hebrew, Aramaic, and Greek, and are attempting to keep the English version as close as possible to that. The purists want, to the greatest extent understandable, a word-for-word translation from the original language to the English. You would think that would be the ideal for everyone, and for people who consider themselves purists, teachers, scholars, and academicians, it is. The downside to that, though, is that it leaves the English a little harder to understand because the original languages don't work in quite the same way the English does. So to stay pure, some of the English becomes a little challenging to say the least. The trade-offs are between purity in accuracy, and understandability.

On the other end of the spectrum are the **interpretations**. An interpretation is where the translators thought about a section of Scripture and essentially rewrote it into their own words to try to capture the essence of what the original languages were trying to convey. These are typically easier to understand, but since they are not pure to the original languages, you have to be very careful about deriving hard-and-fast doctrinal assumptions from them. One of the interpretations doesn't even have verse numbers because the sentences simply don't correspond to the original languages well enough.

Interpretations fall broadly into two main categories: verse interpretation and paragraph interpretation.

In the verse interpretation, the translators took the original language and rewrote the Hebrew or Greek text into more understandable English, but stayed within the parameters of the single sentence or verse. In paragraph interpretation, you won't have verse numbers because the Hebrew and Greek sentences have been lost in the translation. The result is a 'discussion' of what the original languages were trying to convey in more common language.

Then there are the rest of them that fall somewhere in between the two extremes.

Both extremes, as well as those in the middle, have their advantages and disadvantages. I use several different versions that span that gamut and I get a lot out of all of them.

I'm going to repeat my word of caution here, though: There are many examples where the simpler, more 'understandable' versions have lost a great deal of accuracy in the translation. Some of them even come a little too close to heresy for comfort in my opinion. Just be very careful about relying solely on the 'more understandable' versions, and always compare them with the King James Version (KJV), New American Standard Bible (NASB), or New King James Version (NKJV) for anything you are going to take to heart and apply to your life.

So what I'd like to do here is to give you some specific versions and some guidance on the type of studying you can do with each.

The first three Bibles, KJV, NASB, and NKJV, are what I call the 'pure' Bibles. They are pure because the authors were very serious about translating, word for word, from the original languages. The more you deviate from the original languages to achieve understandability, the more you risk inaccuracy and possibly even heresy. The translators have to be very careful, and from what I can glean from the many debates I've heard on this topic, these are the one's most scholars believe are the most accurate.

King James Version (KJV) — The original printed English Bible, printed in the early 1600's under the authority of King James of England. It was written in the language of the day, hence all the "thee's" and "thou's." They understood it because that's the way they spoke. The KJV is extremely accurate to the original Hebrew and Greek, so is a very good one for the purists and scholars. It is reported to be the easiest to memorize because of its poetic nature, and once you get used to it, it is quite beautiful. Beginners find it extremely difficult to understand because of that same feature. My understanding is that this is the only version many Baptist churches recognize as the authoritative Word of God.

New American Standard Bible (NASB) — I have heard radio commentators arguing about whether the King James or the NASB is the most accurate to the original languages. I would suggest that since the authorities can't agree on that, then unless you are going for your doctorate in theology or something, it doesn't matter much. In my early walk, I found the NASB to be easier to understand, so that's what I started with. Since then, however, I've become much more familiar with the language of the KJV, so I go back and forth. So far in my own studies comparing the two to the versions of the Greek Bibles that I have, I have found a dozen or so differences between the KJV and the NASB in the New Testament. For most of them, the differences are insignificant and don't change the meaning much.

New King James Version (NKJV) — This is essentially just the King James Version with the "thee's" and "thou's" changed to "you" and "your." I've never heard anyone address whether this is more or less 'pure' than either the KJV or the NASB, but I have read that it is a very good translation.

If your goal is to become a serious student of the Bible, then I'd recommend you get both KJV and NASB, and possibly the NKJV as well. Read them and compare as you go. The differences you will find are enlightening.

New International Version (NIV) — The New International Version is a translation, and does a reasonable job of staying fairly close to the original languages. I've never heard anyone recommend it, though, for those who see themselves as serious scholars and purists. The target audience for the NIV, in my opinion, is the person who wants to be somewhat close to the original language but isn't as focused on looking up the Greek or doing the other more complicated word studies. Since the translators didn't feel the need to be exactly pure to the original languages, it tends to be the easiest of the better translations to understand. However, I have seen some websites that do a verse-by-verse comparison with the KJV, claiming that some of the differences are fairly extreme and almost heretical, so caution is encouraged. If you want to use the NIV, then

I'd recommend you also get a KJV, NASB, or NKJV, and compare as you go just to be safe.

New Living Translation (NLT) — The New Living Translation, although it is still something of a translation, is starting to creep toward more of an interpretation. You will have verse numbers, but each verse is only loosely tied to the word-by-word Greek. As it turns out, though, there are good examples of verses in the NLT that, in spite of the fact that they aren't as 'pure' to the original language, do a better job of conveying the *intention* of the original language than do the more literal translations. The reason for this is because the English language just struggles trying to duplicate the richness of the Greek and Hebrew languages. If you restrict yourself to only using one or two words to convey what a single Hebrew or Greek word uses, then you might not have any very good choices in the English. They had to make some compromises in depth to stay pure to the verbiage — not accuracy, just depth. The NLT translators, on the other hand, have given themselves license to use as many words as they thought they needed to to convey the essence of the original language rather than the letter of it. I never use the NLT as my primary study Bible because it's just too far from the original languages, but I will use it occasionally to help me understand the NASB and KJV when the pure translation wording is difficult.

God's Word (God) — This is a newer translation/interpretation hybrid that approximates the NLT idea. I find this version to be slightly easier to understand than the NLT in some texts, but as you get more understandable, you tend to get less accurate to the original languages, so again, there's the tradeoff.

New Century Version (NC) — Of all of the interpretation/translation hybrids, I find this one to be the easiest to understand. Remember, though, that it also makes it the least literal to the Greek and Hebrew, and the least accurate of those I've listed here.

The Message

The Message is by far, the book that epitomizes the term 'interpretation.' This book has no verse numbers because the sentences do not approximate the original sentences closely enough. As such, it is the easiest to read, but has lost a lot of the original language. It's a wonderful book to read casually, and I have one, but I would never use it as my primary source of Scripture. Use it as a wonderful narrative and as a way to capture some of the nuances of the original languages, but use one of the pure translations for Biblical study.

Study Bibles

There are also what they call 'Study Bibles.' They are still the versions listed above (plus those I haven't listed), but they have 'helps' with them. These 'helps' are comments, maps, cross-references, concordances, etc. There are women's Bibles, men's Bibles, Bibles for teens, Bibles for children, Bibles for students, Bibles for military people, and more. There are prophesy Bibles, and 'Finding Jesus' Bibles that show you where Jesus is throughout the Old Testament. Each of these has the same original Bible at the core as the versions listed above, but with additional comments and other aids to help the reader understand more. Some also have wide outer margins for jotting down notes as you read. That's what I have, and I love it.

Bibles can be fairly expensive, so spend some time doing some research and looking over several of them before you start buying.

So, let's boil it all down for you:

I am a serious student, and I want to go very deep, possibly into the Greek and Hebrew some: King James Version (KJV), New King James Version (NKJV), or New American Standard Bible (NASB)

I want to study Scripture, but I need something a little easier to understand: New International Version (NIV)

I have a pure Bible (one of the first three), but I'd also like something I can use to help me with difficult passages or gain additional insight: New Living Translation (NLT), or God's Word (God), or New Century Version (NC).

I have a pure Bible, but I'd like something I can read casually when I have some time to just relax in the Word: The Message

My apologies to those versions I have not listed here, and I deeply pray I have not misrepresented any that I have included here. I know each version has its pros and cons, and absence from this list should not imply in any way that they have no value. The reader is strongly encouraged to go on-line to get more information and talk to your pastor about the versions that are available and the one that's right for you.

APPENDIX D — HOW TO USE THE BIBLE

Getting Started

When I first started reading the Bible, I was a bit overwhelmed at what I was reading. It was *huge*, and I had no idea where to start. I'd tried a few times in my life starting at Genesis (Don't you start reading a book at the beginning?), only to get bogged down half-way through Abraham, not understanding what I was reading, having no idea how my life would be changed by it, and just couldn't maintain the energy it took.

That's probably a familiar story to some of you. Some of you might have actually made it all the way to Exodus or Leviticus before you crashed and burned, but I don't know too many people who started their Bible study that way who got beyond Leviticus. Some boring, nasty, bloody stuff if you don't know what you're reading.

So I'd like to spare you that misery and give you some guidance on where to start. But before we get there, there are a couple of things you need to know.

As I said in the text of the book, the Bible is organized into the Old Testament and the New Testament. The word 'Testament' means Covenant, or Promise. The Old Covenant is that God would make Israel a great nation and give them Canaan, 'the land of promise,' the land flowing with milk and honey. The New Covenant is with the Christians, and says that God has given us Jesus, the Messiah, to die to save us from our sins. The Old Testament is the Jew's Bible, and the Old Testament and the New Testament together comprise the Christian's Bible.

If you've never compared the size of the Old Testament with the New Testament, it's an interesting exercise. Grab your Bible, divide it up in your hands with the Old Testament in your left hand the New Testament in your right. The difference in size between the two will surprise you if you've never done it before.

Now, understand that you will definitely be getting to the Old Testament in your reading, but you need to start with the New Testament. If you don't understand the end of the book, the beginning of the book will just be a bunch of boring, bloody history about the Jews. It is so vastly more than that, but the richness and the depth of it will be lost on you if you don't have as your foundation the Gospel of Jesus Christ. You already know that if you've read the body of this book, and if you haven't, you'll get there. If you don't know Christ, then you won't know what to look for in the Old Testament to find Him there.

So start with the Gospel of John. It's the fourth book in the New Testament, after Matthew, Mark, and Luke.

Then, and this is fairly important, you need to learn a little history about the Apostle Paul. The Gospel of John will introduce you to the other Biblical authors, but the Apostle Paul doesn't show up until Acts. If you don't read about him, you won't know one of the primary writers of the New Testament.

So start your reading in this order:

- ➢ Gospel of John to learn that Jesus is God in the flesh, and learn about the disciples
- ➢ Acts Chapter 7 to learn about Stephen (the first martyr)
- ➢ Acts Chapter 8 verses 1-4 to learn who Saul was and what he did
- ➢ Acts Chapter 9 verses 1-30 to learn about the Apostle Paul

Actually, starting from Chapter 9 and then all through the rest of Acts is mostly about Paul. The book of Acts is about the early church, so it wouldn't hurt you to read the entire book of Acts after you've read John to get a bigger picture of the early church. The sections in the above list are pretty pivotal, though, so don't skip them.

Once you've read John and the story of Paul, the exact order you take to read the rest of it is up to you. You can make your decision based on your church's direction, the book where your pastor is preaching from right now, or the Bible study you're in. Don't skip the above readings first, though. They're very good stuff.

And don't just skip around chapter by chapter or verse by verse. When you select a book, read from Chapter 1 verse 1 through the end of the book before you move to another book. If you don't do that, you miss way too much of the context and you'll never get to know the authors, or the Great Author, God.

I heard a sermon on-line that suggested you read a long book, then a short book, then a long book, and then a short book until you've made your way through the entire New Testament. I thought that was good advice, so I pass it along to you.

As a new Christian, spend most of your early time in the New Testament. When you get a little more familiar with it and who Jesus is, then the Old Testament can come alive to you if you know how to find Jesus there. There are many sections in this book to help you do that, if you haven't already read it.

Some general information about the books of the Bible might be helpful.

The New Testament is divided loosely into the following sections:

> ➤ Gospels — The stories of Jesus, from four different perspectives to four different audiences for four different purposes.
> ➤ Acts — The history of the early church of Christ and how the Gospel was spread throughout Asia, and then to the rest of the world.
> ➤ Paul's Letters (called The Pauline Epistles) — The letters written by the Apostle Paul to churches and to specific individuals. Paul wrote these letters to instruct, encourage, admonish, and guide the people of God.

- Hebrews — a letter written to the Hebrew, or Jewish, people to help them see how the New Testament fits into the Old Testament. Scholars aren't sure who wrote Hebrews.
- Remaining Letters — Letters written by the Apostles John, James, Peter, and Jude to the Christians that were living in the area to encourage them through their trials and to give them guidance.
- Revelation — The revelation directly from Jesus to the Apostle John, showing us how the world is going to end, how Satan and his minions are going to be defeated, and the glory of the return of Jesus Christ. If you're not a believer, it's a very frightening book. If, however, you are bound for the Kingdom of heaven, it's the most exciting book in all of Scripture. Whenever you have tough times and a battle with the enemy, you can proudly and confidently say, "Yeah, but *I know the end of the story, and we win!*"

Bible reading is the window into seeing and getting to know Jesus Christ, and your opportunity to have Him as your Counselor, your Comforter, and your Friend. In falling in love with Him, you will experience that profound joy and peace that He alone offers. If you view and have an approach to reading in the right manner, you will find it to be extraordinarily comforting, fulfilling, and exciting. If you don't find that to be true for you, then find people who *do* feel that way and study with them. Their knowledge and their enthusiasm will rub off on you, and you will never regret it.

What's A Verse?

Okay, you've bought a Bible and flipped it open. What on earth are all those numbers at the beginning of sentences?

When the original authors, way back in the mid first century, wrote the individual books of the Bible, those numbers didn't exist. As a matter of fact, the chapter numbers didn't exist. Each 'book' was actually just a letter written to someone, and was one long dialogue without any divisions of any kind. You would never divide a letter you've written to a friend up by chapters and the like, and neither would they.

The chapters and verses were added centuries later. They added them because we needed some way of organizing our study and communicating our thoughts to each other. Adding the chapter divisions helped us do that, and then later adding a chronological number at the beginning of each cohesive thought added significantly to that communication.

So the numbers at the beginning of those thoughts are the 'verse' identifiers. Notice that the verse isn't necessarily a complete sentence, and sometimes a verse will actually have more than one sentence or combinations of partial sentences. Some of the sentences in the Bible are fairly long and complicated and actually comprise several distinct thoughts, so they divided the sentences up that way. You'll notice that many of them start with the word "and" or "but." As a matter of fact, you'll even find some chapters starting with the word "and."

So when I say, "John 3:16," I'm saying go to the book of John, which follows Matthew, Mark, and Luke in the New Testament, flip over to Chapter 3, and then within that chapter, go to verse 16. It says:

> "For God so loved the world, that He gave His only begotten Son, that whosoever believes in Him shall not perish, but have eternal life."

So what about the letters behind the verse designation in some things I've read, like "John 3:16b." They're not in the actual Bible, but you might find them in commentaries and the like. The "b" refers to the second part of the verse. In the case of John 3:16, the "b" would refer to "that He gave His only begotten Son." In this example, there may be "a," "c," and "d" as well.

Now, when I say, "go to the book of John," you might say, "That's easy for you to say, but where *is* the book of John?!"

Great question. Actually, you'll eventually get used to where the books are in the Bible, but for now, the Bible has what every good book has: a table of contents. Flip to the beginning of your Bible and you'll find the table of contents with page numbers. Skim down the 66 books listed until you see "John," or "The Gospel of John." Remember that the Old Testament is a whole lot bigger than the New Testament, so John will be close to the end of the Table of Contents, relatively speaking, even though it's early in the New Testament.

Also, some Bibles have small black indents in the edges of the pages with shorthand for each of the books. John would be listed as "Jn" or "Joh" or "Jno." You'll get used to it after a while.

If your Bible doesn't have that, then you can go to a Christian Bookstore and get pre-printed tabs that you can add to your own Bible. I have to tell you, though, that I did that when I was a new Christian, and I found that they tore the pages of my Bible. I guess you can be careful and not do that, but I found them to be a problem, so I took them off. Again, it's about preference and trade-offs.

Why Are Some Words In Italics?

As you read, you'll notice that some of the words in the text are in italics. This has to do with the Greek.

The translators of the Bible tried to convey the clearest meaning of the Greek and Hebrew into English the best they could while staying pure to the original languages. The problem, as I've stated before, is that the Greek and Hebrew are very rich, and there are occasions when there simply *was* no English word that adequately conveyed the subtle nuances of the original language. When that happened, they would sometimes insert an additional word in the text to further explain what was originally meant in the text. When they did that, they would put the inserted word in italics so the reader would know that there was no Greek or Hebrew word from which this word was translated, but that it was added by the authors for clarity and depth.

When you run across those words, read the sentence again without the italicized word to see if it makes a difference to the meaning. If it does, then take the time to figure out what the translator was trying to do with the added word and look the root word up in the Greek. That's one of the places I've found some really fun treasures.

Why Are Some Words In All Capital Letters?

When you run across words that are in all capital letters, the translator is telling you that they are quoting something out of the Old Testament. Again, this can be a great source of treasures. When you see that, find out where in the Old Testament that quote comes from and go look it up. You will have some very fruitful treasure hunts that way.

Concordance

Many Bibles have in the back what they call a "Concordance." A concordance is simply an index of the words in the Bible. If you get a "Complete Concordance," which is a separate book, then you have the work of some wonderful individuals who went painstakingly through the Bible and made a list of *every single word in the Bible* and grouped them in alphabetical order. Then, for every word, they listed *every single verse* where that word appears.

So, for instance, you'd have the following as one of the words in your concordance (this is the NASB version):

> Offense   Lev 19:7
>   Eza 10:19
>   Mat 11:6
>   Mat 13:57
>   Mar 6:3
>   Luk 7:23
>   Act 25:8
>   Rom 5:14
>   Rom 9:33
>   Rom 14;20
>   1 Co 10:32
>   2 Co 6:3
>   1 Pe 2:8

So if you were to read your NASB Bible, cover to cover, and count the number of times you found the word "offense" in the

English, you'd find thirteen of them. The full concordance will list all thirteen verses where that word is found.

The concordances will often have a short segment of the actual verse itself as well, so you can more easily find what you're looking for. So, if you were interested in how the word "offense" is used, or if you wanted to find a particular verse and you knew the word "offense" was in the verse, then you would go to the Concordance to find out where it is in the Bible.

The Concordance you have at the back of your Bible is a condensed version of the full one. You won't have all the words listed, and you won't have all of the verses listed for the words it does have, but it is still handy and it will serve a purpose. If you think you're going to want to be doing that a lot, though, getting a complete concordance will be a good investment.

The other thing the Concordance provides is the "Strong's Number." For almost every English word in the Bible (barring those in italics), there's a Greek word that that English word was translated from. The Strong's Numbers are in the right-hand margin, to the right of the column where the verse is provided.

To use the Strong's Number, go to the back of the Concordance. The numbers are in numeric order. Look the number up on that list, and you have an abbreviated definition of that particular word in the Greek. You'll notice that sometimes the same English word actually has a few different Strong's numbers. That's because the Greek is an extremely rich language, and there is often more than one Greek word that can be translated into a single English word. That's why looking it up in the Greek can be so helpful. Sometimes there are subtle nuances in the Greek that the English cannot convey. Spend time looking them up, and you'll be thrilled at some of the treasures you can find.

Margin References

Many Bibles have margin references on each page. You'll see them, usually on the inside or outside margin, of every page that has Scripture. Sometimes they contain comments, and sometimes they are just references to other passages of the Bible that might have something to do with this one. It could be that the same story is located in another Gospel and it will tell you where it is; it could be that a specific word is used somewhere else in the same way; it could be that the idea is represented in a different section of Scripture in addition to this one.

In any event, there are too many of them to stop each time and look it up, but if you are on a specific verse and it has some special meaning to you today, then you might want to take a minute to check out the referenced passages as well.

One way I have found my treasure-hunting to be particularly fruitful is to go to the references to the Old Testament when I'm reading in the New Testament, or to references to the New Testament when I'm in the Old. I highly recommend checking out those references whenever you come across them. You may end up with an empty hole, but more often than not, there's a nugget for your efforts.

There's a lot of information online about how to read the Bible, and your church small group and Bible study will be an invaluable source of information. Avail yourself of those rich resources and really learn how to use your Bible.

For a comprehensive, practical Bible reading program, go to http://www.opnhrt.com/ohcc/biblepgm.php.

APPENDIX E — REFERENCES AND RECOMMENDATIONS

Here I'd like to share with you some of the resources I've used in my years of study of Scripture. The books are all available on-line at Amazon.com or at your Christian book store and a host of others sources. The web sites are the web addresses that were in place as of this writing.

Commentaries

> Application Commentary of the New Testament, by Jon Courson
> Application Commentary of the Old Testament Vol I, by Jon Courson
> Application Commentary of the Old Testament Vol II, by Jon Courson
> Bible Knowledge Commentary by the Dallas Theological Seminary
> Jamison-Fawcett Brown Commentary
> Matthew Henry Commentary

Resource Books

Zodhiates, Spiros; *Complete Word Study Dictionary: New Testament* AMG Publishers, Chattanooga, TN 37422
- Also available in Old Testament, plus
- The Complete Wordstudy Dictionary: New Testament (Word Study Series)
- The Complete Wordstudy Dictionary: Old Testament (Word Study Series)

Web Sites — All *highly* recommended

http://bible.crosswalk.com — On-line Bible resources
http://joncourson.com — Jon Courson
http://www.gospelcom.net/ — Ravi Zacharias
http://www.gty.org/index.php — John MacArthur, Grace to You
http://www.oneplace.com/ministries/Truth_for_Life — Alistair Begg
http://www.calvarychapelradio.com/listen.asp — Calvary Chapel Radio on-line
http://www.walkthru.org/ — Chip Ingram, Living on the Edge
http://www.leadingtheway.org/ — Michael Youseff, Leading the Way
http://www.mcleanbible.org/ — Lon Solomon, McLean Bible Church
http://www.frontline.to/ — Frontline, a Youth-oriented branch of McLean Bible Church

There are many other fabulous resources. Hunt around, but be careful. There are also many "false prophets" masquerading as God's sheep and shepherds. Be discerning, and if you have any doubt, talk to your pastor.

APPENDIX F — INTRODUCTION TO THE AUTHOR

By Way Of Introduction…

As I said in the introduction of this book, a friend of mine said that before anyone is going to trust what I have to say, they have to know who I am. By way of submission to her judgment, I offer here a little information about me.

As I write this book, I have been a licensed Social Worker in the state of Maryland for over 10 years and I am currently a full-time private practice Christian Mental Health Therapist. After spending nearly 30 years in the computer industry, I left that career so I could devote my full-time attention to my mental health practice. I work out of my home office in a semi-rural setting of Southern Maryland.

My Testimony

I dedicated my life to the Lord in September 2001, ten days prior to the Twin Towers attacks. I was 48 years old at the time. My sister-in-law had given her life to the Lord a year earlier, and in April of that same year, my husband had re-dedicated his life again to Christ after asking God 24 years earlier to forgive him as he went through college with an 'open' mind. Both of them had grown up in a Christian home, but my Christian roots were thin and not deeply set. In fact, through my High School and College years,

I had become an analytical and scientifically-minded academic, and finally, a devout Atheist.

After I went into cardiac arrest with the announcement that my husband was now a "Jesus freak," he, in the most gentle and humble tone imaginable, *invited* me to attend church with him. I threatened him with divorce if he tried to "shove that stuff down my throat." He assured me that was not his intention, but hoped I would be supportive of him "as my wife" he said, in something so terribly important to him. I relented, but literally announced myself as a "non-believer" when I went into the building.

To make a several-month-long story short, it started to threaten me less and intrigue me more, and I bought some books. I spent a good amount of money on what I called my "Is there a God?" books. I read, asked my husband and my sister-in-law endless questions, and finally, that first Saturday morning in September 2001, I ran across something profound in one of the books I was reading and just shattered into a million pieces. It felt like Jesus Christ Himself had just swooped into my living room on a waterfall. I was hooked — transformed. I was a new person and I knew it. I didn't understand yet what had happened, but I knew I would never be the same. It was almost like someone had just plugged in the power-cord of my life.[49]

I became ravenous for the company of Christian women and the Holy Bible. I wanted to know everything there was to know as fast as I could. At 48 years old, I had a lot of catching up to do, and I didn't want to waste any time.

My Background

Ok, I need to share this with you: I'm not a formal Bible scholar: I'm a Mental Health Therapist. As I indicated in the last section, I'm a relatively young Christian, all things considered, and I've had no accredited training. Initially, I wondered about my qualifications to write a book of this nature. I prayed to the Lord and sought guidance from people I trust. After those discussions and some additional prayer and reflection, I've come to see my background in a different light. I've come to see it as a real asset.

You see, my 'lack of qualifications' should be an encouragement to you. Like me, you don't have to have a Seminary education for the Bible to be a life-changing experience for you. You don't have to go through formal training to understand what God is trying to tell you. Like me, you only have to have a love for the Lord and a passion to know Him better. I'm no different from you, and no smarter. Regardless of your educational background, God wrote the Bible so that everyone can understand it and be transformed by it. He loves us way too much to make it above our heads. It's there for us. It's there for you.

My Master's Degree and state license allow me to practice mental health. My Biblical knowledge comes from weekly church sermons, endless sermons on radio and CD by masters such as Michael Youssef, Charles Stanley, Lon Solomon, Billy Graham, James Kennedy, Robert Schuler, R.C. Sproul, Alistair Begg, Ravi Zacharias, John Bevere, Jon Courson, and many, many others. In addition, I have attended many Bible studies developed by such notable teachers as Henry Blackaby/Claude King, Bill Gothard, Beth Moore and others. However, my knowledge is cultivated from my daily Bible reading, cross-referencing with other versions of the Bible, referring to different commentaries, and spending a little time in the Greek.

The real credit, however, goes to the Holy Spirit. He has given me an insatiable desire to learn Scripture and draw closer to the Lord, and He guides me every step of the way.

Thank you, Lord, for your love, for your coaching, and for rescuing me from bondage.

Visit me at http://www.TherapyWithGod.com.

NOTES

NOTES

NOTES

TESTIMONIALS

"This book reads exactly like what it is; a deeply meaningful conversation between you and someone who loves you and wants you to be healed. Sue McHenry gives you the spiritual medicine you need, straight from the Great Physician Himself. You will be comforted, confronted, and brought to a place of peace you thought did not exist on the opposite side of pain. This book truly can change your life." Kristin Ballou.

"This book is an excellent resource offering practical examples of how to deal with everyday struggles. What I love most is that it shows us how to utilize the Bible as our personal instruction manual and provides a step by step approach to making Jesus Christ the focal point of our life." Mary Ellen Tancreto, Entrepreneur.

"Sue McHenry does an excellent job in inviting the reader to come in, sit down, learn about and experience first hand how God is our Comforter that we long for and need in every area and situation in our lives. Sue guides the reader in exploring the Bible to uncover life's changing truths to set the captives free to live the abundant life God intended for all of us." K. Walston, Christian support group leader.

FOOTNOTES

* * * * * * * *   * * * * * * *   * * * * * * *   * * * * * * *

1. A 'blessing' in this context is referring to a fullness in Him and Him alone, a sense of great inner peace, contentment, and joy, and a closeness to Him. I discuss this at length in the section, "Treasure," in Chapter XIV - Bible-Based Therapy.
2. I wholeheartedly acknowledge that God is fully capable of miraculously restoring anyone to full health, regardless of the illness, and I would always pray for that. These are Scriptural principles that would be applied if He responds, "No, I want you to learn to trust Me and lean on Me through this illness."
3. This section assumes the mental health issues are environmental or a dysfunctional lifestyle, not pathological, or that the pathology has been stabilized through medication.
4. Ferentz, Lisa LCSW-C, DAPA. 2006. Trauma Therapy Certification Program. University of Maryland School of Social Work, Baltimore, MD
5. There's also R&R – Rest and Relaxation. If you're in that phase, sing praises to God, but be mentally prepared for the next phase of training or battle.
6. Pastor Dave Huffman. 2006. South Potomac Church, White Plains, MD
7. I know, your agape love isn't pure or consistent, but if your intention is to agape love Him, He will work with you to perfect it.
8. Go to http://bible.crosswalk.com. Search around and you can get definitions of the Greek terms.
9. See the Appendix, "I'm a new Christian – Now what?" for suggestions as to how to go about that.

10 This was the standard operating procedure for the armies of that day.
11 From Courson, Jon. 2003. Application Commentary, Old Testament, Vol I, and many sermons I cannot now recall.
12 This is not to say we should just sit around and wait for God to solve our problem. We have responsibilities and are partnered with God. I deal with this in more detail in the chapter called "Victory in Trials."
13 Southerland, Mary. 2006. Coming Out of the Dark: A Christian woman's struggle with depression. Highly recommended.
14 There are too many references to this in Psalms to list them here.
15 Bill Gothard has a series called, "The Commands of Christ" you can purchase on-line at http://store.iblp.org/products/COCS/. You can review the list at http://billgothard.com/bill/teaching/commandsofchrist/
16 http://bible.crosswalk.com for Greek definitions of 'lust.'
17 John Bevere wrote a book entitled, The Bait of Satan that dramatically illustrates this concept. I highly recommend it.
18 The term 'saint' means "holy one," or "set-apart one." Paul refers to believers as 'saints.' If you're a born-again believer, you're a saint!
19 Piper, John. 1986, 1996, 2003. Desiring God: Meditations of a Christian Hedonist. Sisters, Oregon. Multnomah Publishers, Inc. Great Book, highly recommended reading.
20 Internet article entitled Valley churches celebrate Thanksgiving. (accessed 10/14/07). http://findarticles.com/p/articles/mi_qn4176/is_20061117/ai_n16863221.
21 See note 13 above.
22 Blackaby, Henry and King, Claude King. 2004. Experiencing God: Knowing and Doing the Will of God. Nashville, TN: Holman Publishers. Refer to this book for a full explanation of this.
23 Concept taken from The Call of the Wild, by Jack London.
24 See note 19 above.
25 Quoted from Angel Cartegena in a sermon at South Potomac Church, Waldorf, MD on April 23, 2006.

26 Calvert, Rick. 'Greek Thoughts.' (Accessed December 15, 2007) http://www.studylight.org/col/ds/.
27 For more supporting information regarding this idea, check out the Amplified Bible (Matthew 5:3) and the Bible Knowledge Commentary from the Dallas Theological Seminary (Malachi 3:10).
28 Dye, Lee. May 10, 2006. Laughter May Indeed Be the Best Medicine. ABC News. (accessed July 14, 2006). Also see The Association for Applied and Therapeutic Humor website at http://www.aath.org/.
29 Examples include Martin Luther, Charles Spurgeon, and many others.
30 I am convinced that there are those who have been given an extra dose of faith as a gift from God for His purposes. The rest of us have to build ours over time.
31 Refer back to the section on "Thank Therapy" in Chapter 14, "Bible-based Therapy" if you need to.
32 From Stroebel, Lee. 1998. The Case for Christ: A Journalist's Personal Investigation of the Evidence for Jesus. Grand Rapids, Michigan: Zondervan Publishing House.
33 Pastor Rick Warren is the author of A Purpose-Driven Life.
34 Don't do this if it causes more pain to the victim. Be honest about this and pray about it, but if it will hurt them for you to approach them, just confess it to God and ask His forgiveness.
35 Jesus, predicting Peter's denial of Him during His trial, and telling him how he must grow and strengthen through it.
36 For instance, I memorized Psalm 40, John 1:1-14, Ephesians 3:14-21 and others
37 Pastor Mike Hilson, New Life Wesleyan Church, Waldorf, MD
38 See note 15 above.
39 See note 22 above.
40 Ibid., page 50.
41 Ibid., page 55.
42 I have seen Mr. Bakker on television several times since his release from prison. I certainly can't judge his heart, but it is my belief that he has recommitted his life to Christ and has a wonderful teaching ministry on television now. I hear none of

his prior messages of "prosperity" or see anything close to the pomp and arrogance you see with so many of the "prosperity preachers" of today.

43 "Abba" is an extremely personal, intimate name of God as Father.
44 The Prisoner in the Third Cell by Gene Edwards does an amazing job of explaining this.
45 This was traditional in ancient Jewish culture at the direction of God. If a woman's husband dies and he has no children, she is to marry her dead husband's brother and their first son inherits her dead husband's estate.
46 Leviticus 1:3, 1:10; 3:1, 3:6, 4:3, 4:23, 4:28, 4:32, 5:15, 5:18. There are 33 specific instances in the Law. Go to http://bible.crosswalk.com and do a search on "without defect" to see them all.
47 A religious leader in Jesus' day.
48 A single denarii is a full day's wage.
49 Be aware that not everyone who has legitimately received the Holy Spirit has that "Road to Damascus" experience as I did. Billy Graham did not. It took him several months to find the "fire" he sought. If that's you, you're in good company. Immerse yourself in Scripture and it will happen.
50 Message received from the Holy Spirit, December 3, 2007